Vermont Barn Quilt
Coloring Book Two
John H. Lettau

Barn Quilts of Franklin County Vermont

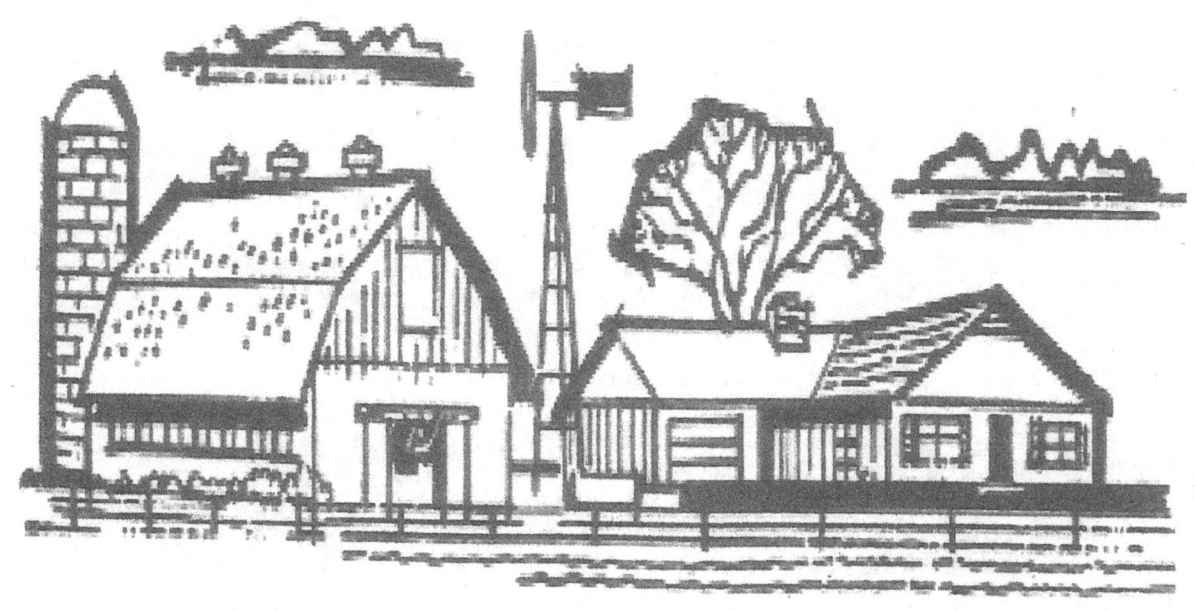

Cover Barn Quilts

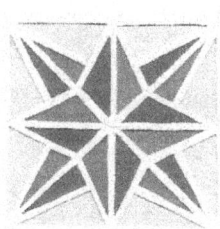 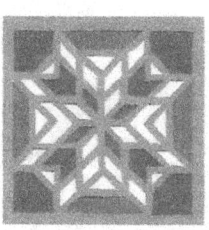 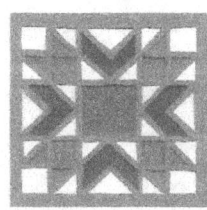 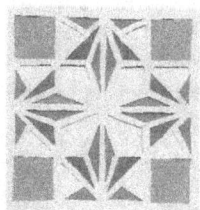

Star Shadow   Lone Star   Blueberry Pie   Complex Star

Franklin County Vermont Barn Quilts

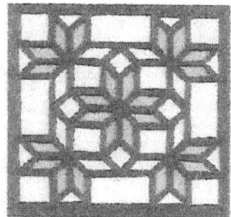 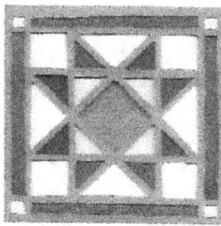 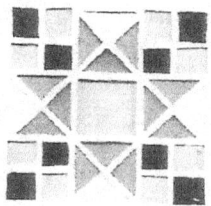 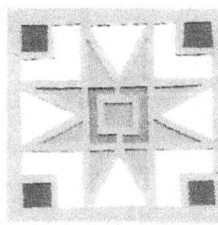 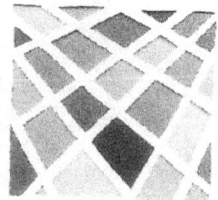

A drive through Franklin County, Vermont is very colorful today because many brilliant "quilt blocks," called barn quilts, are displayed on barns and other structures throughout the area. Five sample barn quilt patterns located in Franklin County are pictured above...Carpenter Wheel, Sawtooth Star Variation, Garden Patch Star, Sun, and Broken Glass. The idea for the Barn Quilts of Franklin County was suggested by Sheldon Raider's Homemaker's Club in 2009.

This coloring book features "quilt blocks" located in the following areas of Franklin County. Swanton, Berkshire, Enosburg, Franklin, Richford, Sheldon, Bakerfield, Georgia, Hero, Highgate, Montgomery and St. Albans..

Objectives of Barn Quilt Projects

Barn quilt groups around the country try to educate, promote and celebrate the unique agricultural heritage through the visual combination of barns and quilts. Barns are vital to the economic well-being of any rural community and provide warmth, beauty, and an outlet for artistic expressions. Projects in Vermont are based on similar projects in Ohio, Indiana, Wisconsin and the Appalachian states. Franklin launched its own version to promote scenic agricultural area to tourists. Note...The Swanton Arts Council embraces the idea of creating barn quilts to encourage public art that adds the beauty of the Swanton area.

What is a Barn Quilt?

A barn quilt is made by painting a barn quilt pattern on two 4' by 8' sheets of ¾ inch plywood then mounting them on barn to form an eight foot square. Two coats of primer are applied to both sides of the boards and the edges. After the pattern is drawn out Frog (painter's) tape is applied. Three coats of each color are applied, with each coat being allowed to dry overnight. After the quilt is finished, it is allowed to cure for at least two weeks before it is put upon a barn or other structure. Barn quilt blocks can be found of different smaller sizes depending on the specific architecture of the various structures.

Making a barn quilt allows individuals and volunteer groups the opportunity to create and paint their own barn square. The design that is chosen may represent a family pattern from a beloved quilt or perhaps new pattern meaningful to the creator(s).

Objectives of Franklin County Barn Quilts
1. Reflect the agricultural heritage of the county
2. To be visual form the road
3. To bring pride to the area
4. To promote tourism in the county
Individual Objectives
5, To sharpen math and drafting skills
6. To promote creativity on a personal level
7. To share public art

Franklin County Barn Quilt Information
www.franklincountyquilters.org
www.trailmapfranklinquilters.org
www.swantonartscouncil.org
*swantonartscouncil@gmail.com*e
fmercure@myfairpoint.net

Special thanks to Swanton Arts Council for their interest and assistance !!!

Barn Quilts of Franklin County Vermont

Prosperity	Main St	Montgomery, Vermont
Star Explosion	Bullock Rd	Georgia, Vermont
Mariner's Star	Valentine Dr	Enosburg, Vermont
Bicycle Wheel	Hill West Rd	Montgomery, Vermont
Shadow Star	Little County Rd	Swanton, Vermont
Star Variation	Upper Welden Rd	Swanton, Vermont
Complex Star	Sheldon Rd	Swanton, Vermont
Dean's Delight	Russell Rd	Swanton, Vermont
Cross & Crown	Brooklyn St	Swanton, Vermont
Garden Patch Star	Bushley Rd	Swanton, Vermont
Cow in Square	Spring St	Swanton, Vermont
Crowfeet	Grand Ave	Swanton, Vermont
My T Fine	Spring St	Swanton, Vermont
Lone Star Variation	Rte 118	Montgomery, Vermont
Storm at Sea	N Main St	Montgomery, Vermont
Buggy Wheel	N Main St	Montgomery, Vermont
Log Cabin	Hanna Rd	Franklin, Vermont
Sawtooth Star	Bushley Rd	Swanton, Vermont
Spinning Star	Fuller Bridge Rd	Montgomery, Vermont
Blueberry Pie	Fuller Bridge Rd	Montgomery, Vermont
Maple Leaf	W Enosburg Rd	Enosburg, Vermont
Carpenter Wheel	Bogue Rd	Enosburg, Vermont
Sun	Elm St	Enosburg, Vermont
Maya the Owl	Tyler Ranch Rd	Enosburg, Vermont
Eight Pointed Star	VT Rte 105	Sheldon, Vermont
The Green Mountains	VT Rte 105	Sheldon, Vermont
Star Burst	E. Sheldon Rd	Sheldon, Vermont
Friendship Star Variation	E. Sheldon Rd	Sheldon, Vermont
Chained Star Variation	VT Rte 105	Sheldon, Vermont
Basket of Flowers	Bridge Rd	Sheldon, Vermont
Blazing Star	Kane Rd	Sheldon, Vermont
Pinwheel	Kane Rd	Sheldon, Vermont
Radiant Star	VT Rte 105	Sheldon, Vermont
Pinwheel 2	VT Rte 105	Sheldon, Vermont
Children Take Wing	Poor Farm Rd	Sheldon, Vermont
Follow the Leader	Poor Farm Rd	Sheldon, Vermont
Grandmother's Garden	Guilnette Rd	Richmond, Vermont
Double Star	Lake Rd	Franklin, Vermont
Sawtooth Star Variation	Maquam Shore Rd	St. Albans, Vermont
Rolling Star	Fourier Lane	Swanton, Vermont
Starr & Lilies	Sheldon Rd	Swanton, Vermont
Compass Star	Church Rd	Swanton, Vermont
Ohio Star	Albans Rd	Swanton, Vermont
Broken Glass	Spring St	Swanton, Vermont
Dove Inside Heart	Pinnacle Meadows	Richford, Vermont
Tulips in Bloom	Sheldon Rd.	Sheldon, Vermont
Winter Stars	North Ave	Richford, Vermont
Dachshunds	Grange Hall Rd	Enosburg. Vermont
Sister's Choice	VT Rte 105	Sheldon, Vermont
Wheels	Richard Rd	Franklin, Vermont

Barn Quilt Prosperity
Franklin County Vermont

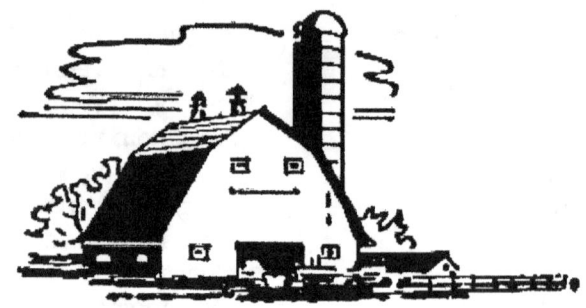

Barn Quilt Location
Main St
Montgomery, Vermont

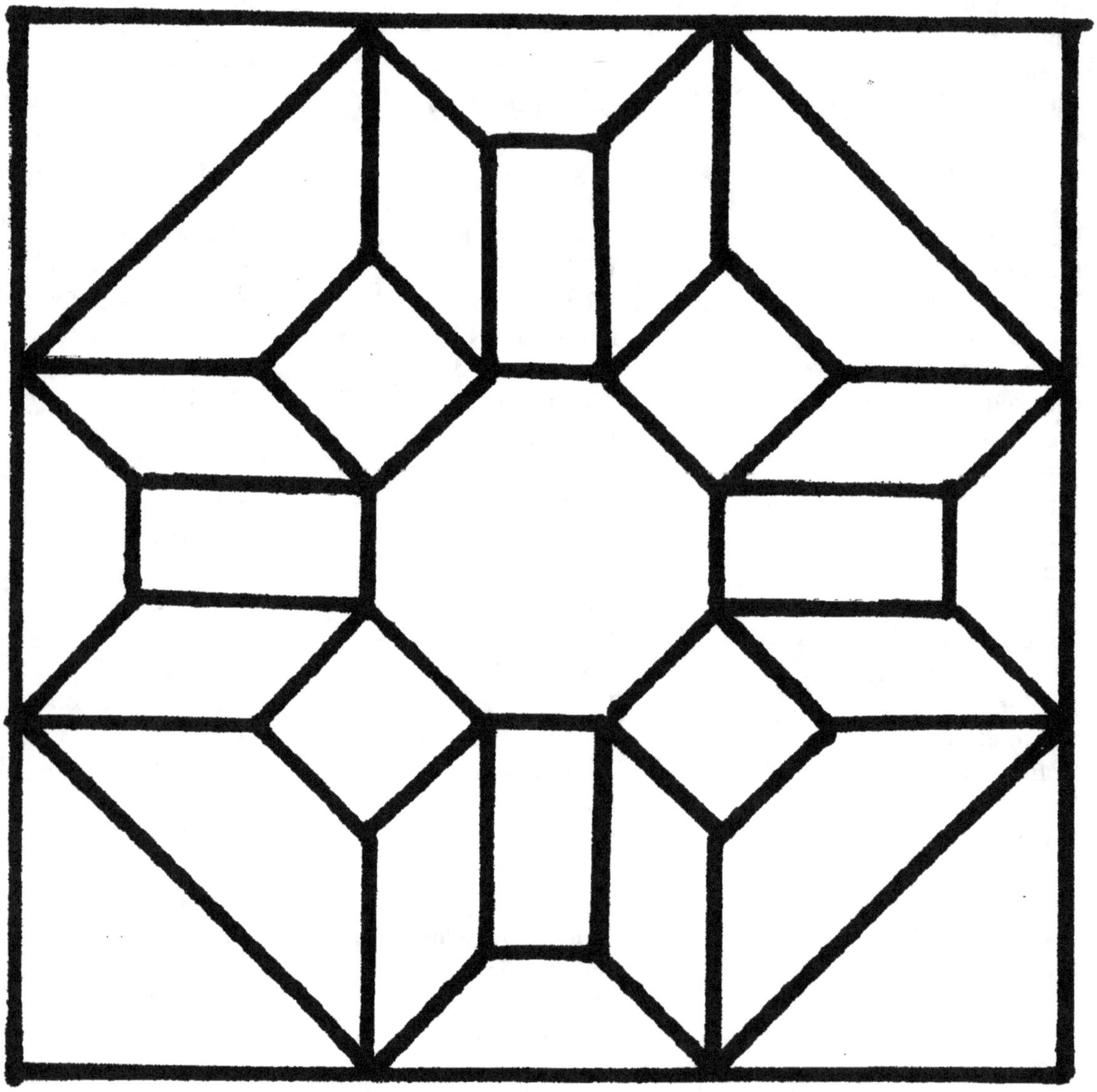

Franklin County Barn Quilt Prosperity

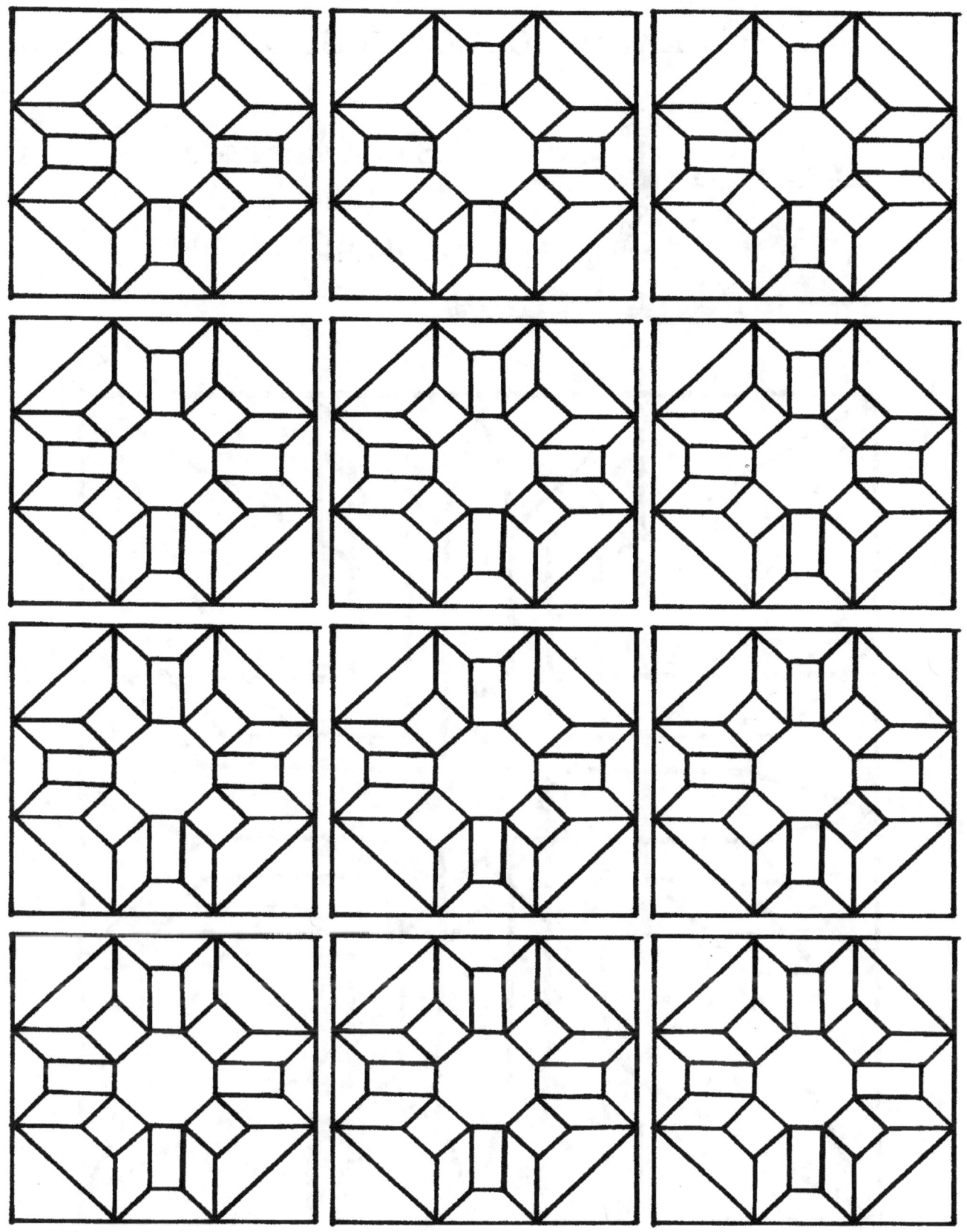

Barn Quilt The Star Explosion
Franklin County Vermont

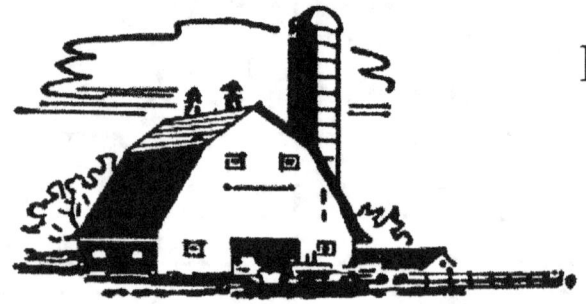

Barn Quilt Location
Bullock Rd
Georgia, Vermont

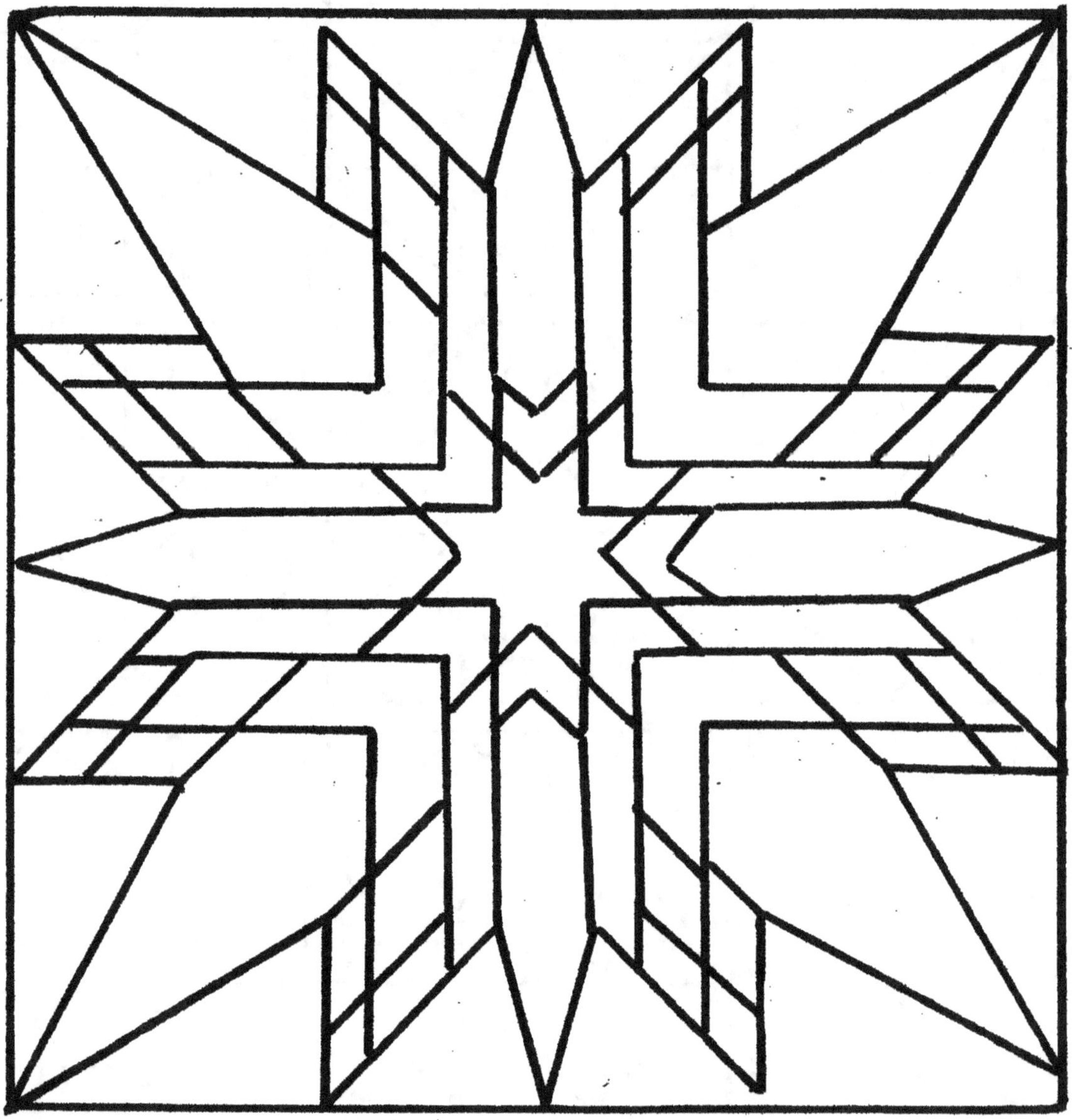

Franklin County Barn Quilt Star Explosion

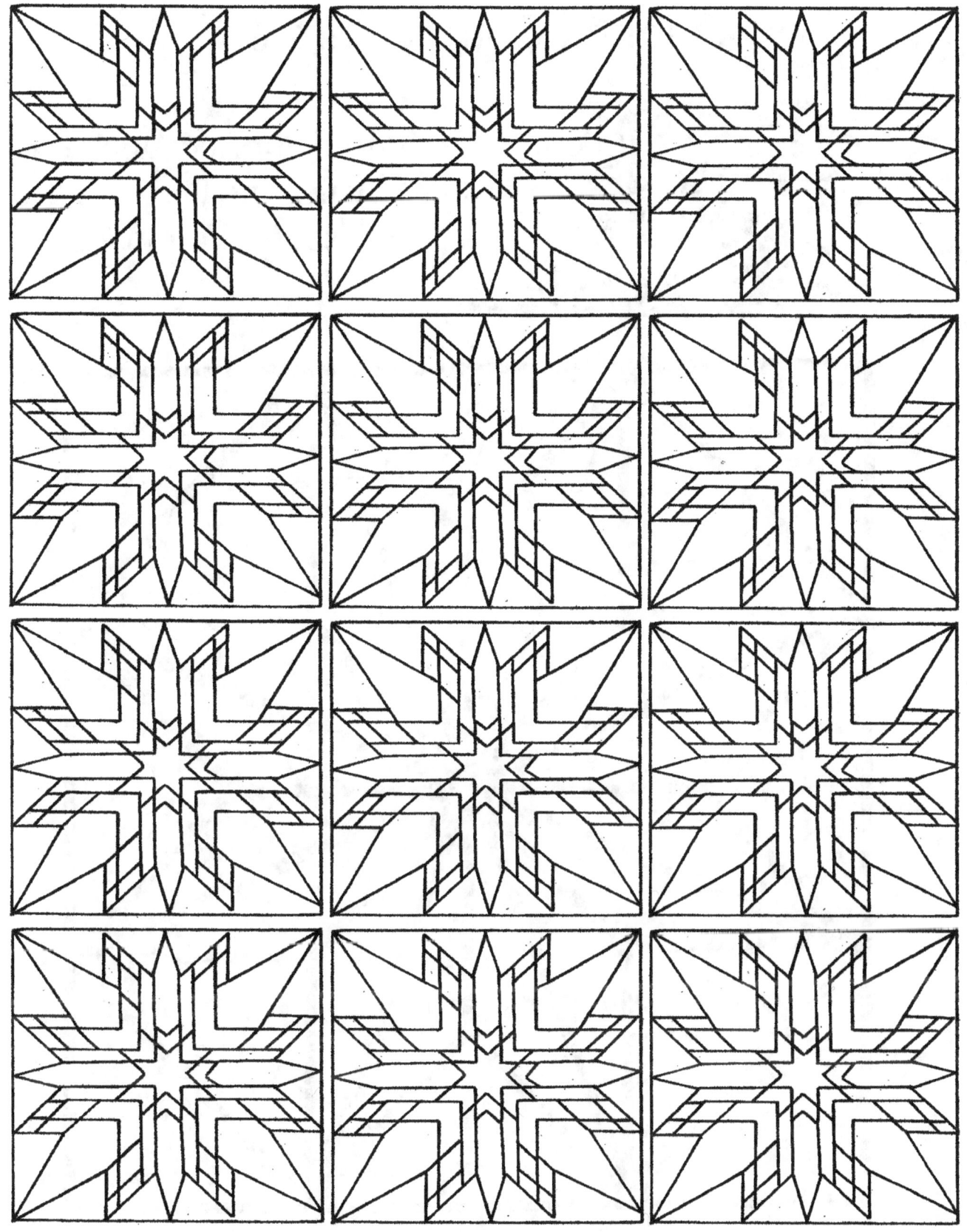

Barn Quilt Mariner's Star
Franklin County Vermont

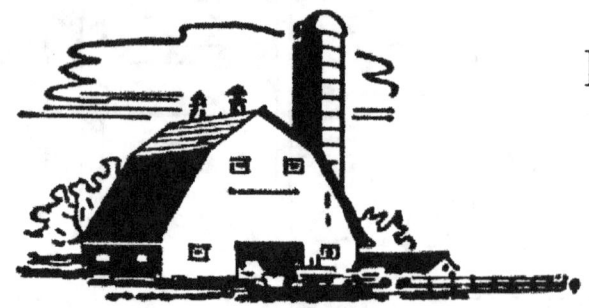

Barn Quilt Location
Valentine Dr
Enosburg, Vermont

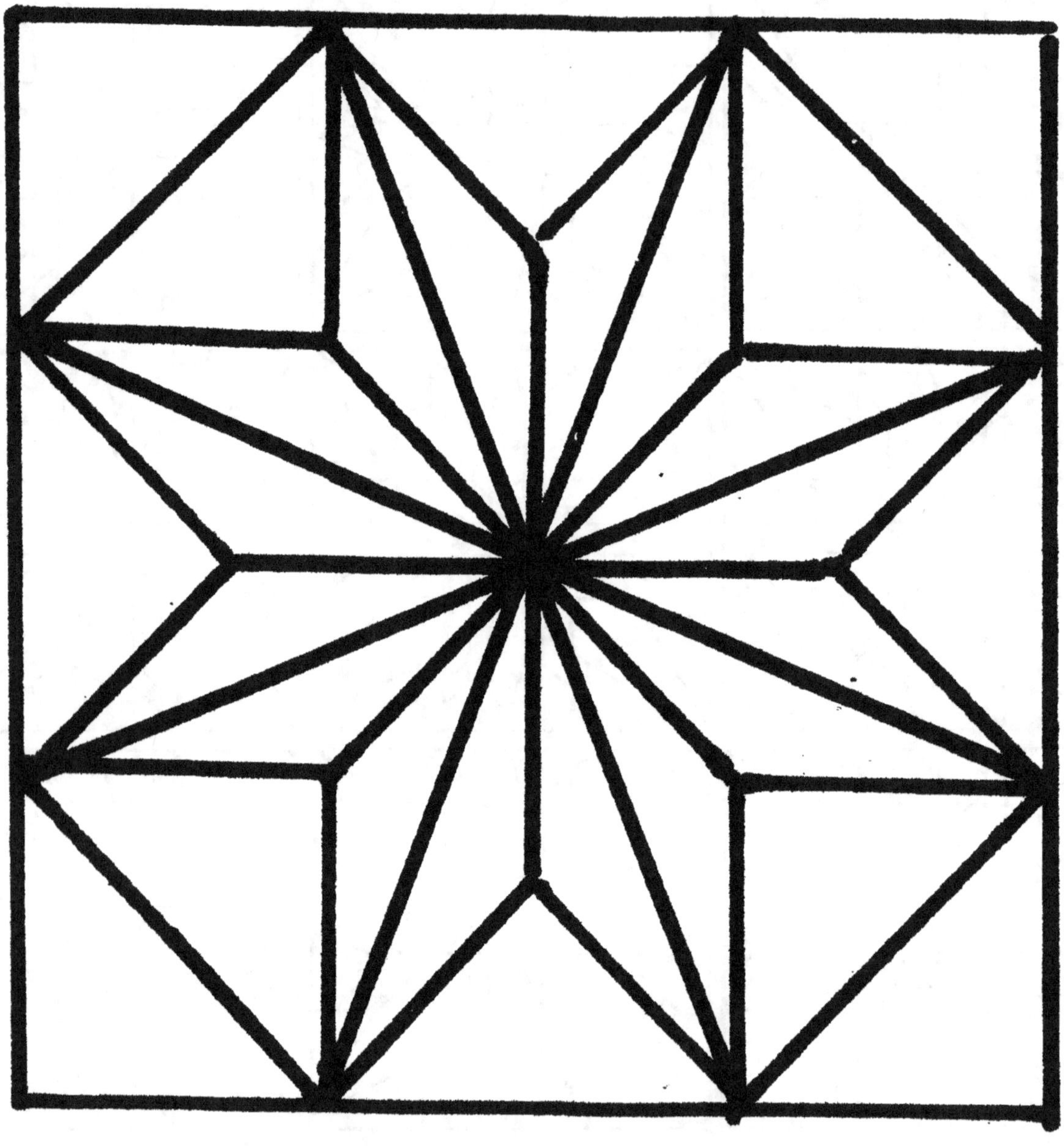

Franklin County Barn Quilt Mariner's Star

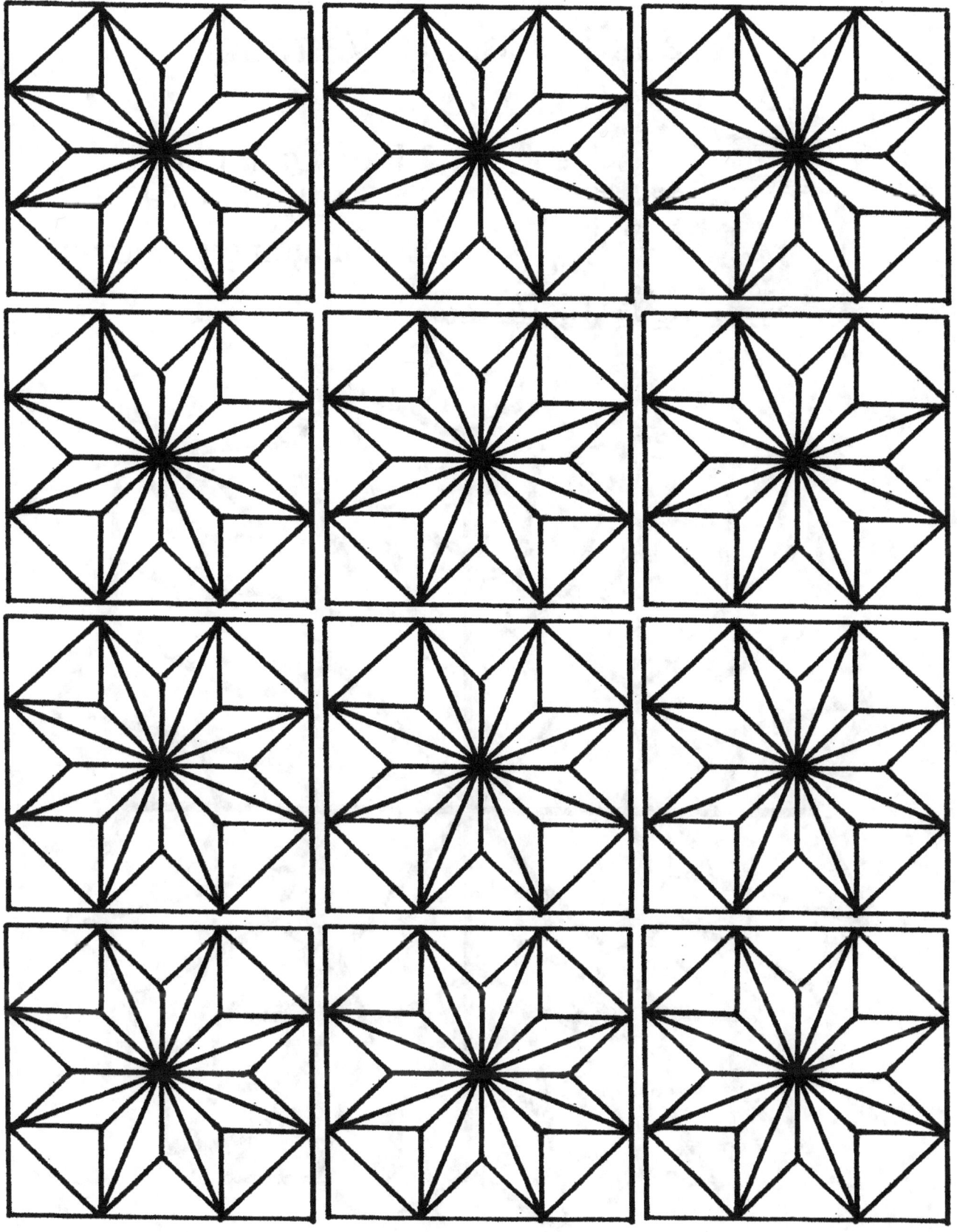

Barn Quilt Bicycle Wheel
Franklin County Vermont

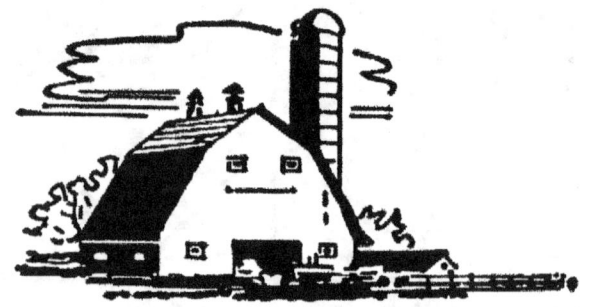

Barn Quilt Location
Hill West Rd
Montgomery, Vermont

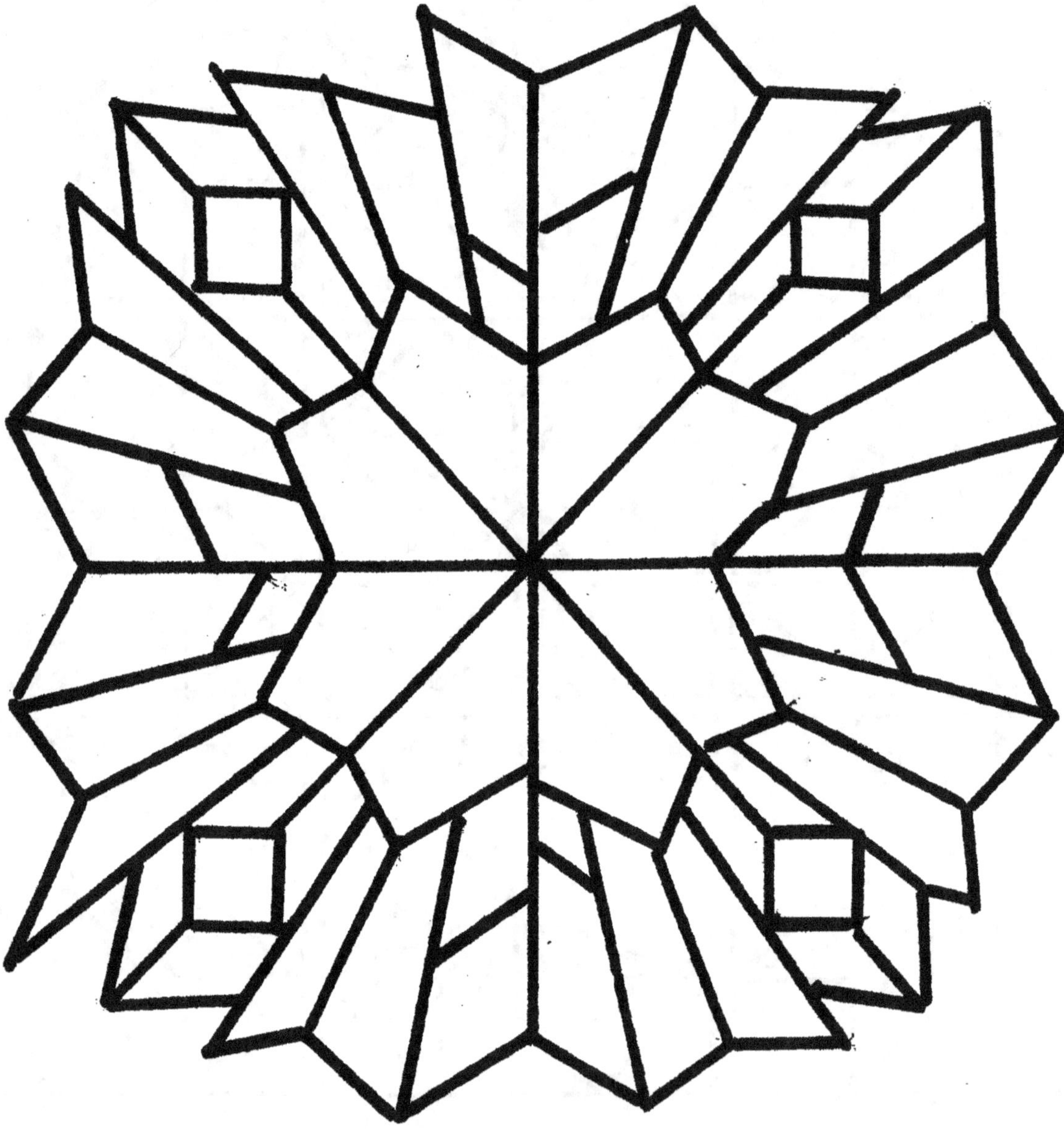

Franklin County Barn Quilt Bicycle Wheel

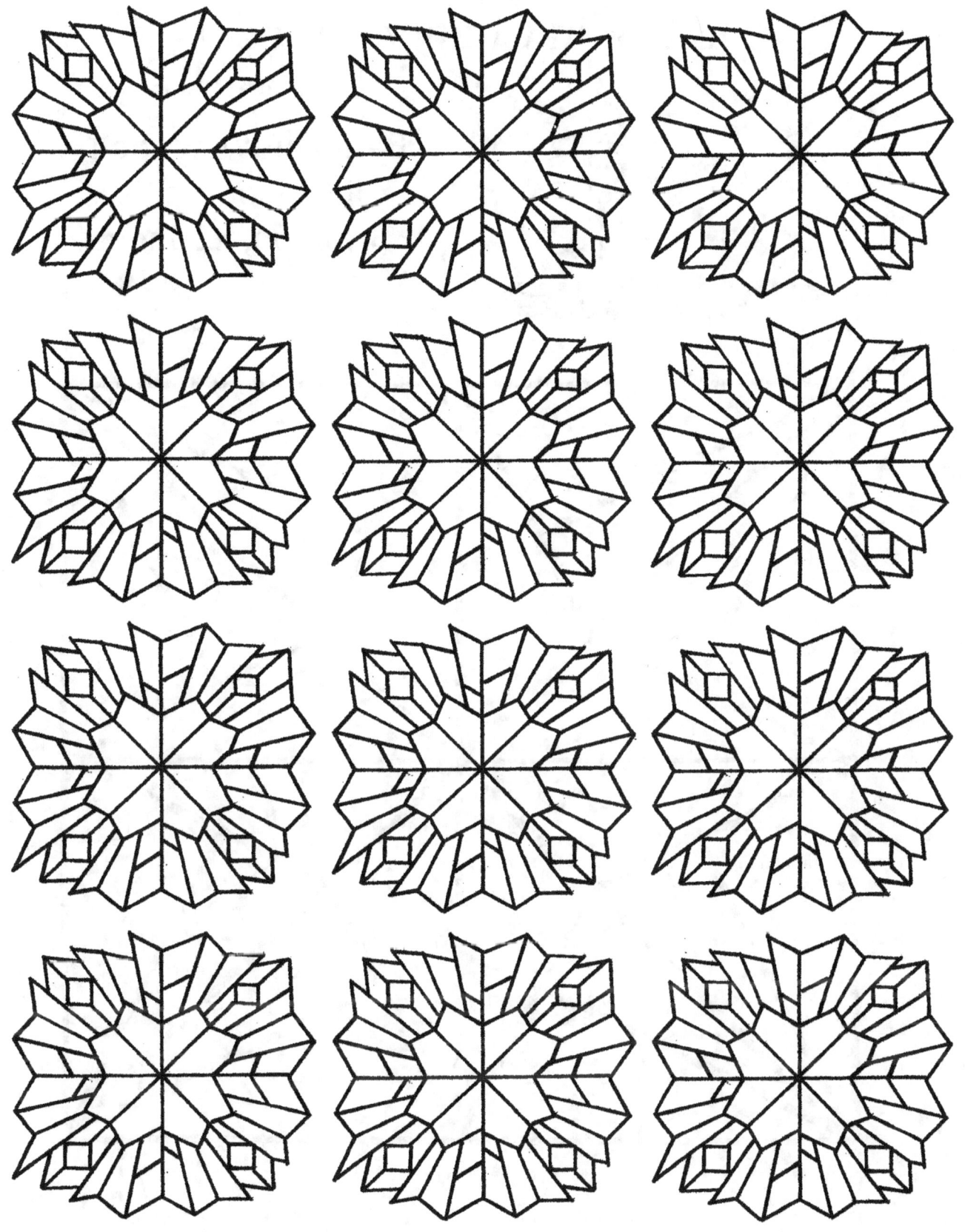

Barn Quilt Shadow Star
Franklin County Vermont

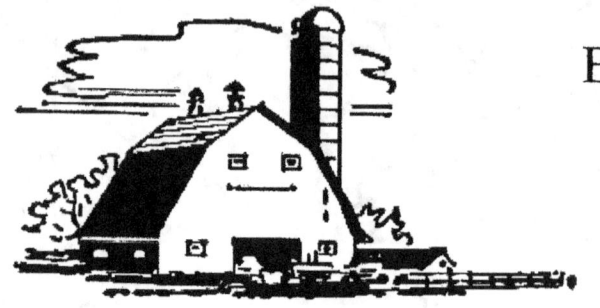

Barn Quilt Location
Little County Rd
Swanton, Vermont

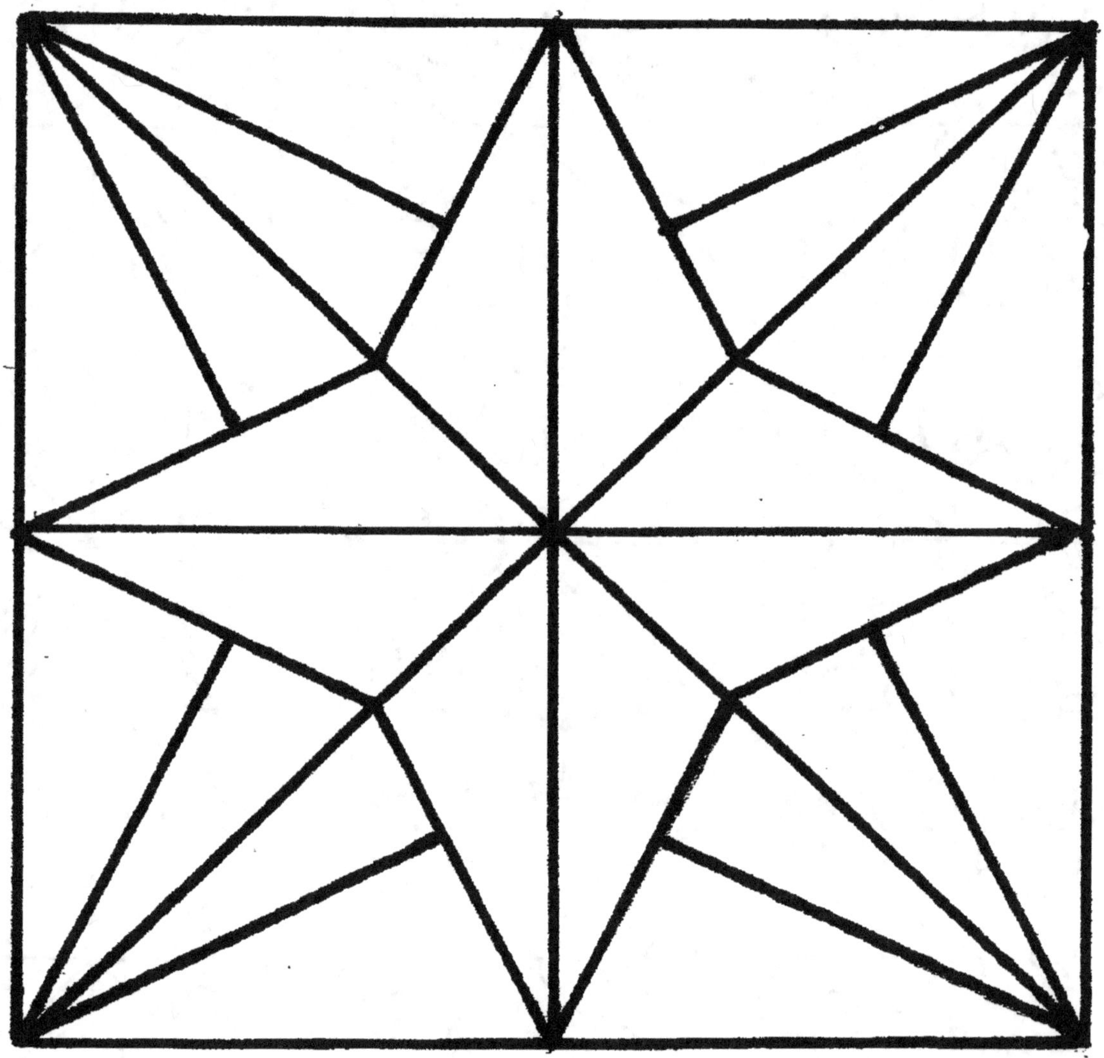

Franklin County Barn Quilt Shadow Star

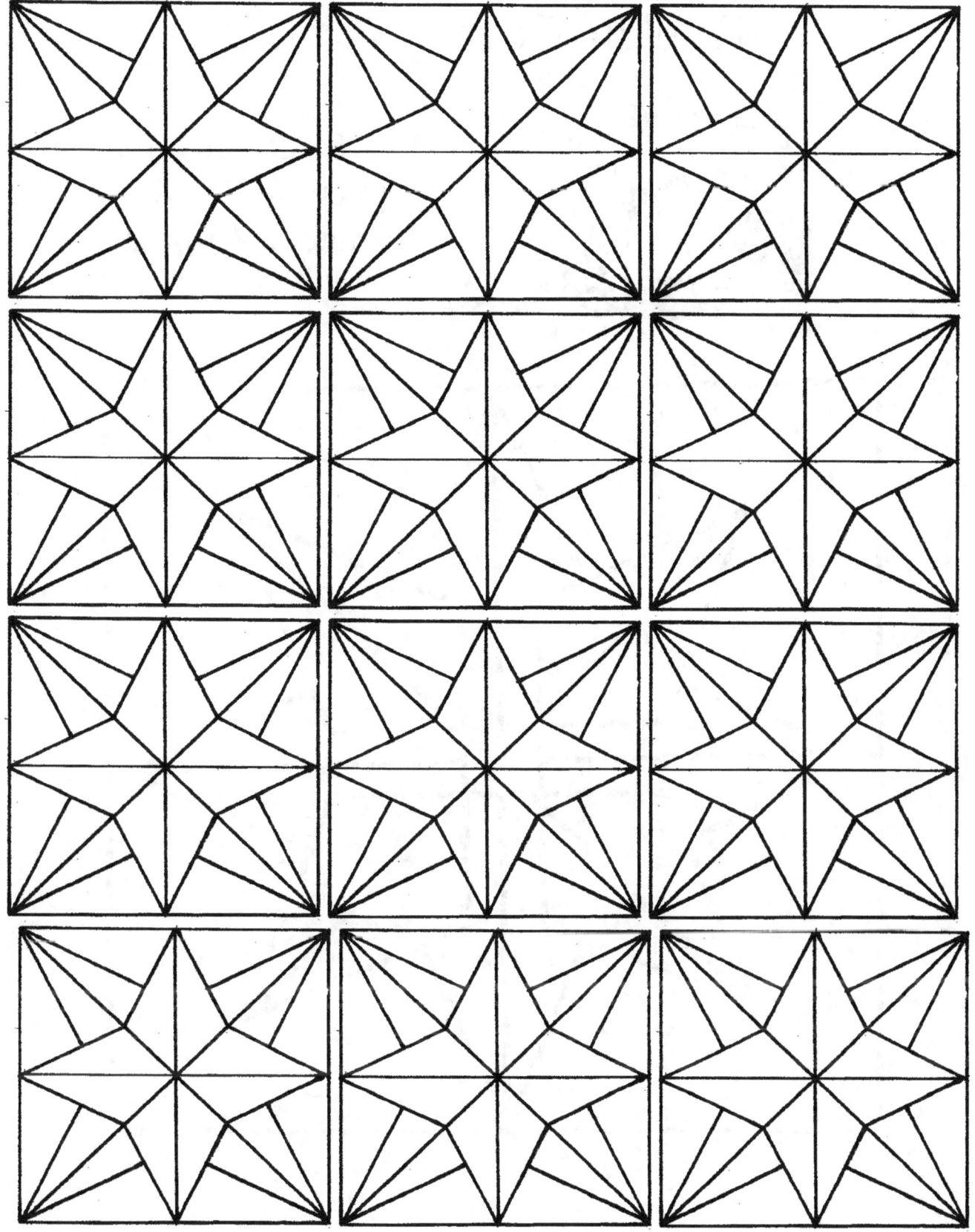

Barn Quilt Star Variation
Franklin County Vermont

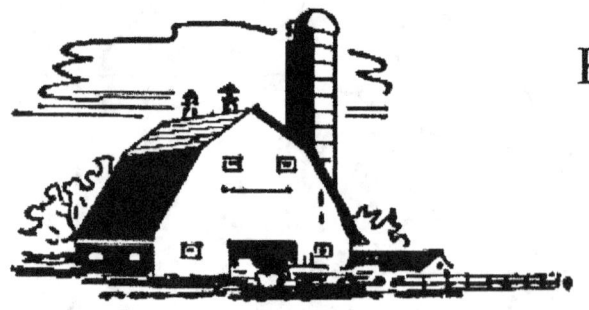

Barn Quilt Location
Upper Welden Rd
Swanton, Vermont

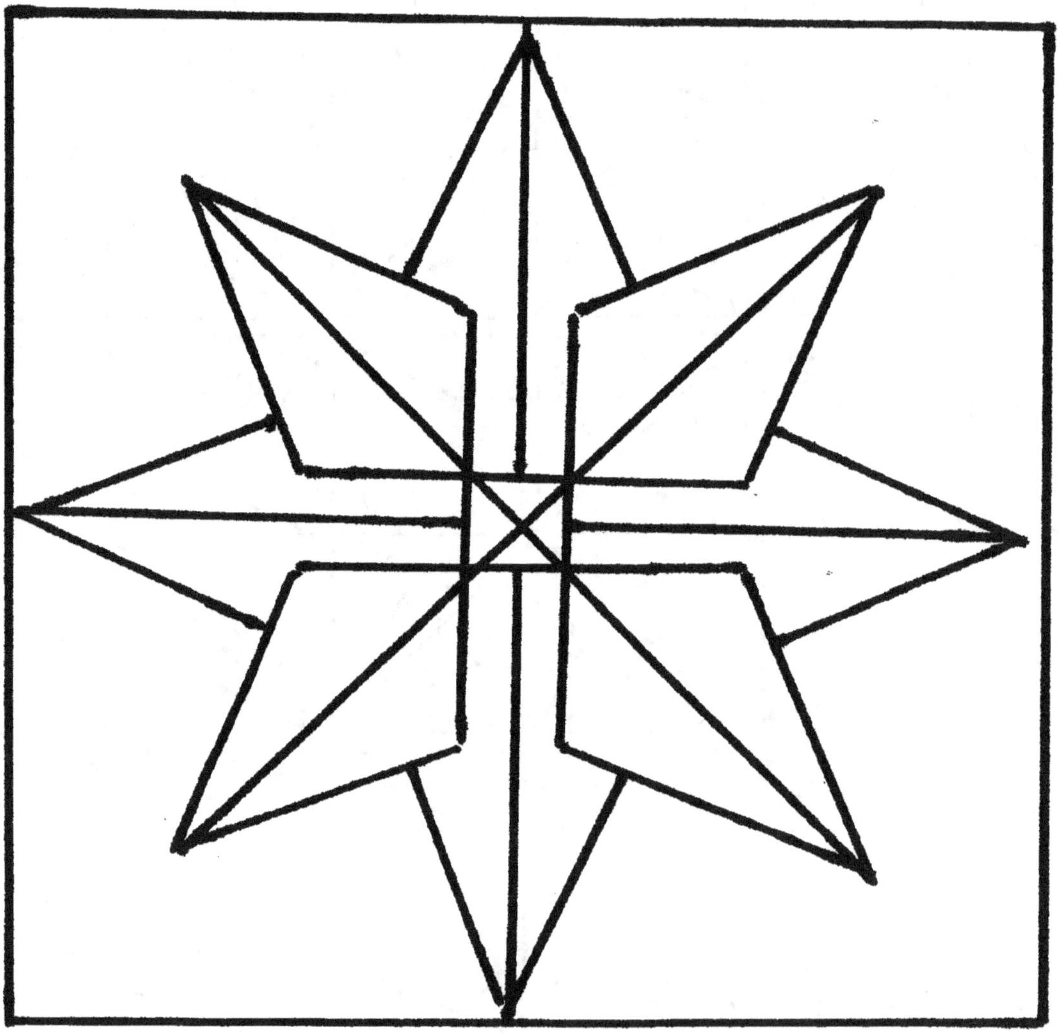

Franklin County Barn Quilt Star Variation

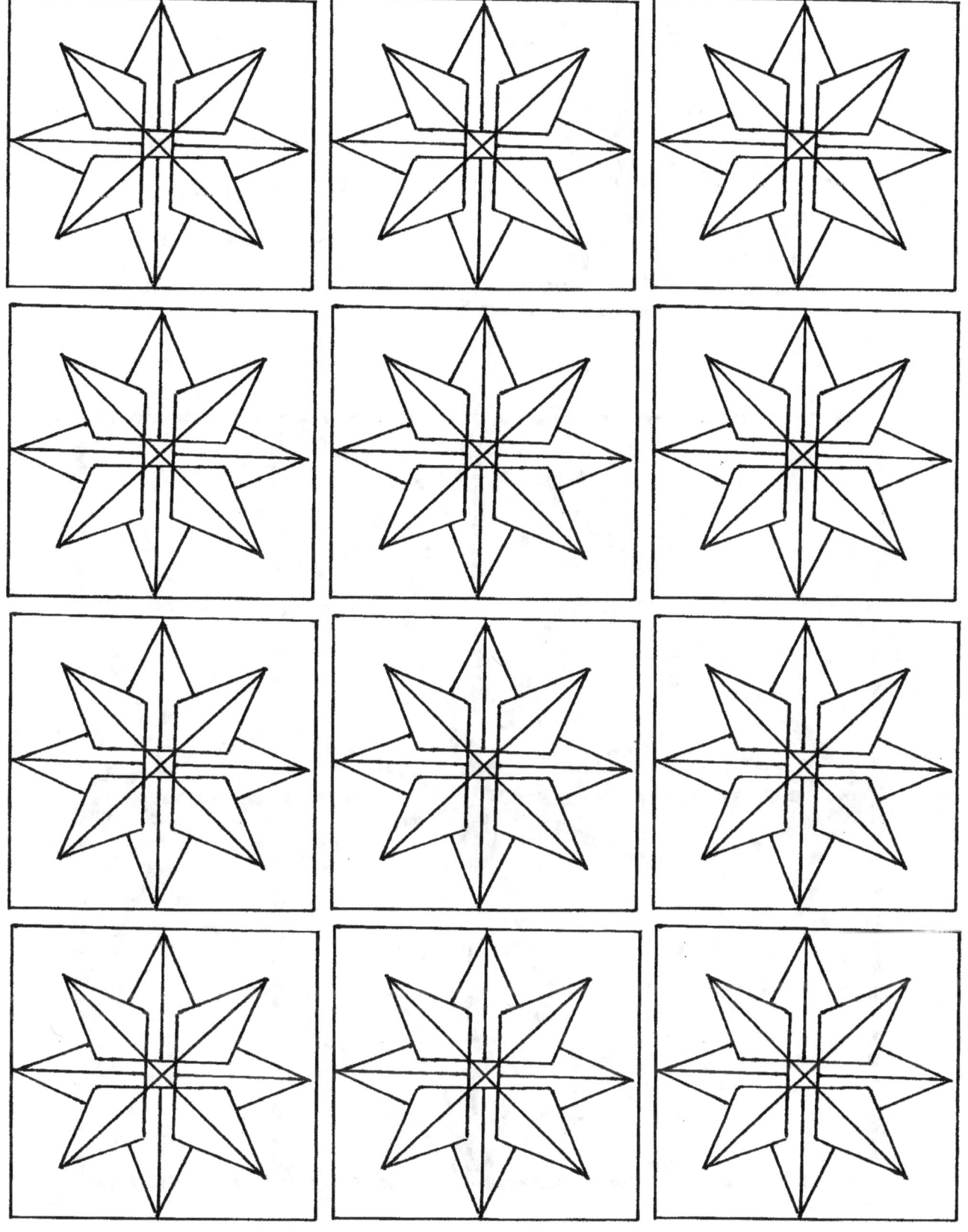

Barn Quilt Complex Star
Franklin County Vermont

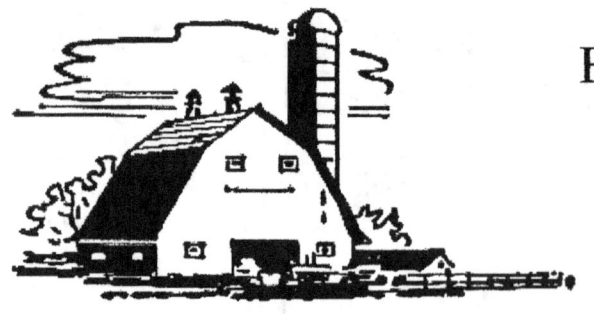

Barn Quilt Location
Sheldon Rd
Swanton, Vermont

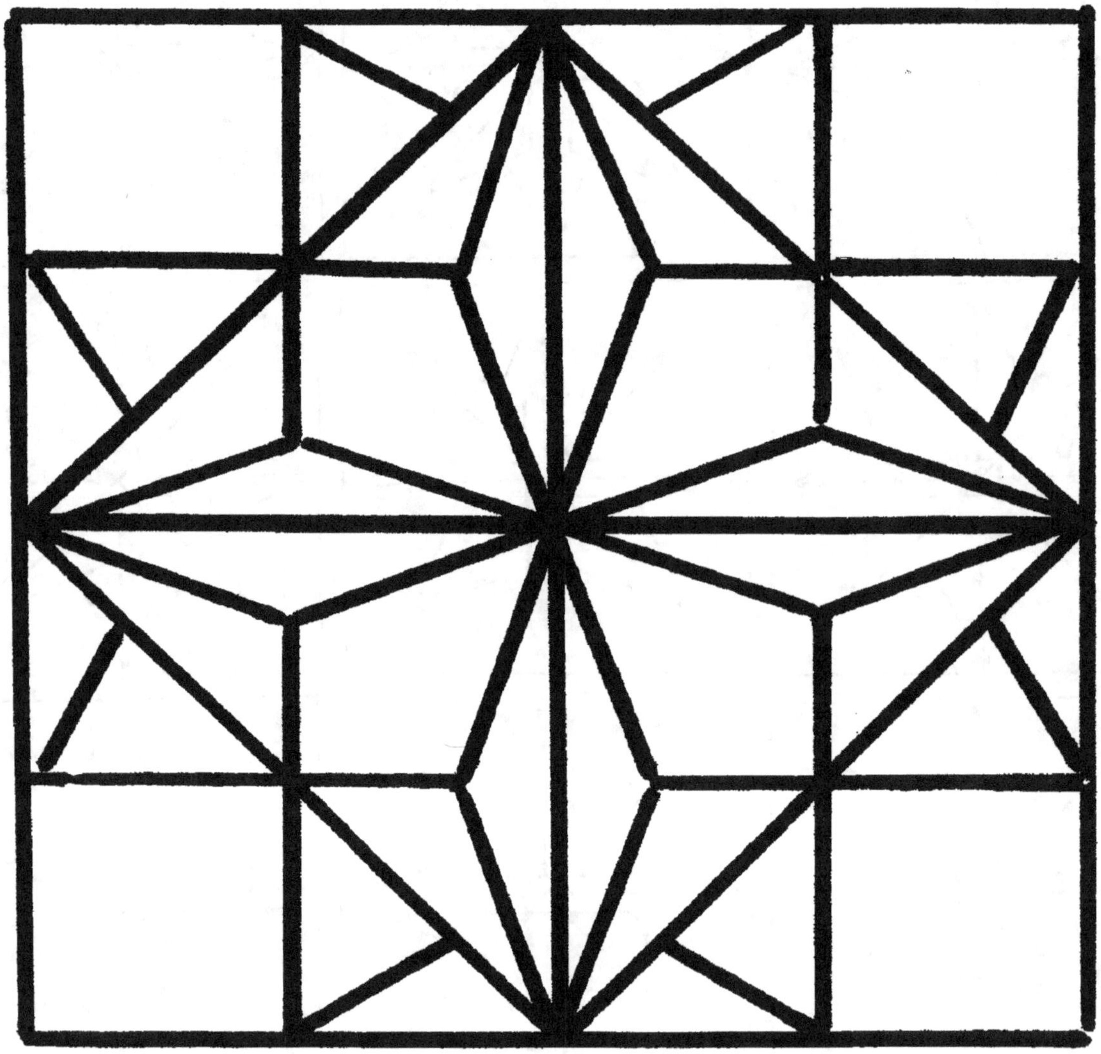

Franklin County Barn Quilt Complex Star

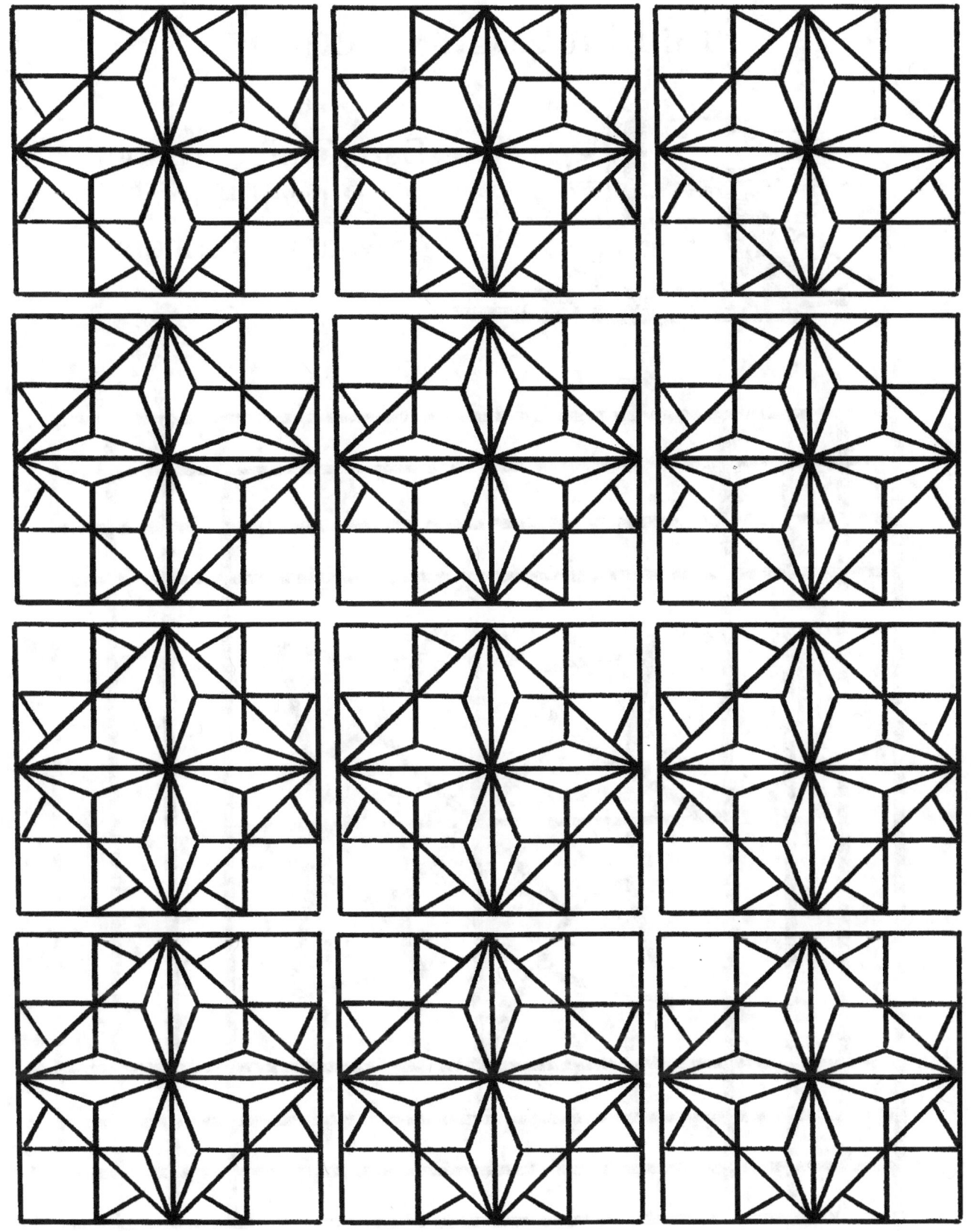

Barn Quilt Dean's Delight
Franklin County Vermont

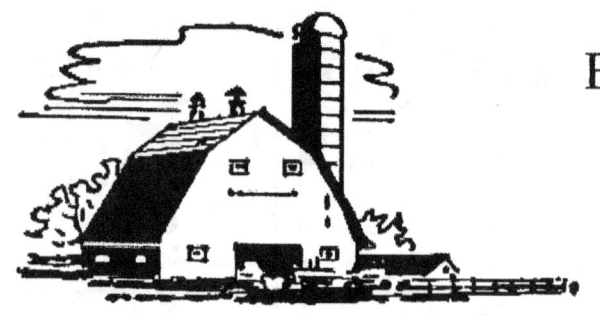

Barn Quilt Location
Russell Rd
Swanton, Vermont

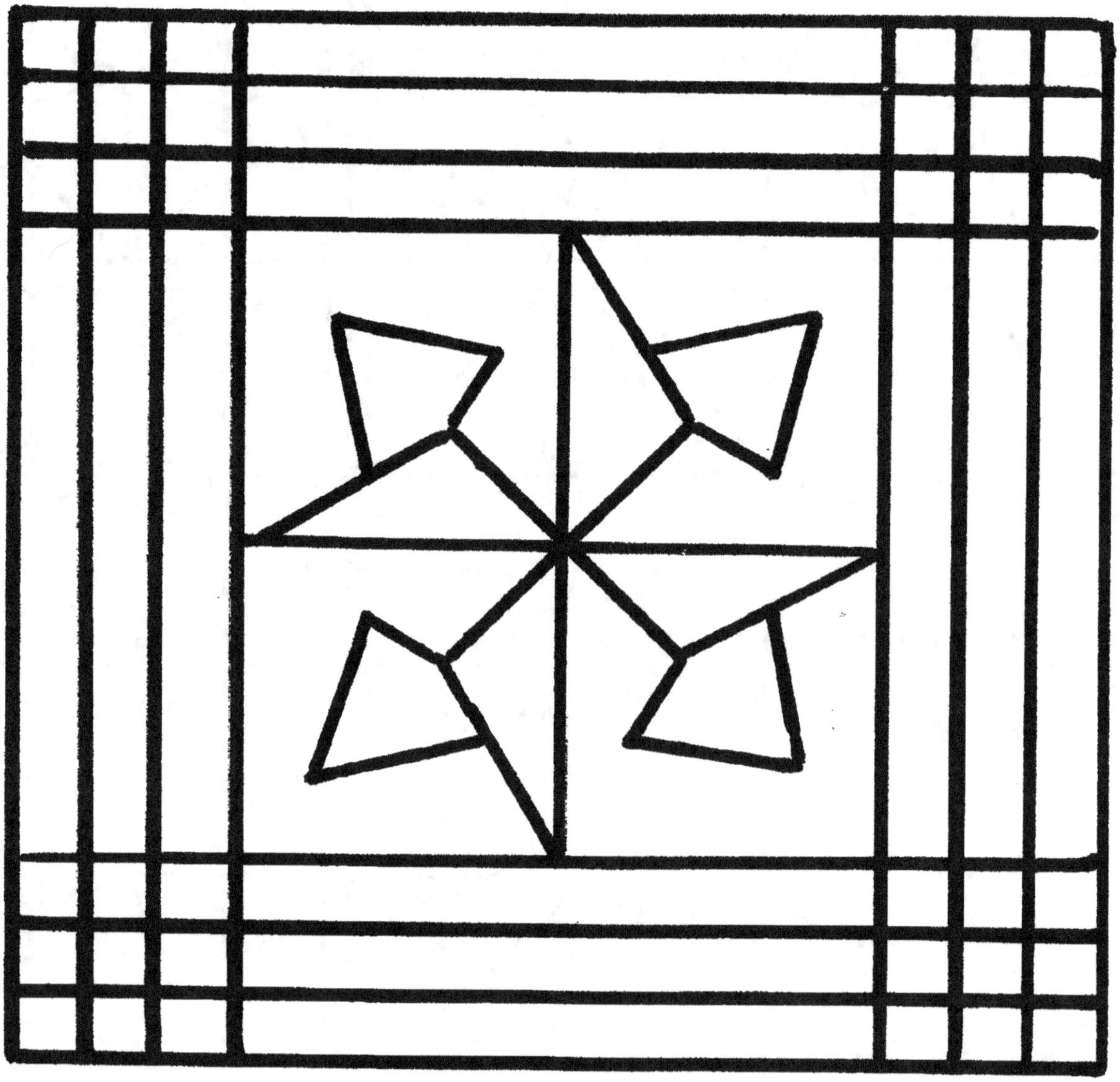

Franklin County Barn Quilt Dean's Delight

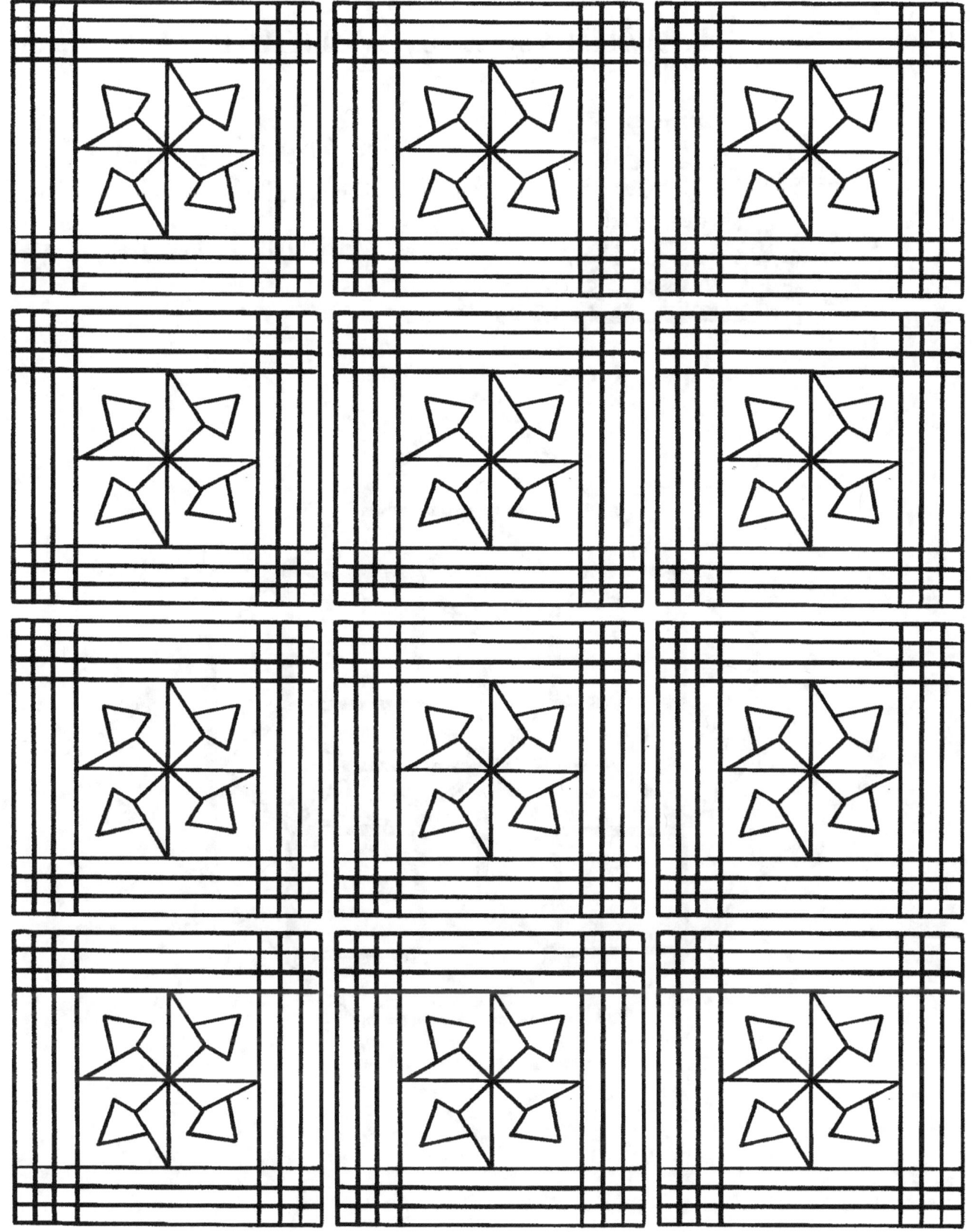

Barn Quilt Cross & Crown
Franklin County Vermont

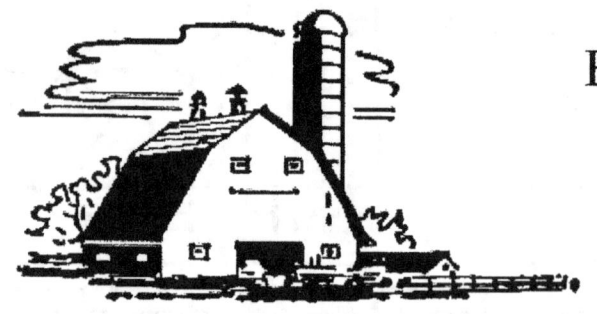

Barn Quilt Location
Brooklyn St
Swanton, Vermont

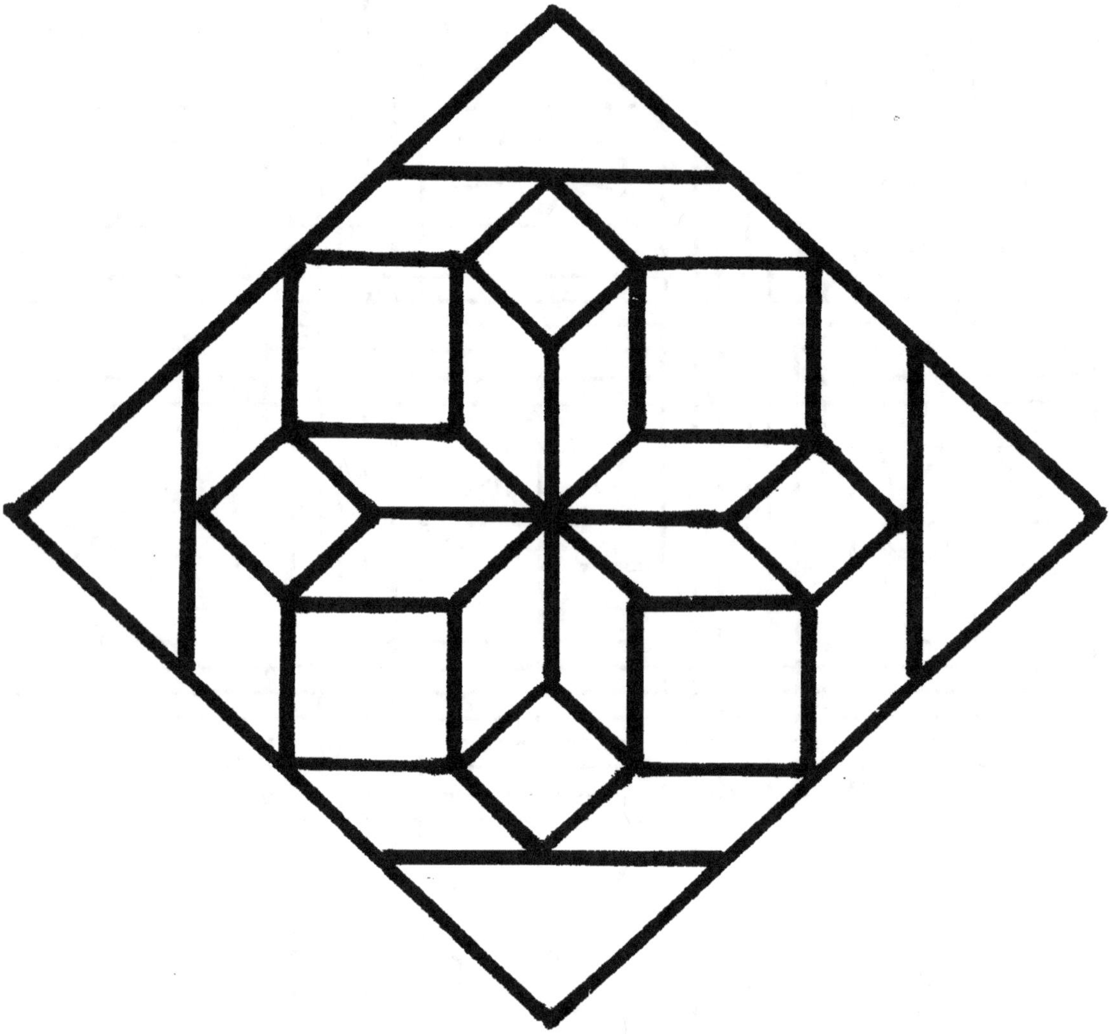

Franklin County Barn Quilt Cross & Crown

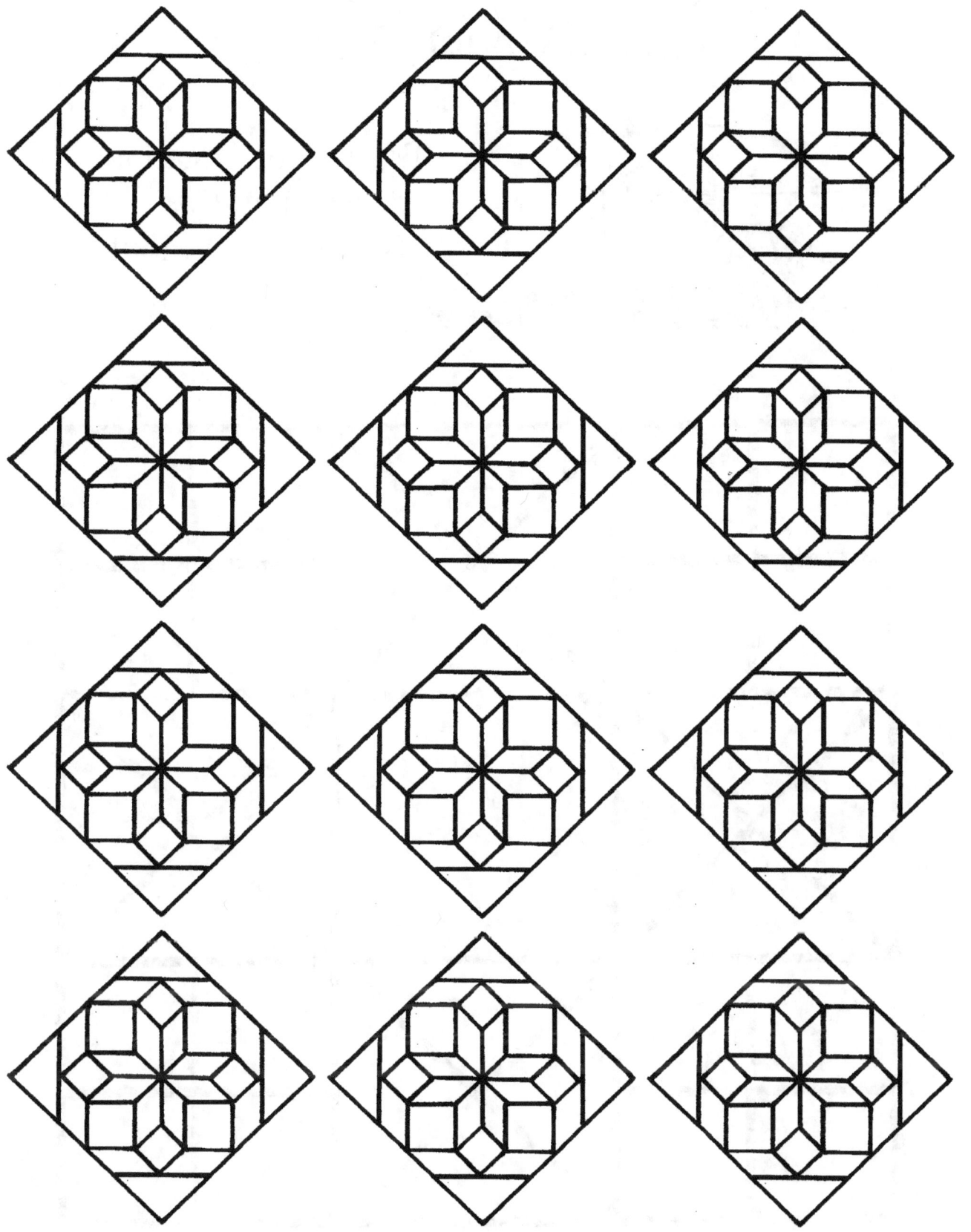

Barn Quilt Garden Patch Star
Franklin County Vermont

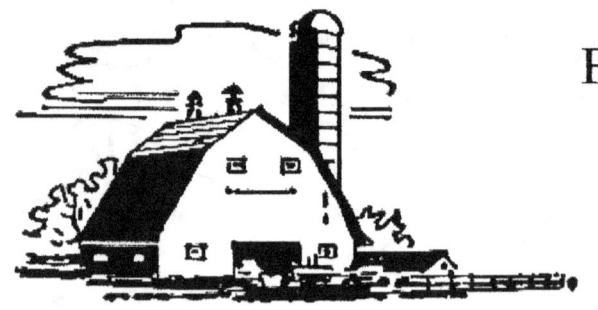

Barn Quilt Location
Bushley Rd
Swanton, Vermont

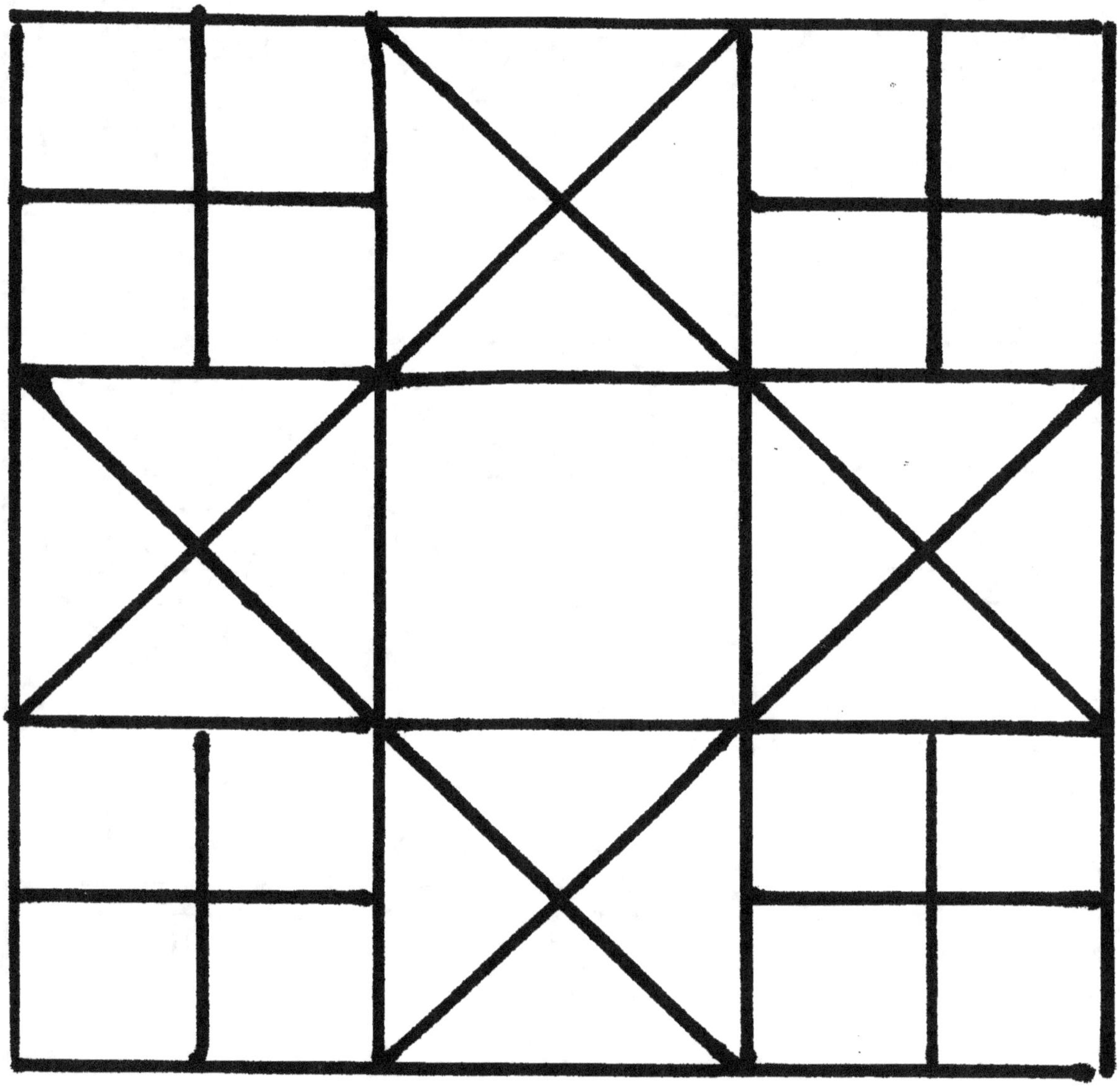

Franklin County Barn Quilt Garden Patch Star

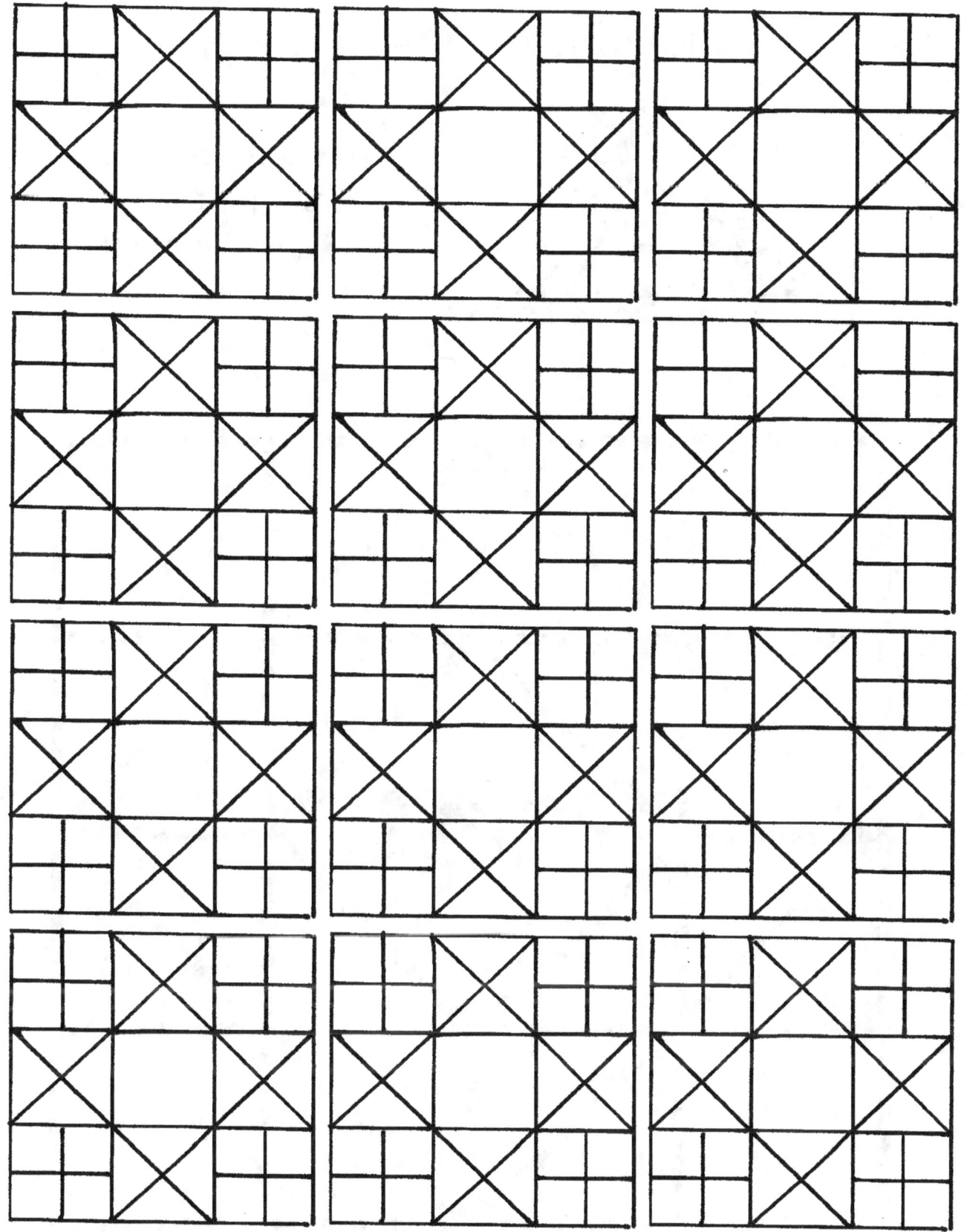

Barn Quilt Cow in Square
Franklin County Vermont

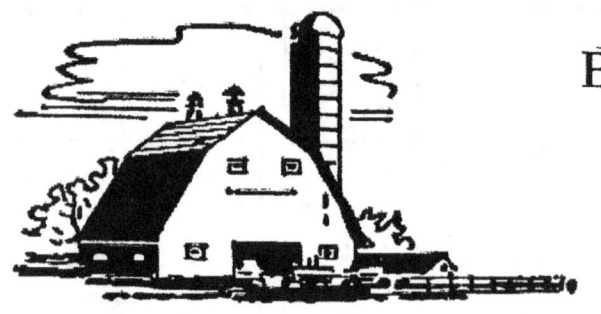

Barn Quilt Location
Spring St
Swanton, Vermont

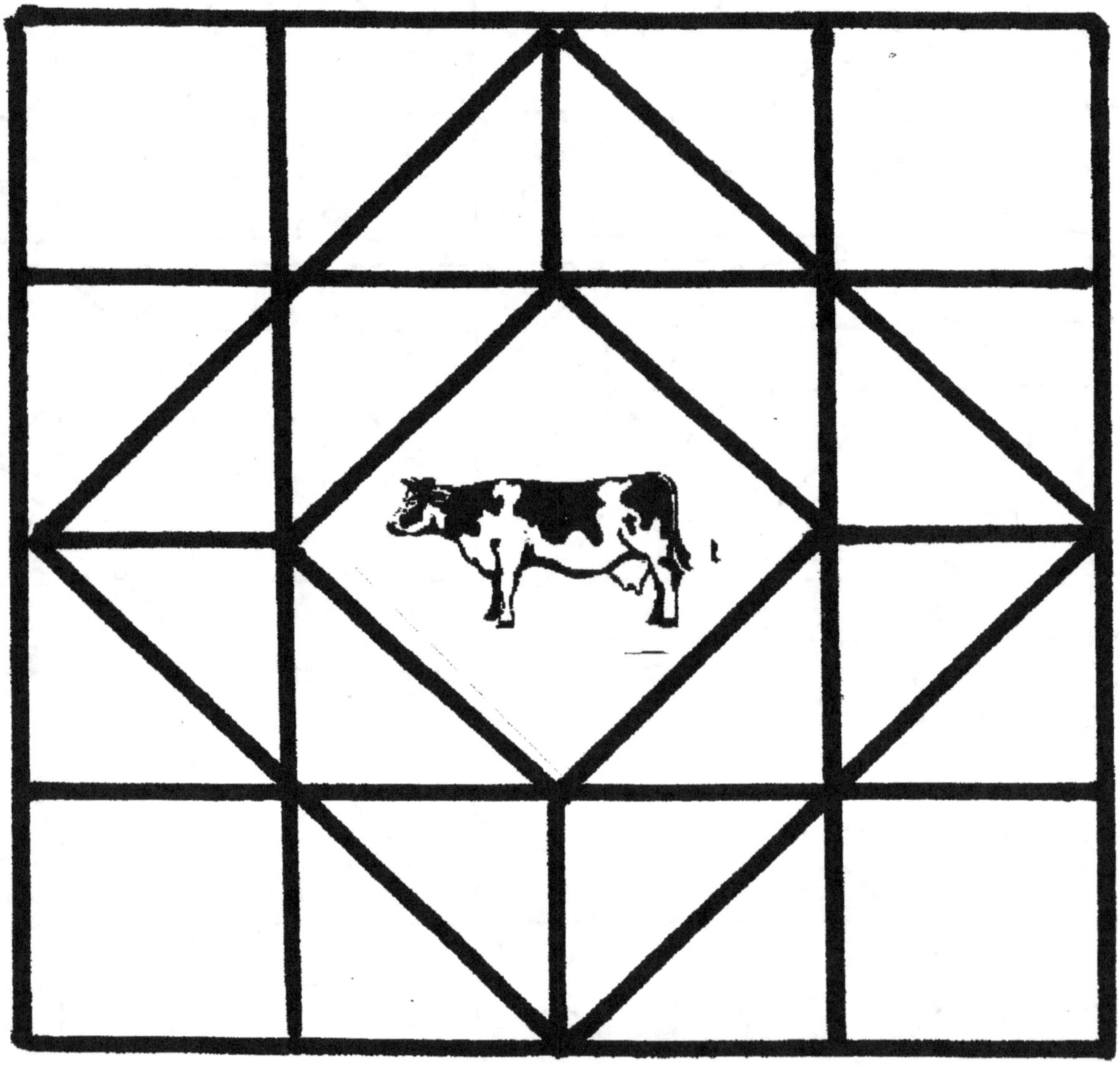

Franklin County Barn Quilt Cow in Square

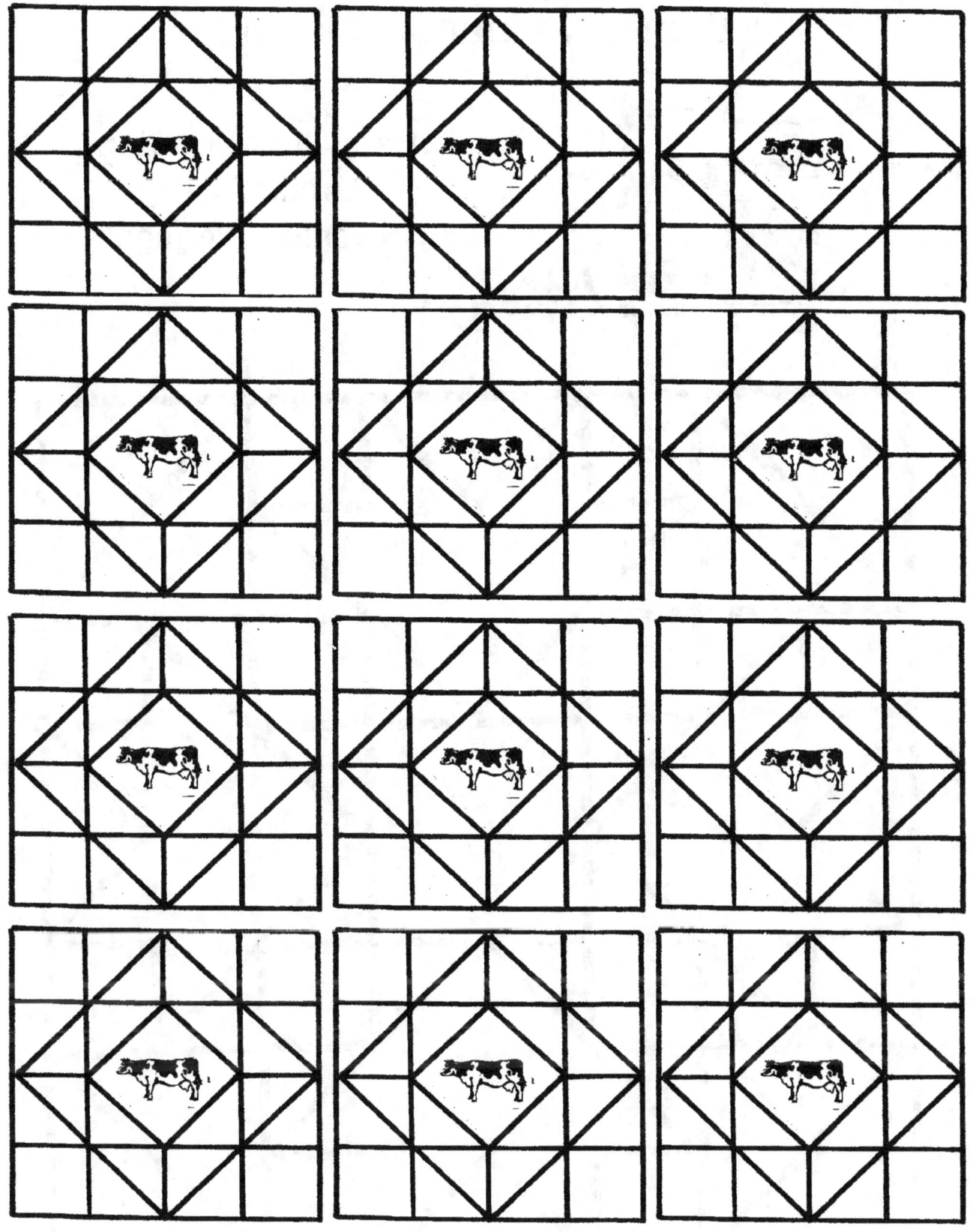

Barn Quilt Crowfeet
Franklin County Vermont

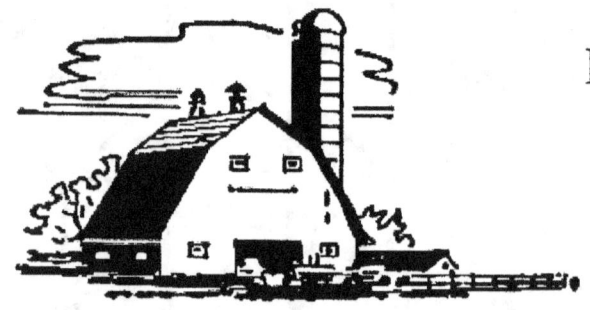

Barn Quilt Location
Grand Ave
Swanton, Vermont

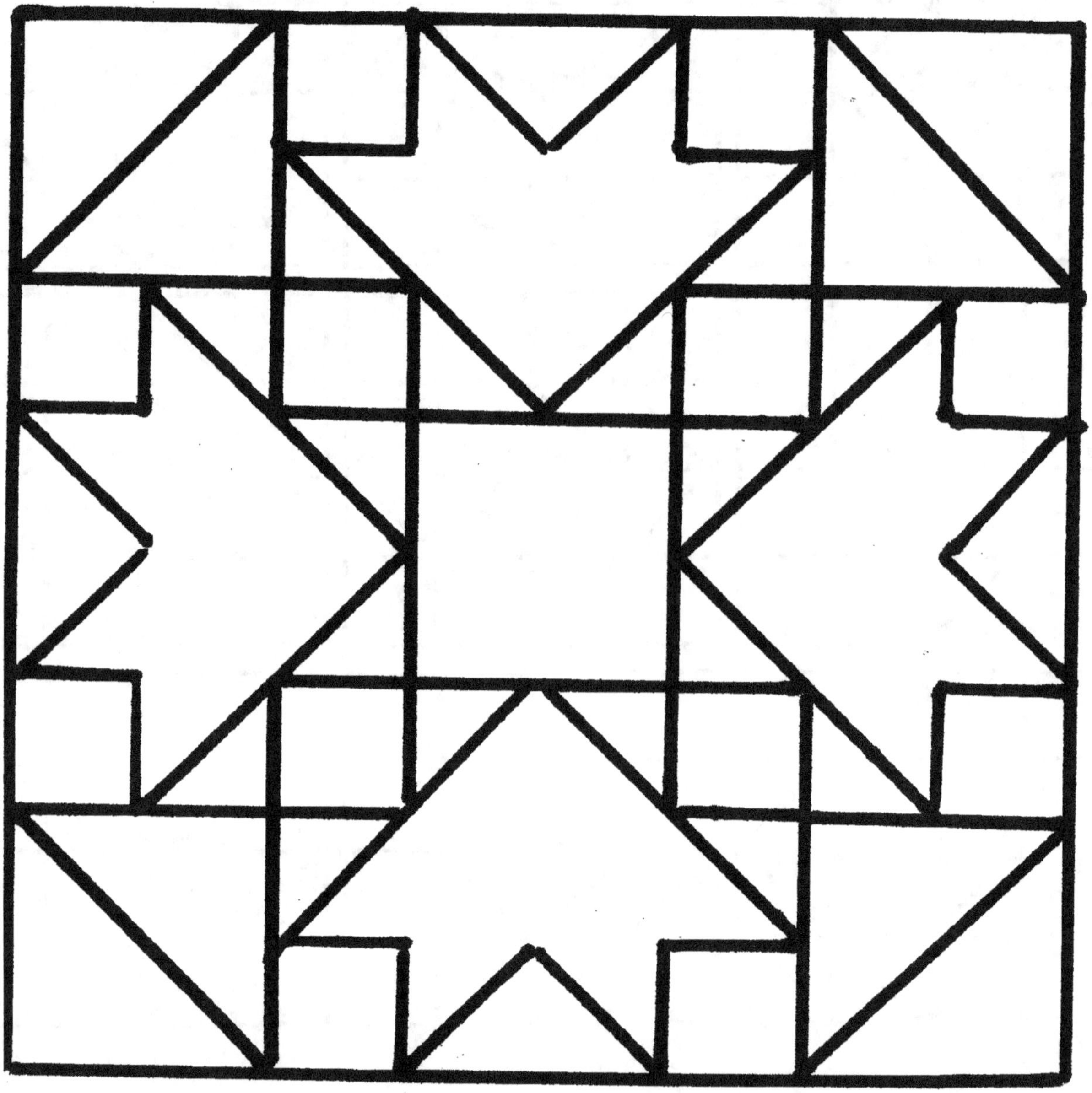

Franklin County Barn Quilt Crowfeet

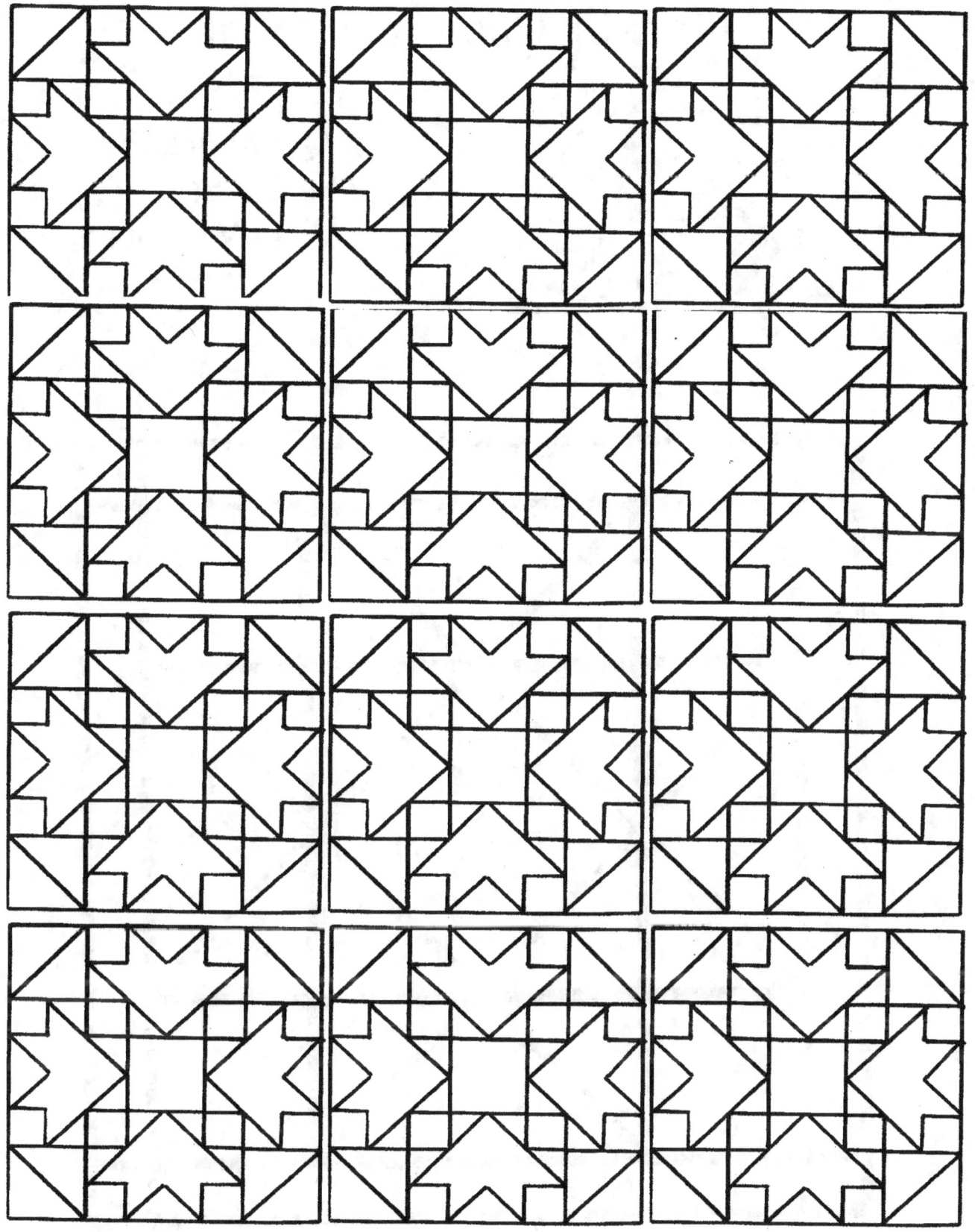

Barn Quilt MY T-Fine
Franklin County Vermont

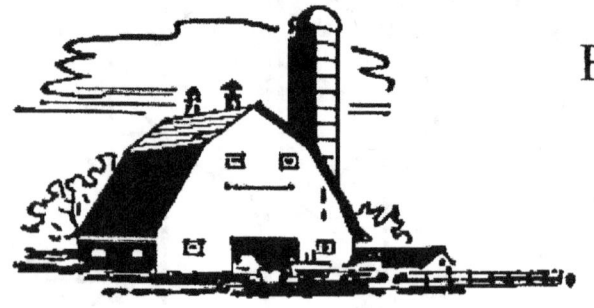

Barn Quilt Location
Spring St
Swanton, Vermont

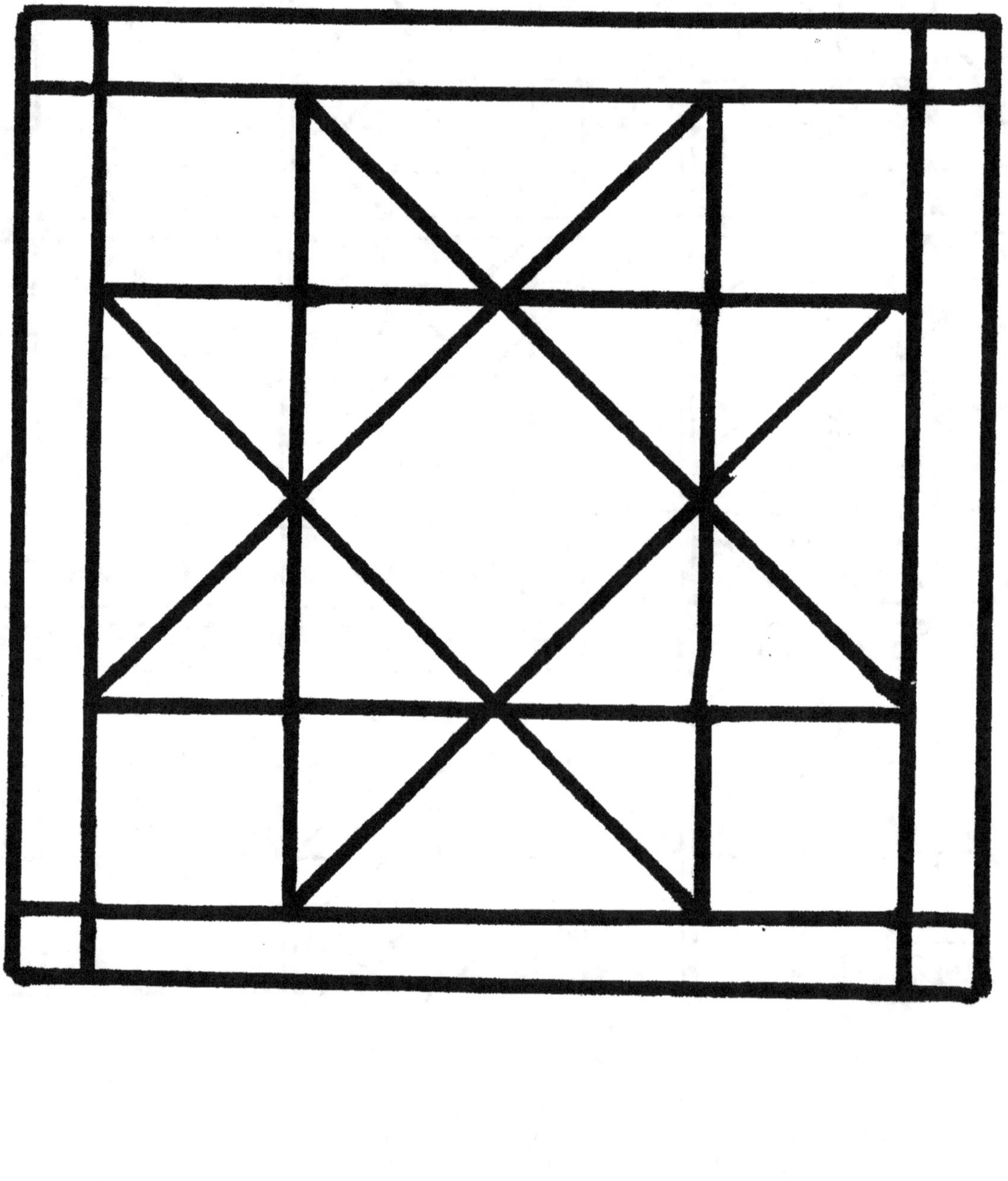

Franklin County Barn Quilt My T-Fine

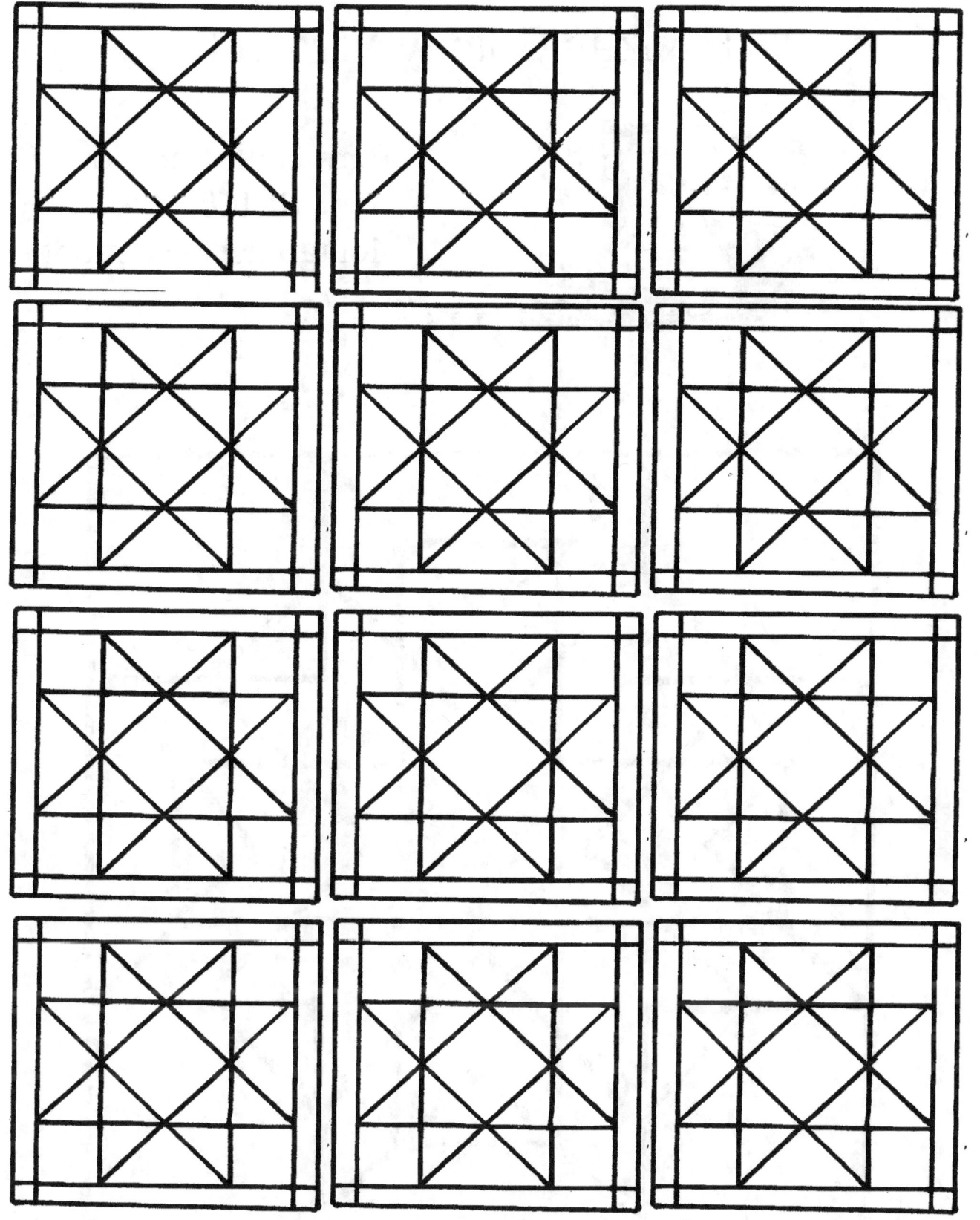

Barn Quilt Lone Star Variation
Franklin County Vermont

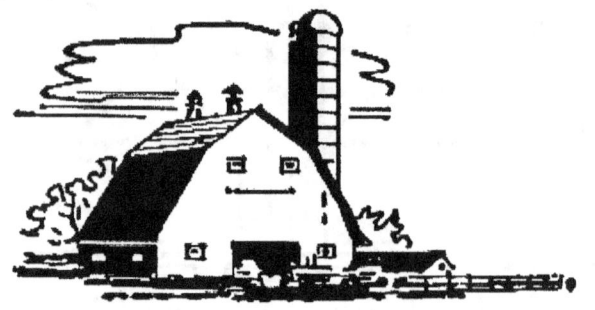

Barn Quilt Location
Rt 118
Montgomery, Vermont

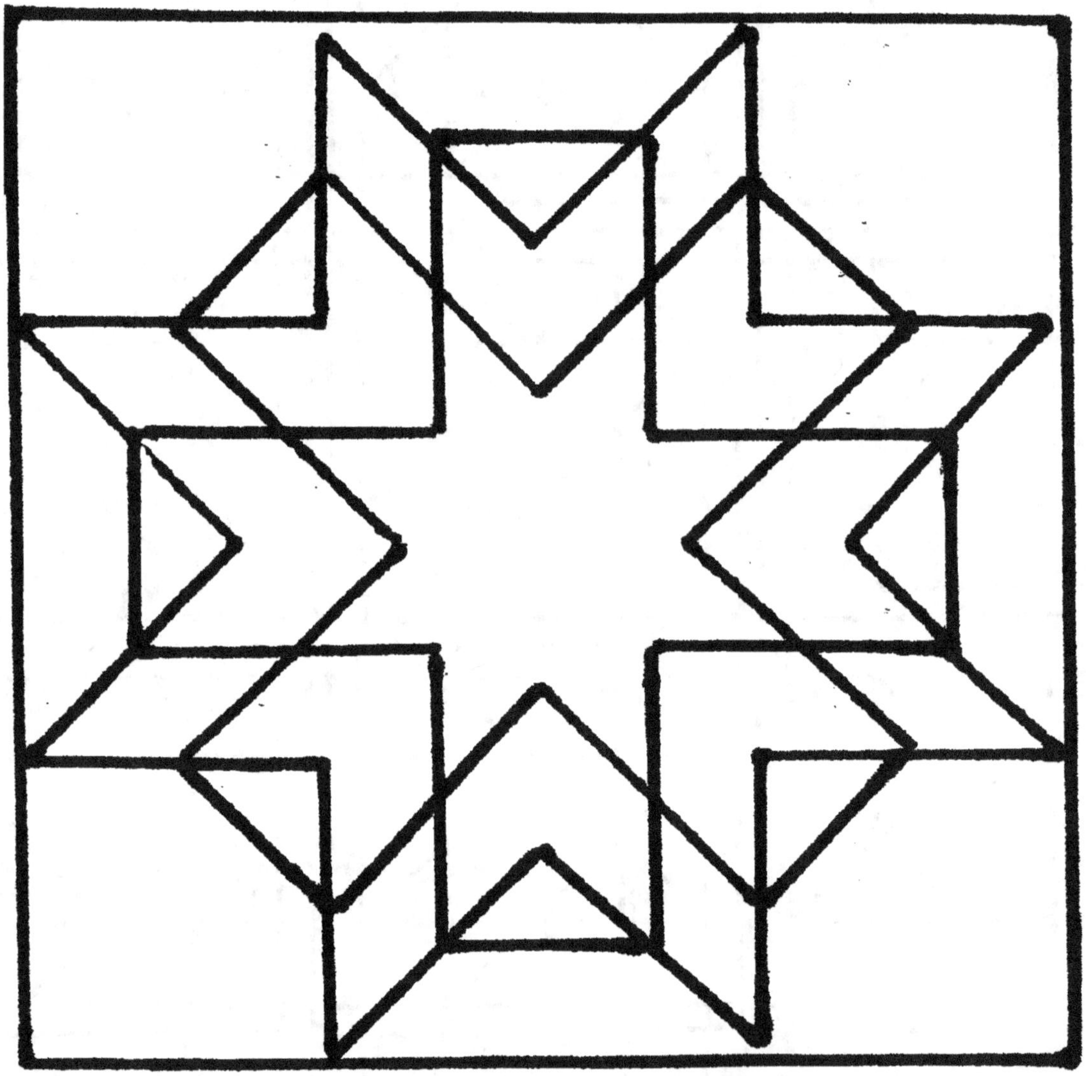

Franklin County Barn Quilt Lone Star

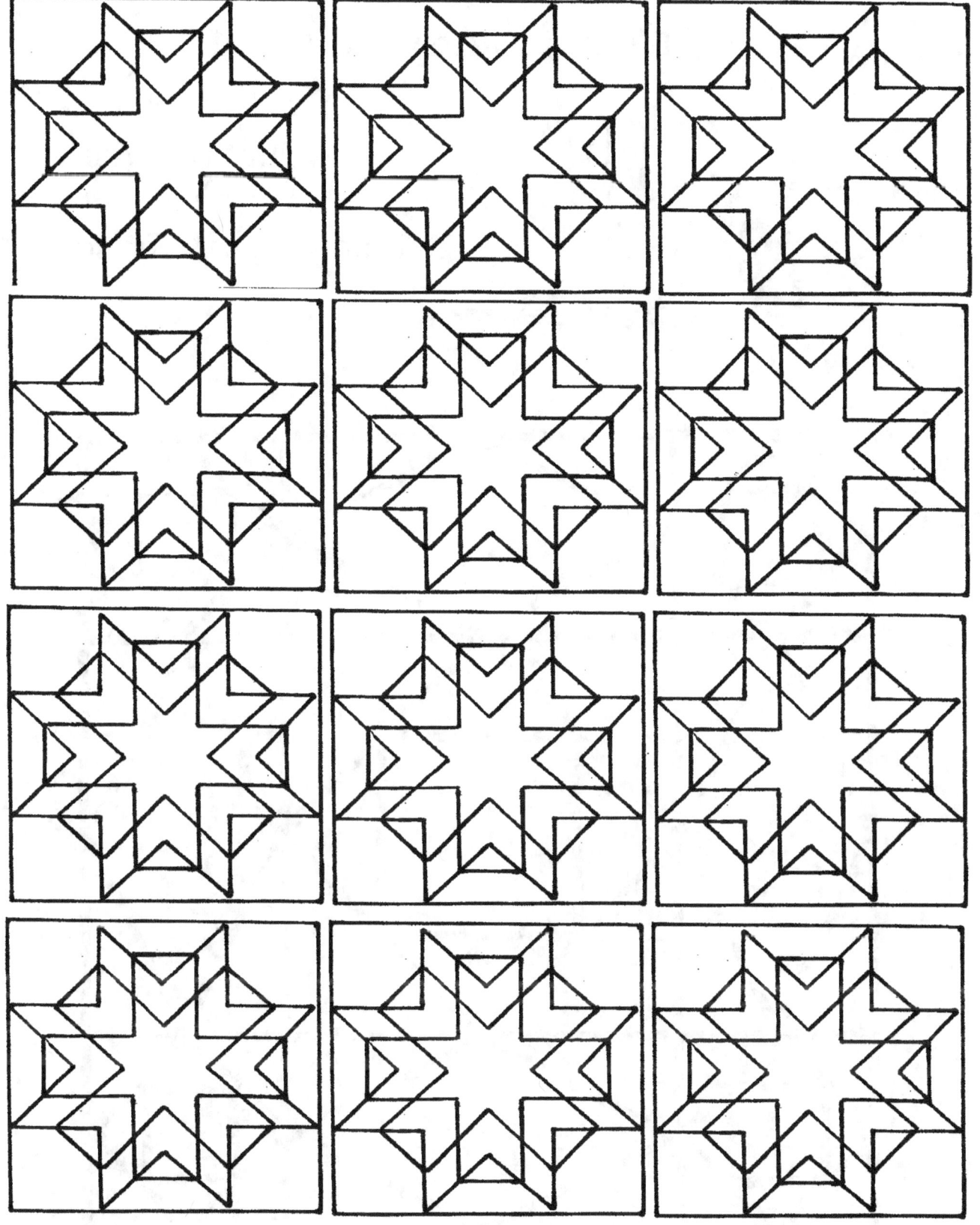

Barn Quilt Storm at Sea
Franklin County Vermont

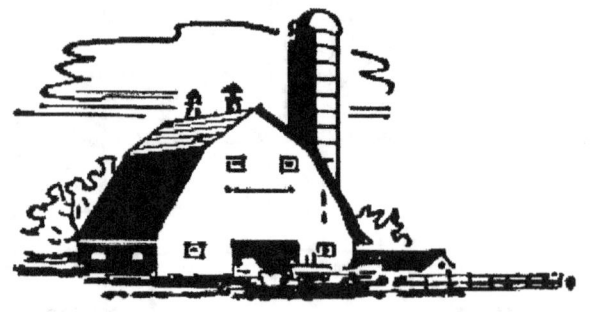

Barn Quilt Location
N Main St
Montgomery, Vermont

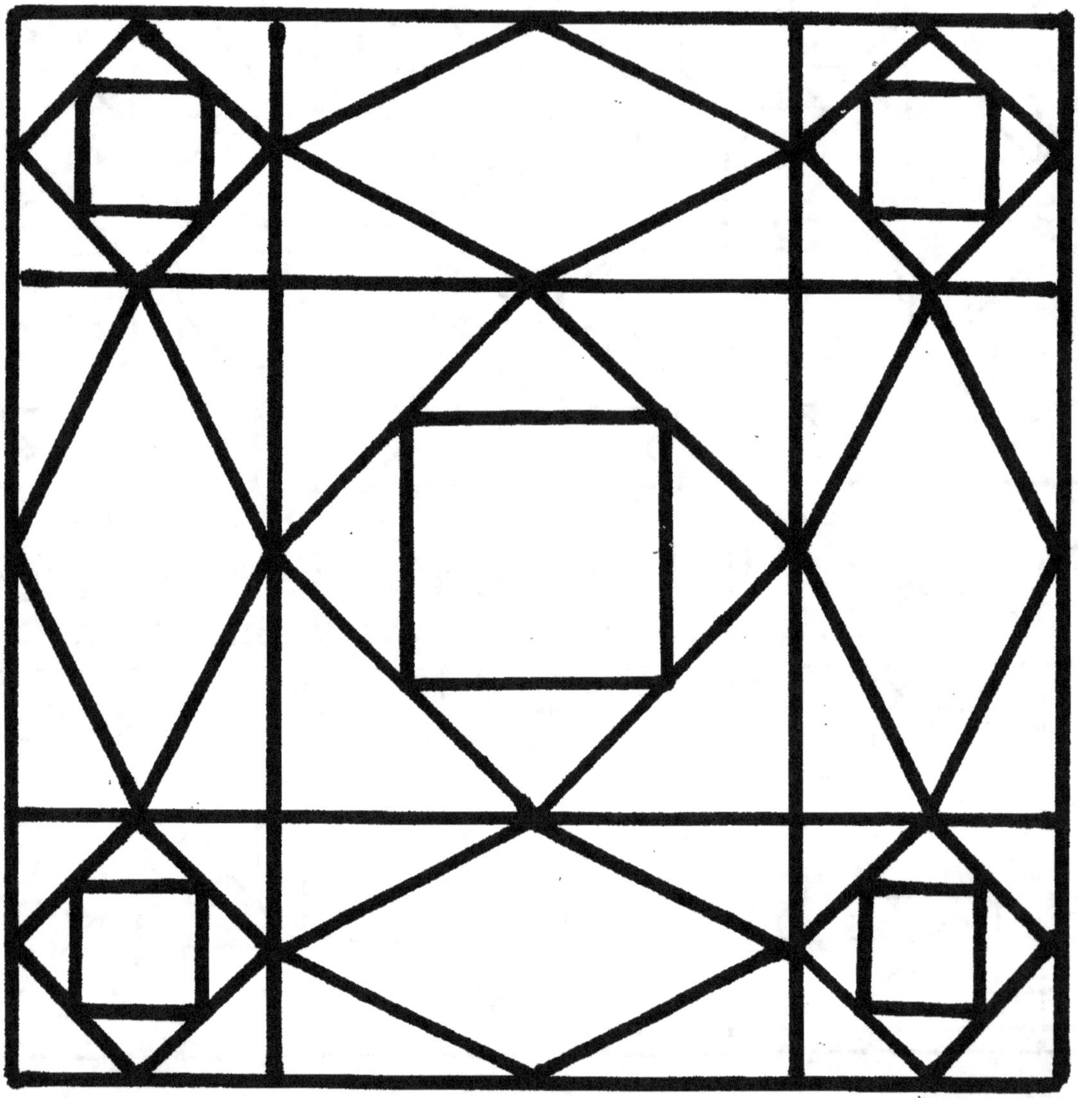

Franklin County Barn Quilt Storm at Sea

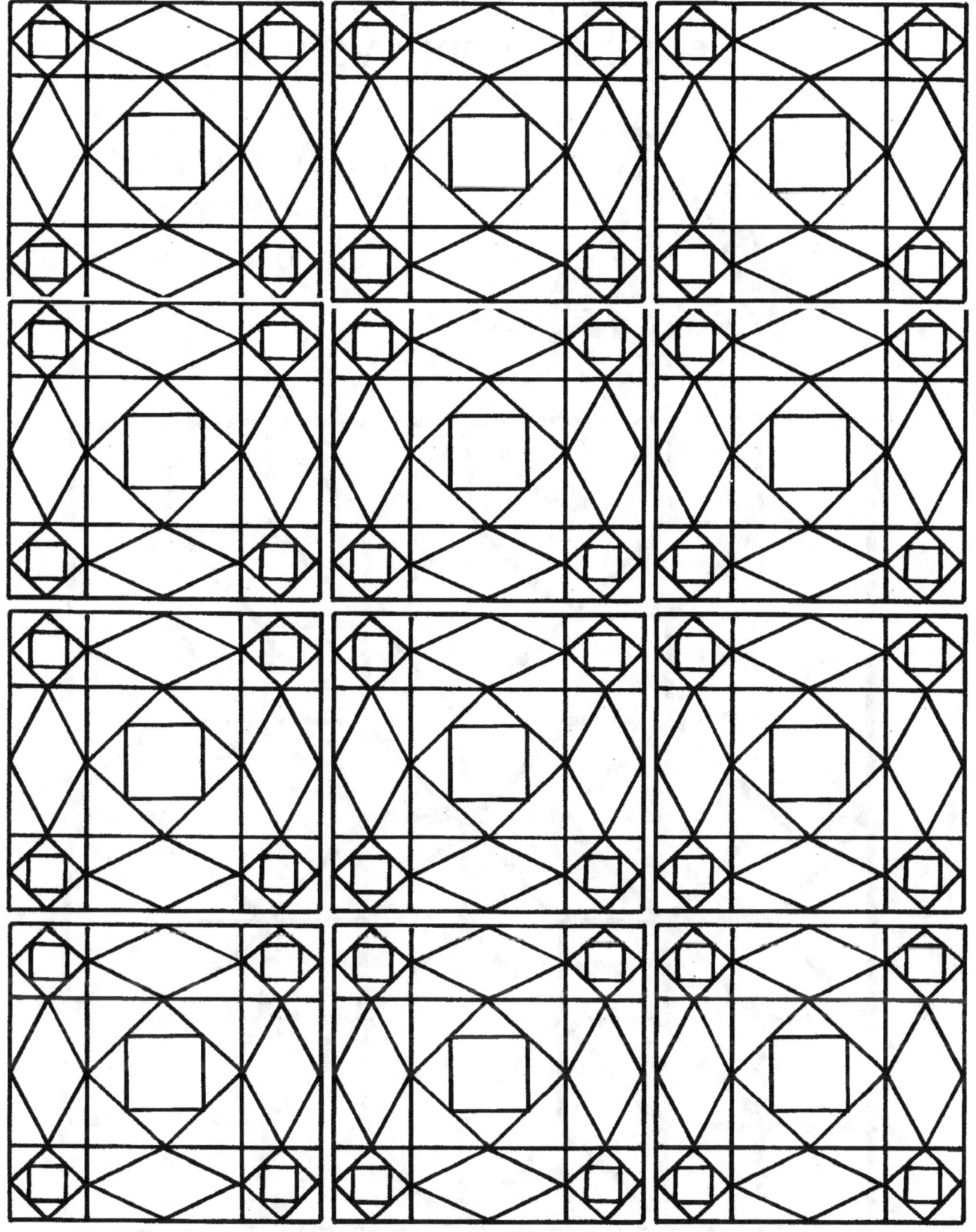

Barn Quilt Buggy Wheel
Franklin County Vermont

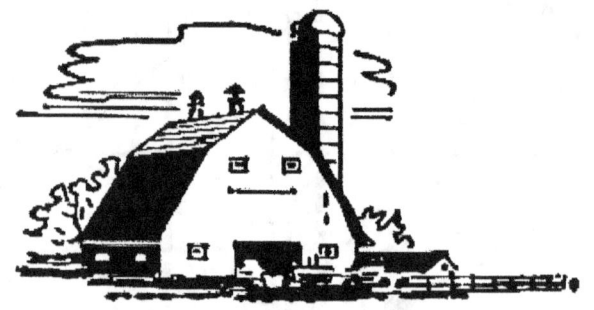

Barn Quilt Location
N Main St
Montgomery, Vermont

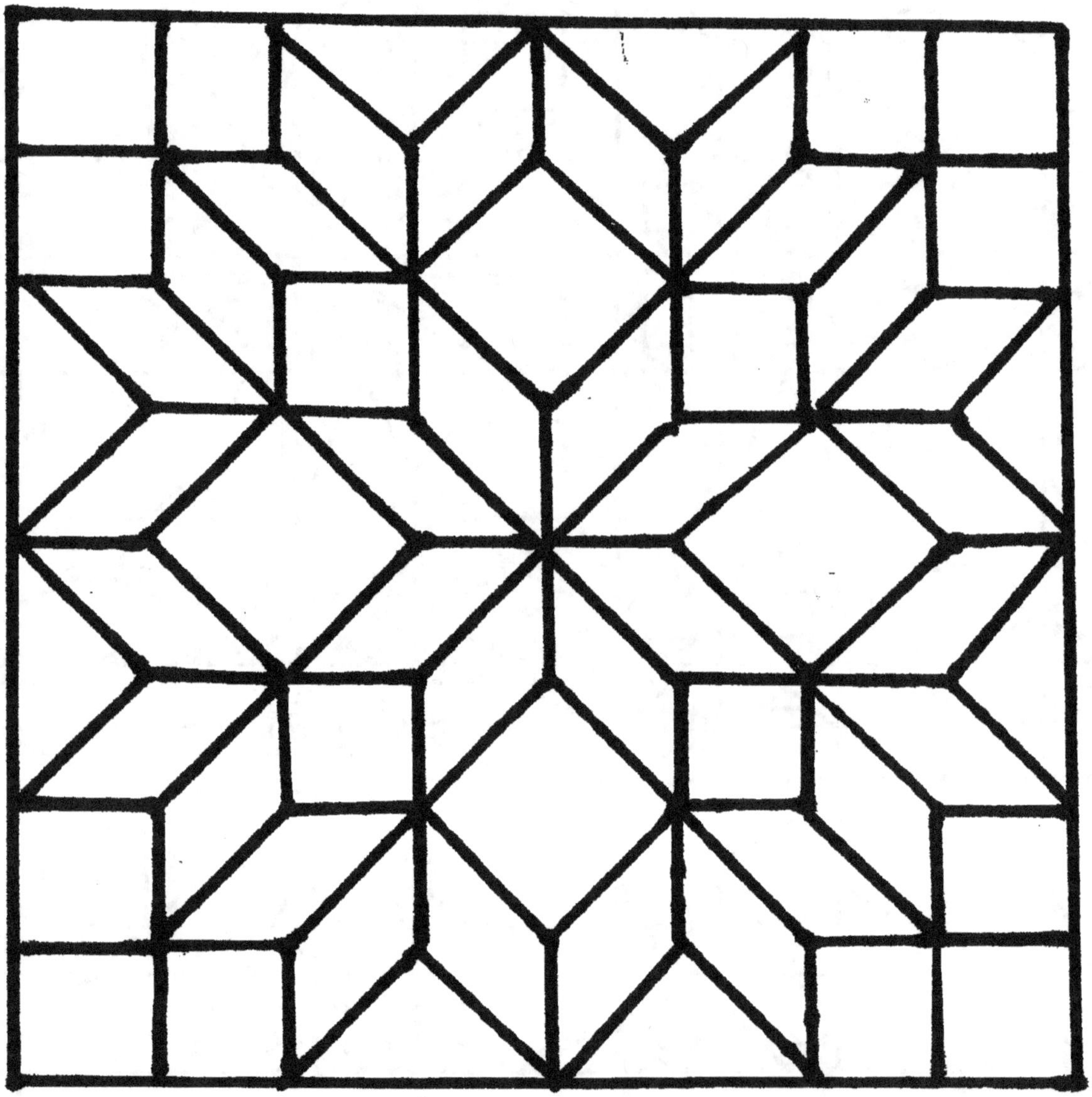

Franklin County Barn Quilt Buggy Wheel

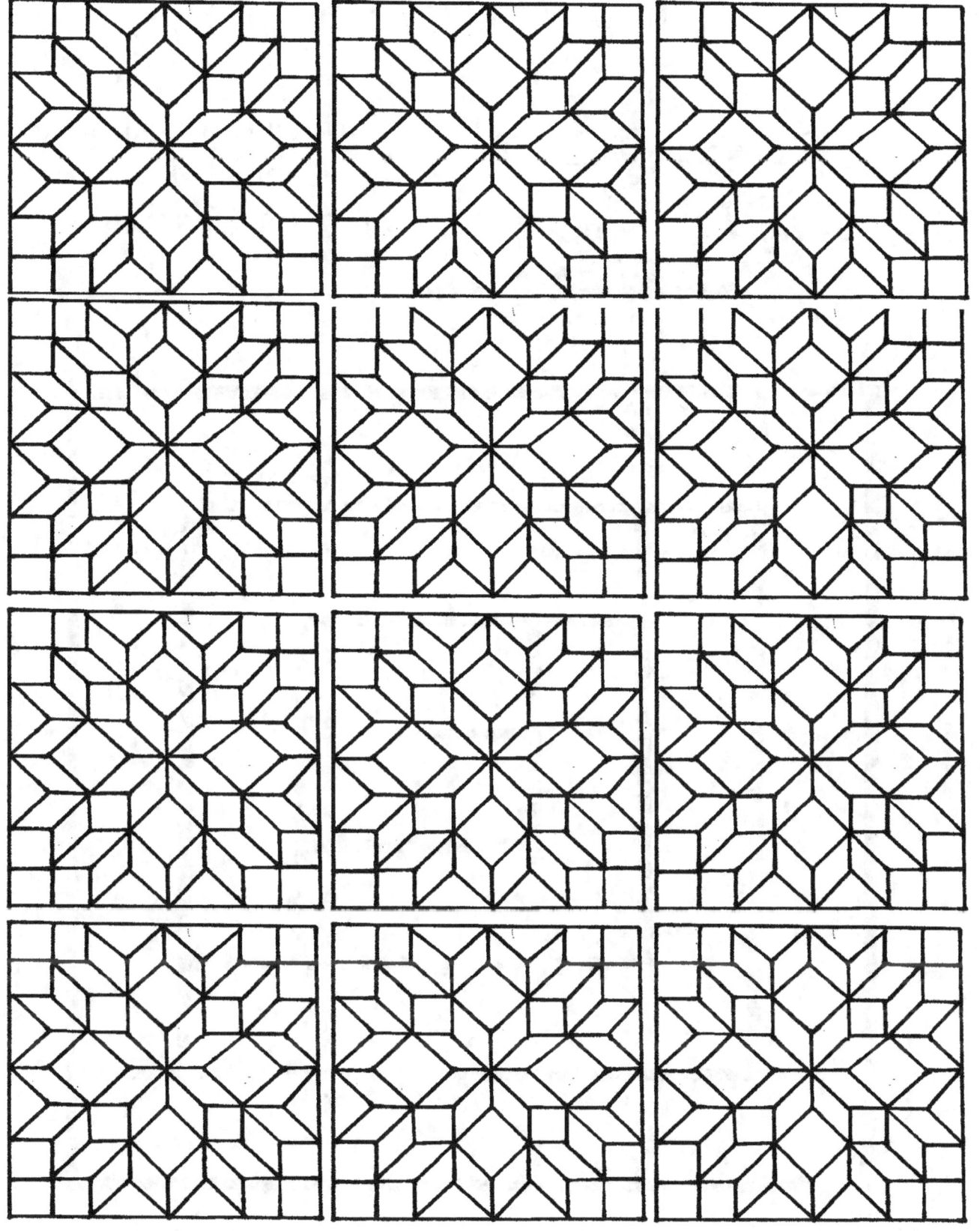

Barn Quilt Log Cabin
Franklin County Vermont

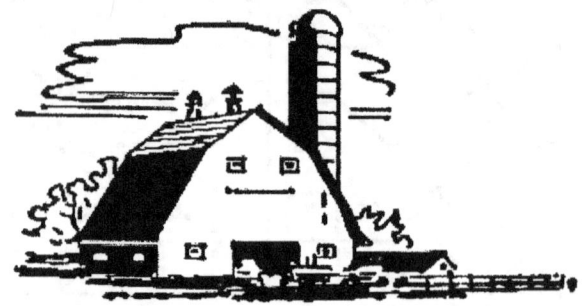

Barn Quilt Location
Hanna Rd
Franklin, Vermont

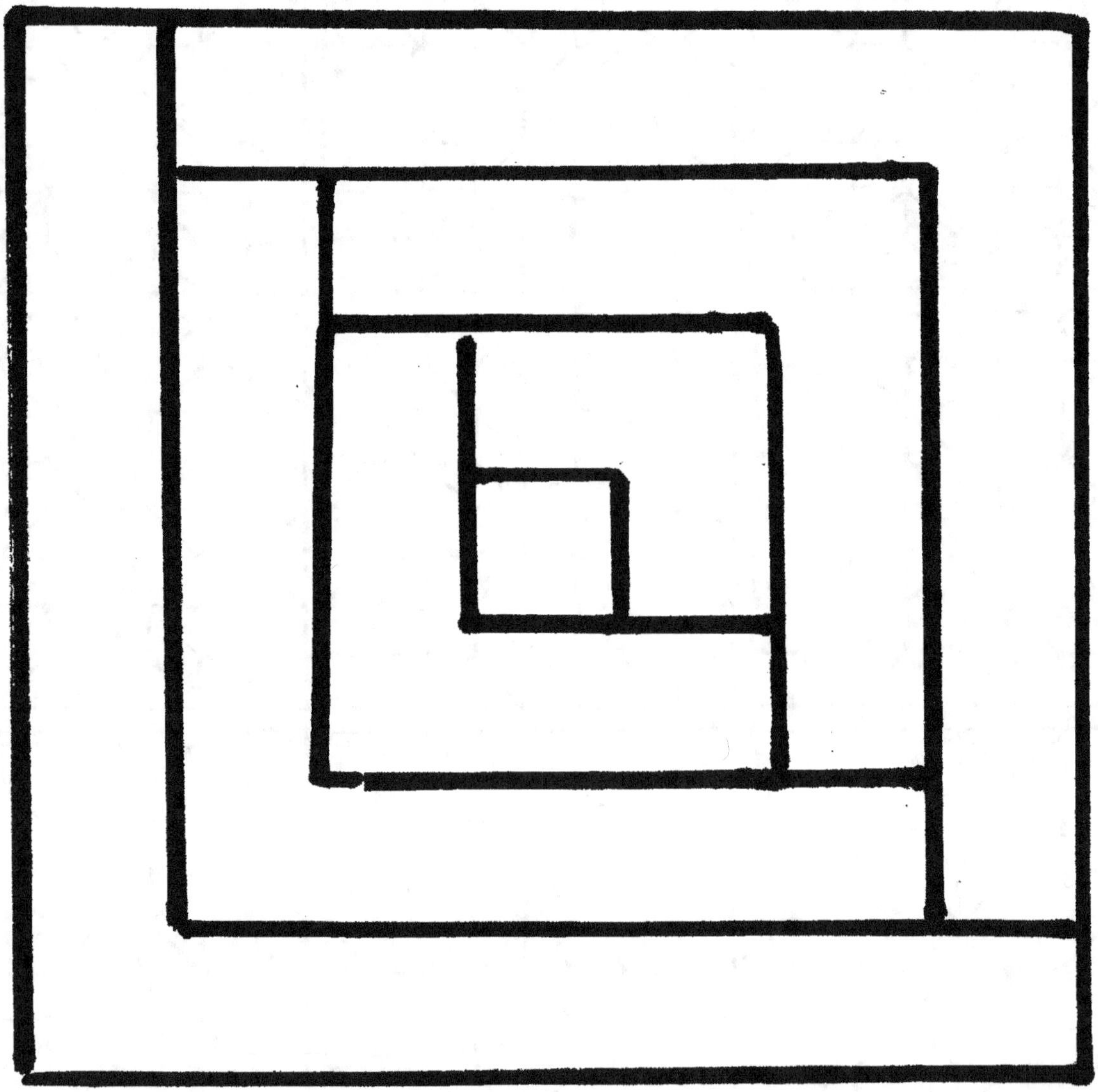

Franklin County Barn Quilt Log Cabin

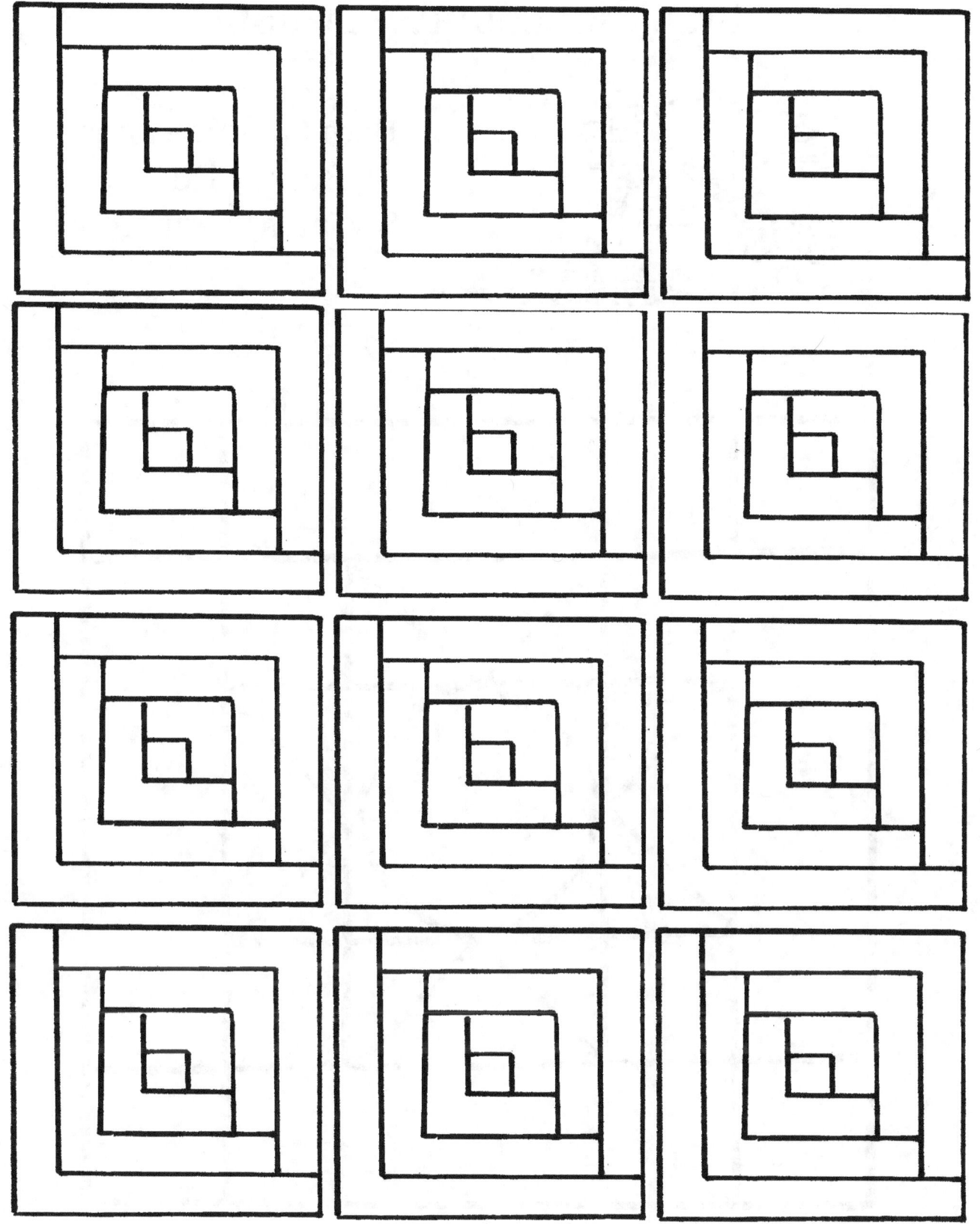

Barn Quilt Sawtooth Star
Franklin County Vermont

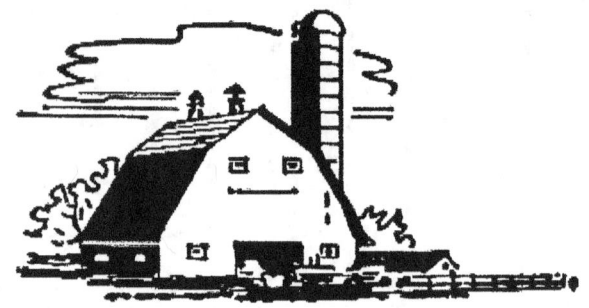

Barn Quilt Location
Bushey Rd
Swanton, Vermont

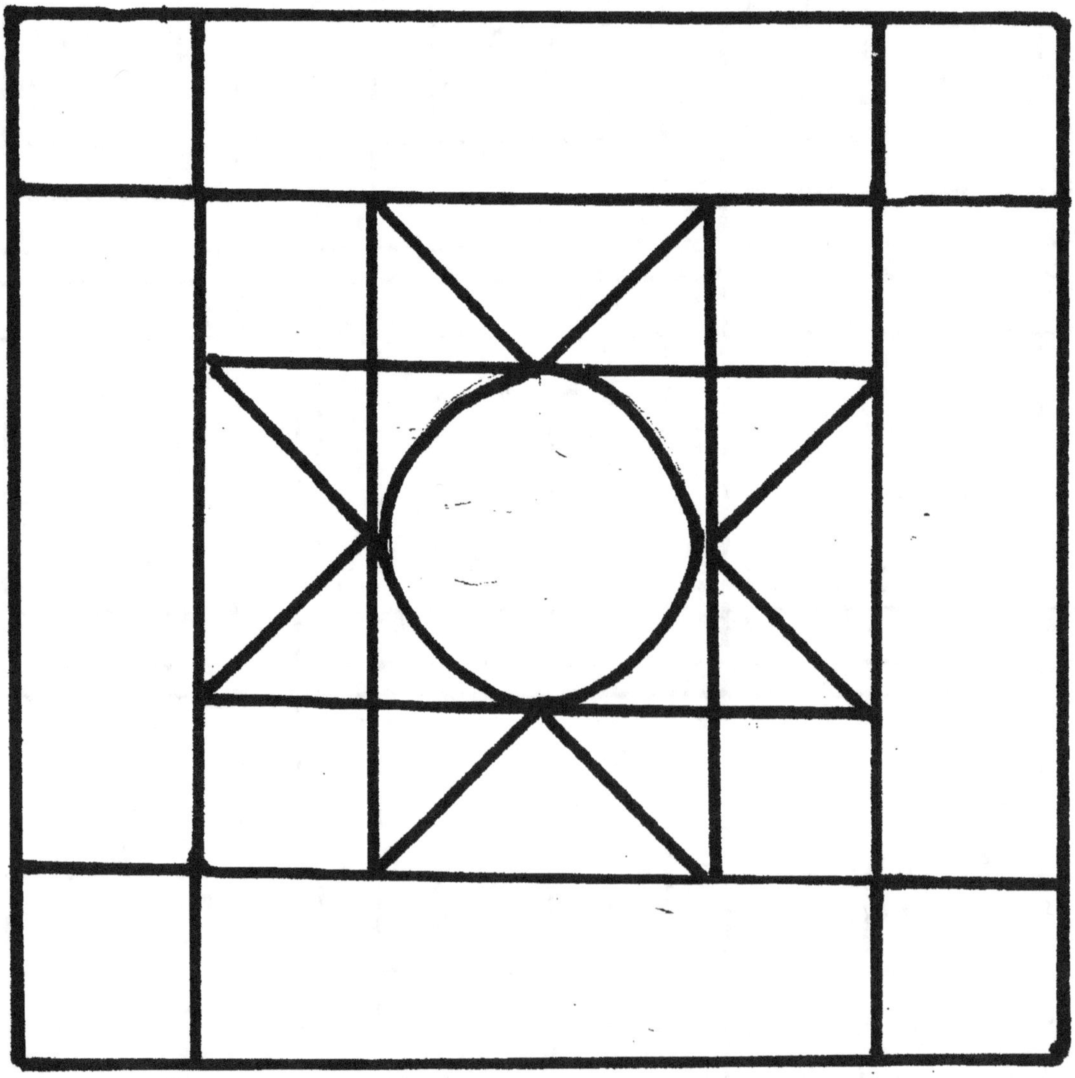

Franklin County Barn Quilt Sawtooth Star

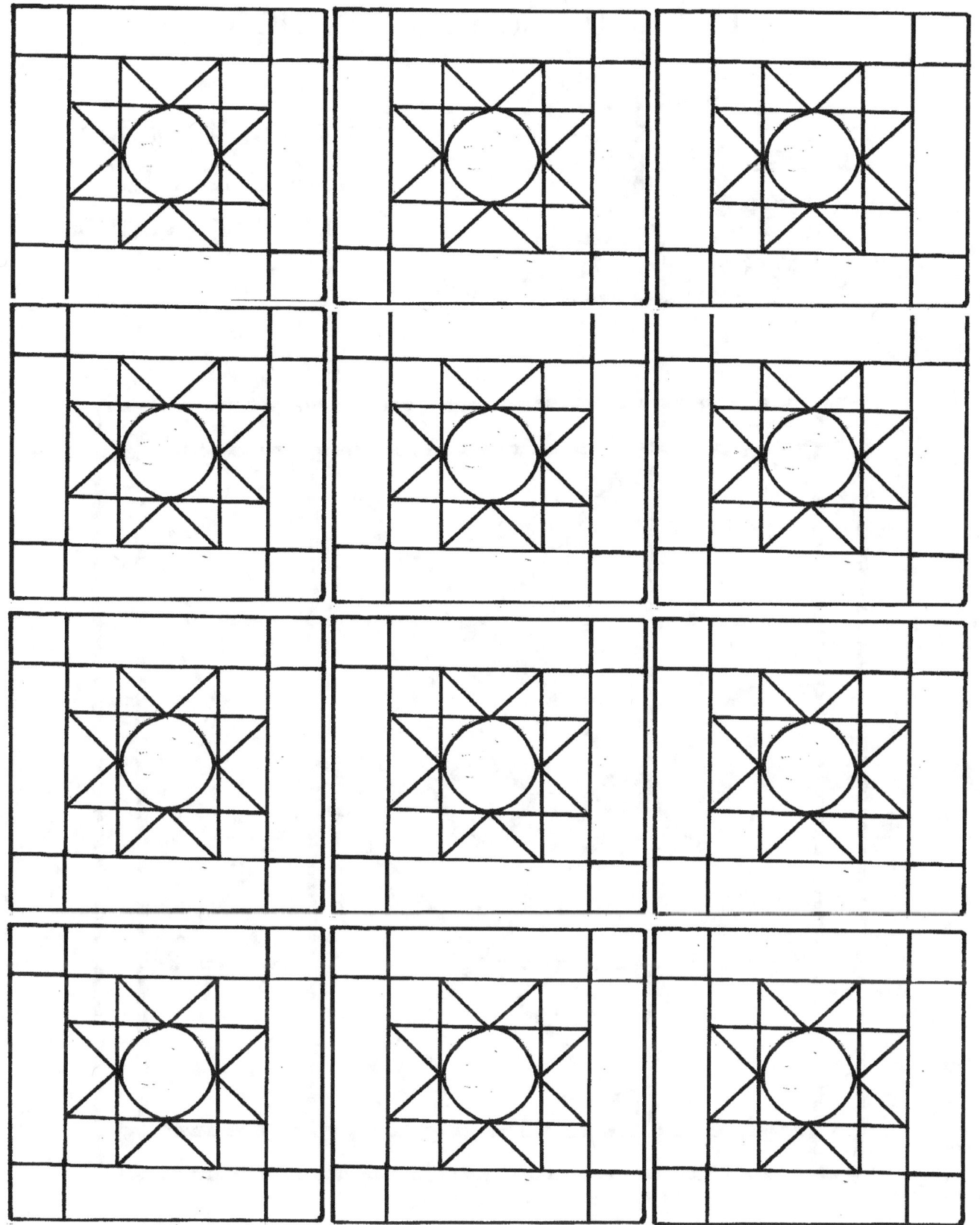

Barn Quilt Spinning Star
Franklin County Vermont

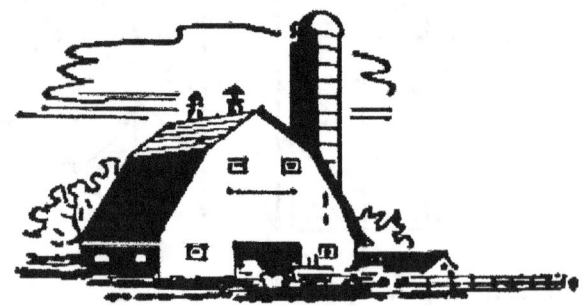

Barn Quilt Location
Fuller Bridge Rd
Montgomery, Vermont

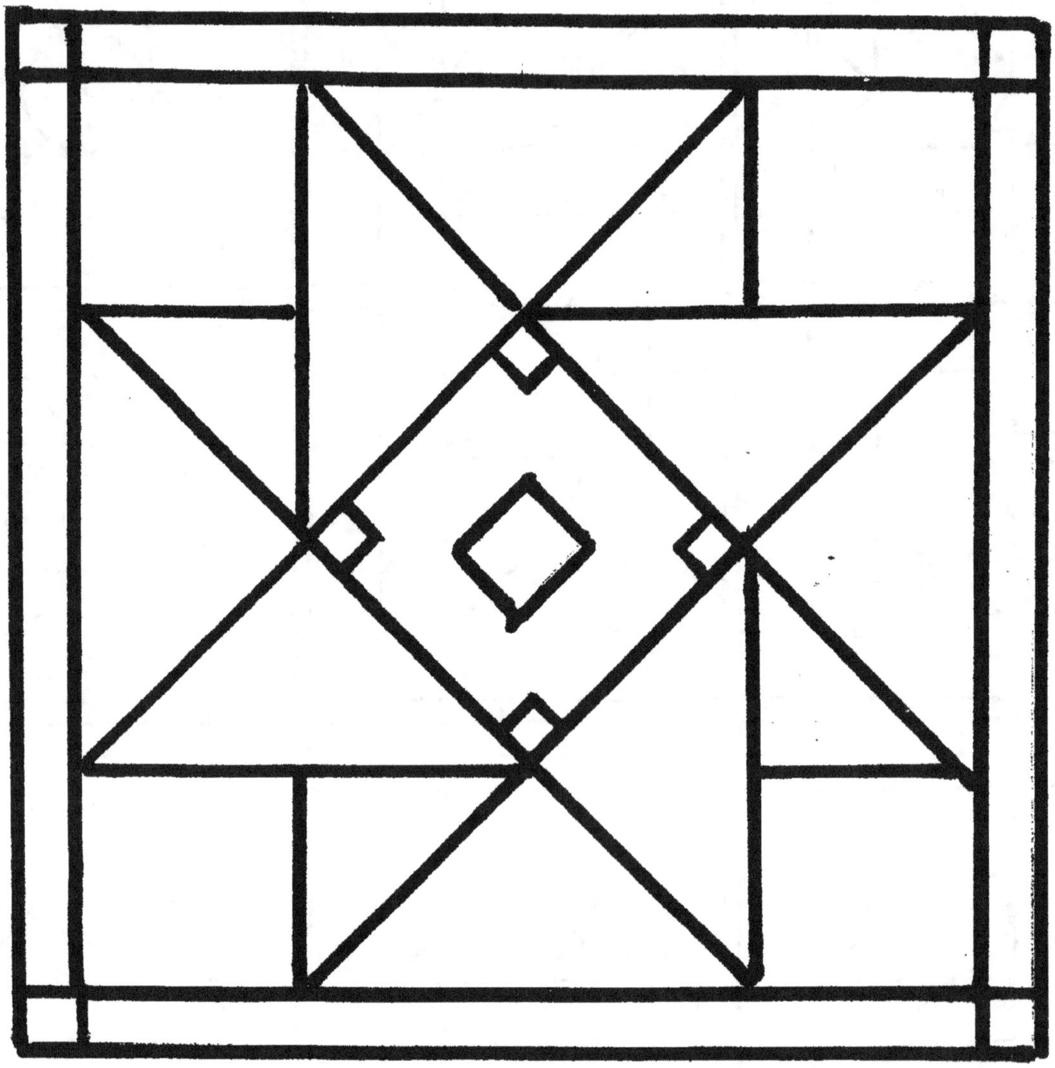

Franklin County Barn Quilt Spinning Star

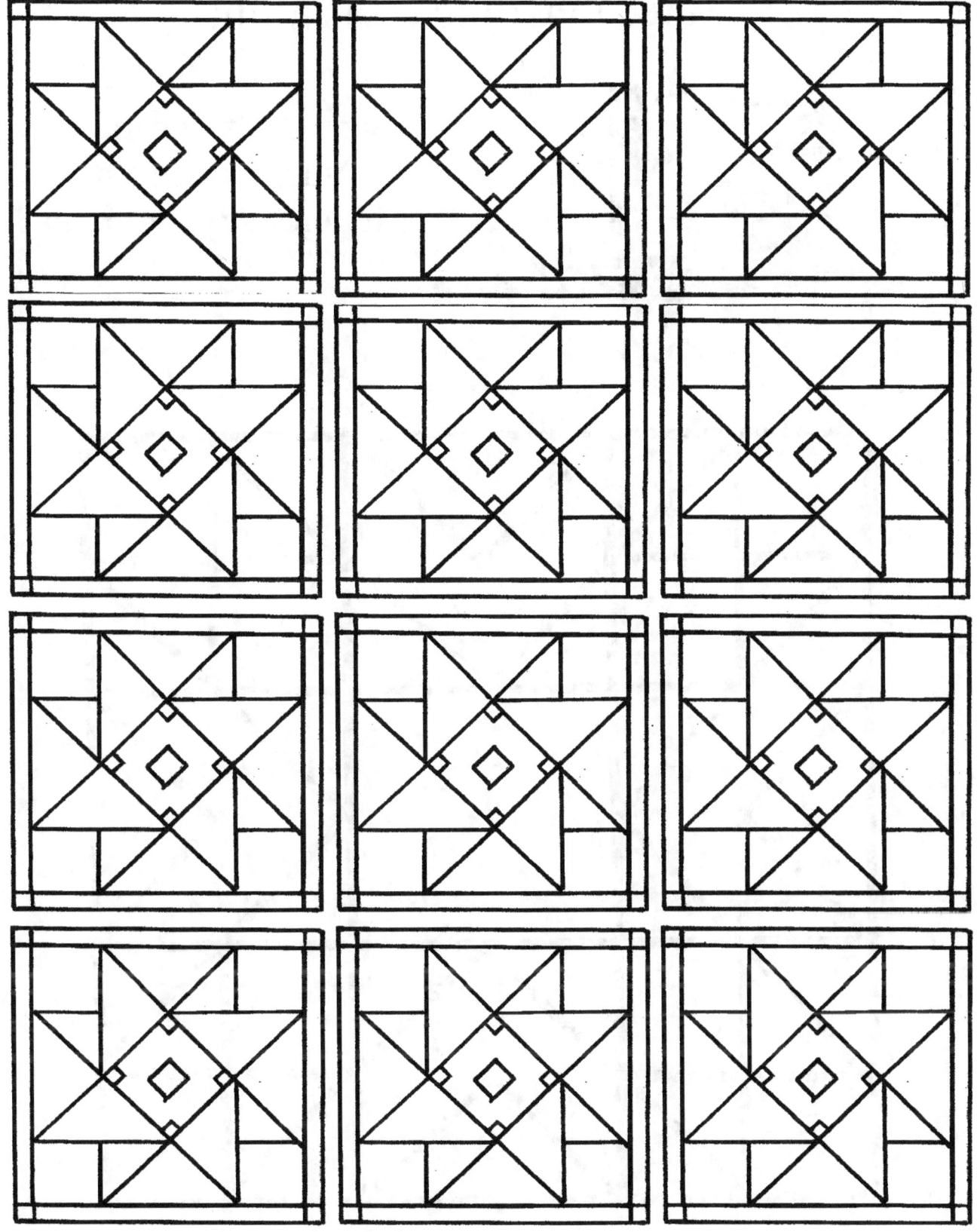

Barn Quilt Blueberry Pie
Franklin County Vermont

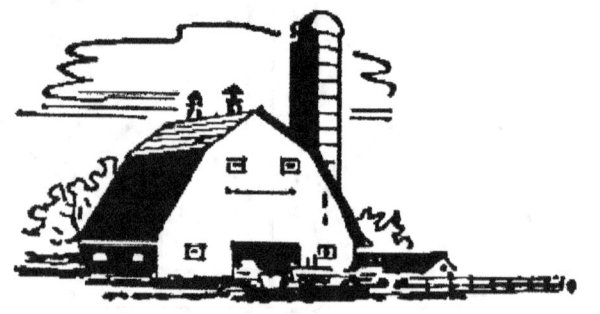

Barn Quilt Location
Fuller Bridge Rd
Montgomery, Vermont

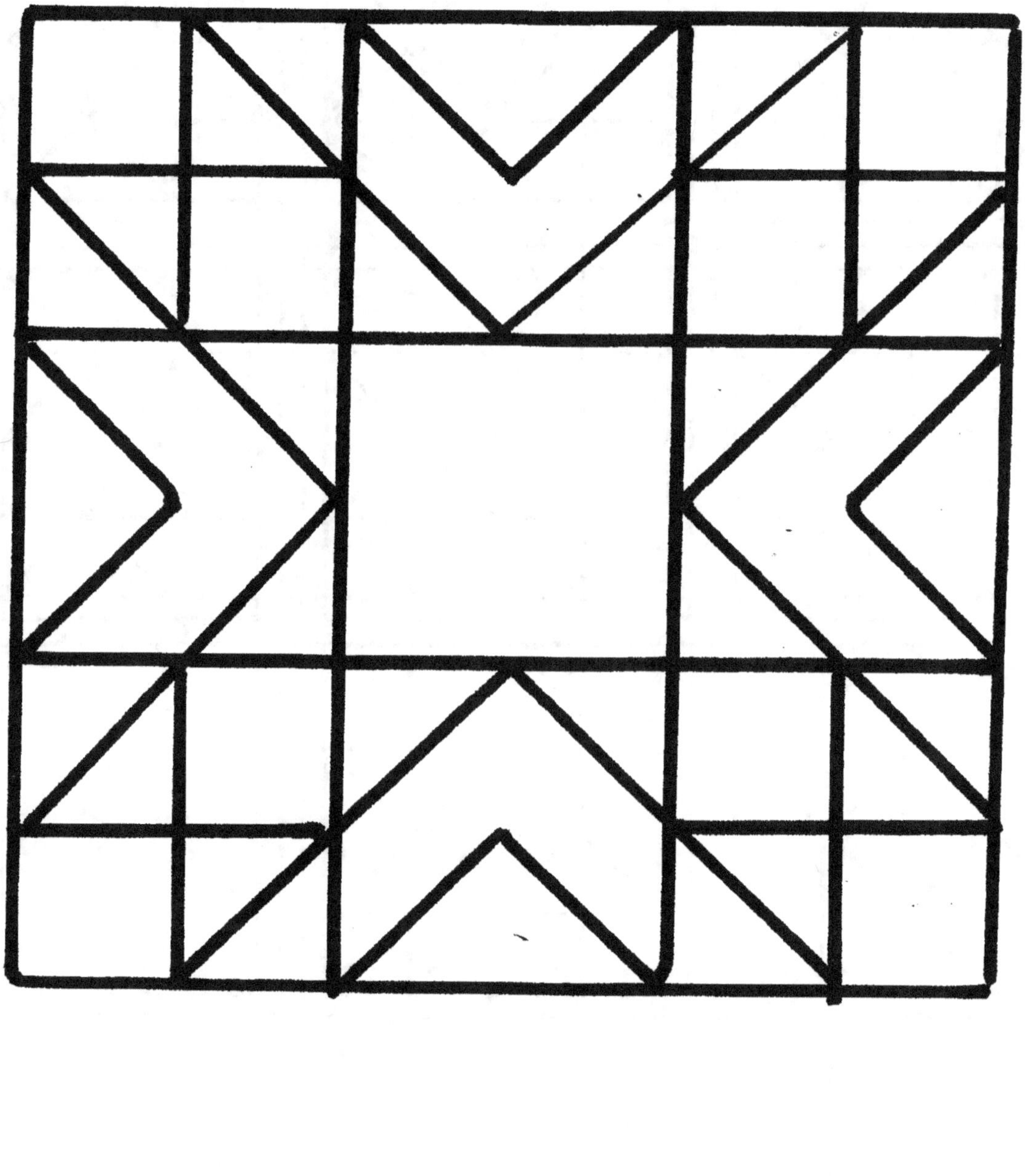

Franklin County Barn Quilt Blueberry Pie

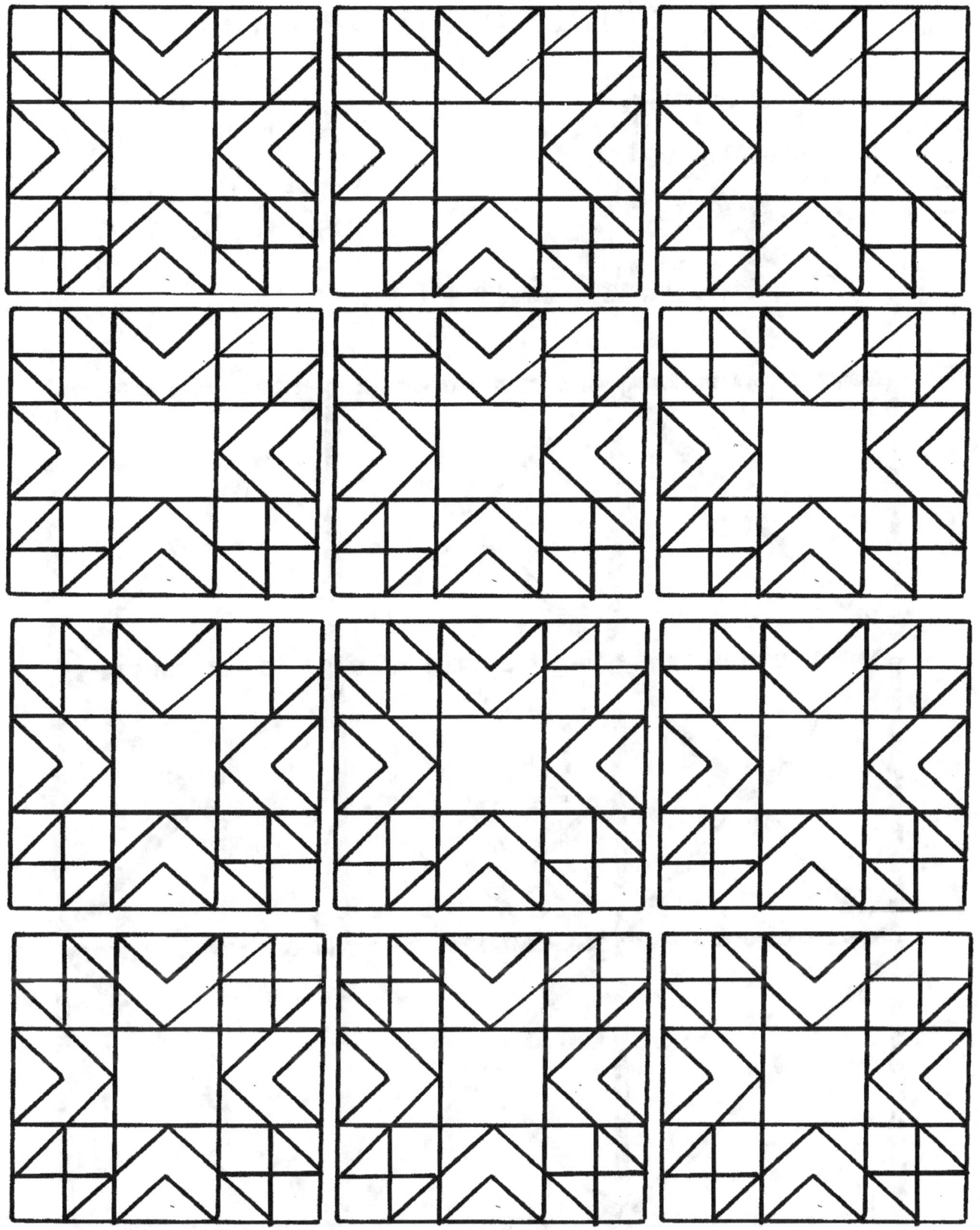

Barn Quilt Maple Leaf
Franklin County Vermont

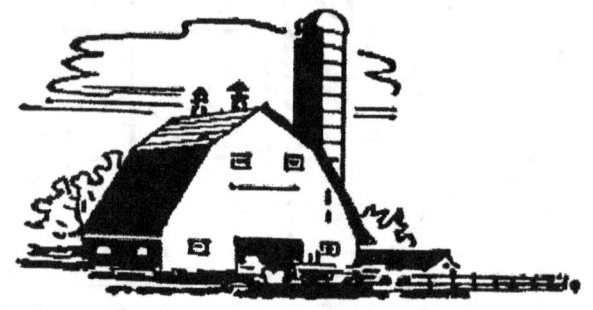

Barn Quilt Location
W Enosburg Rd
Enosburg, Vermont

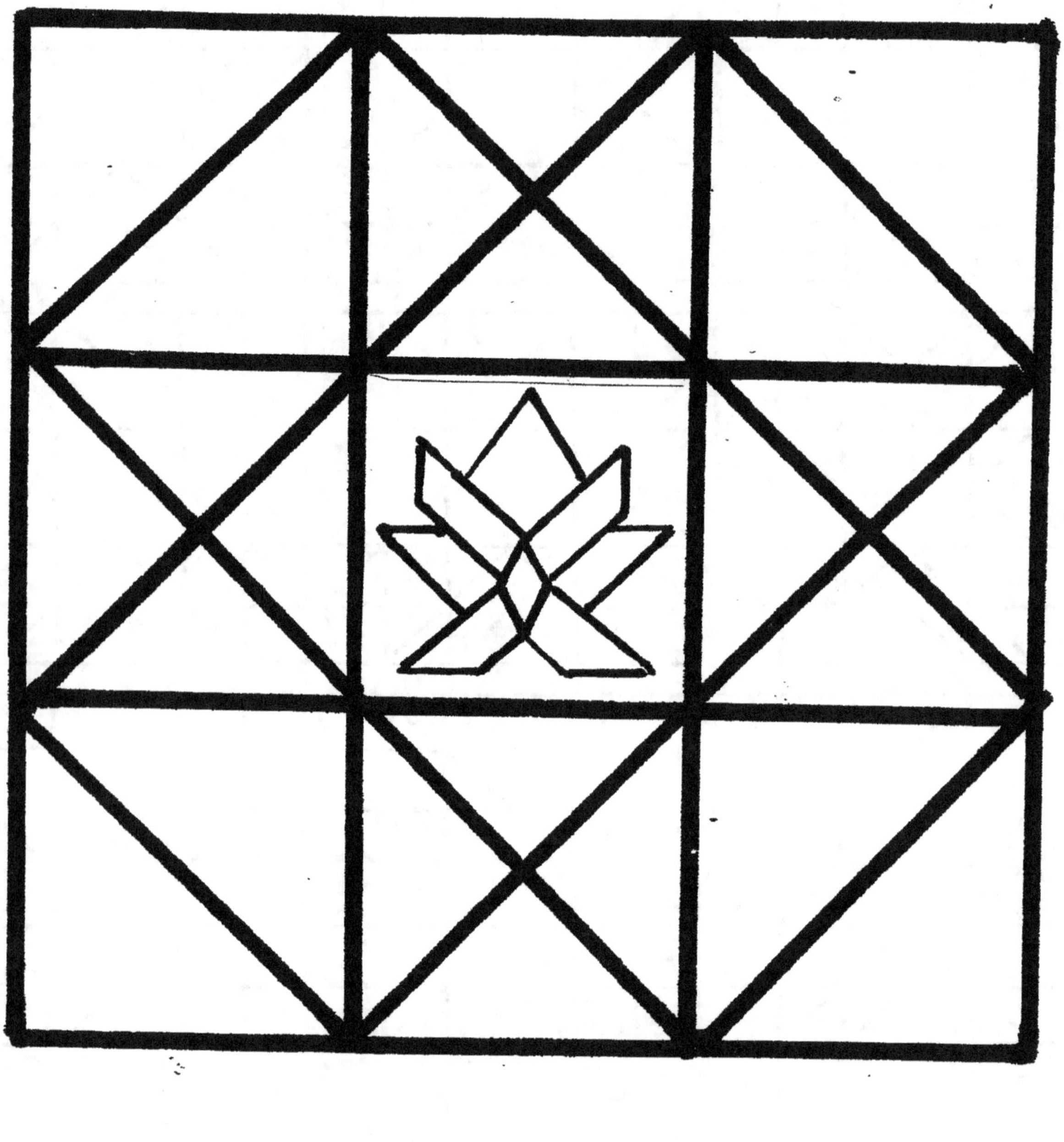

Franklin County Barn Quilt Maple Leaf

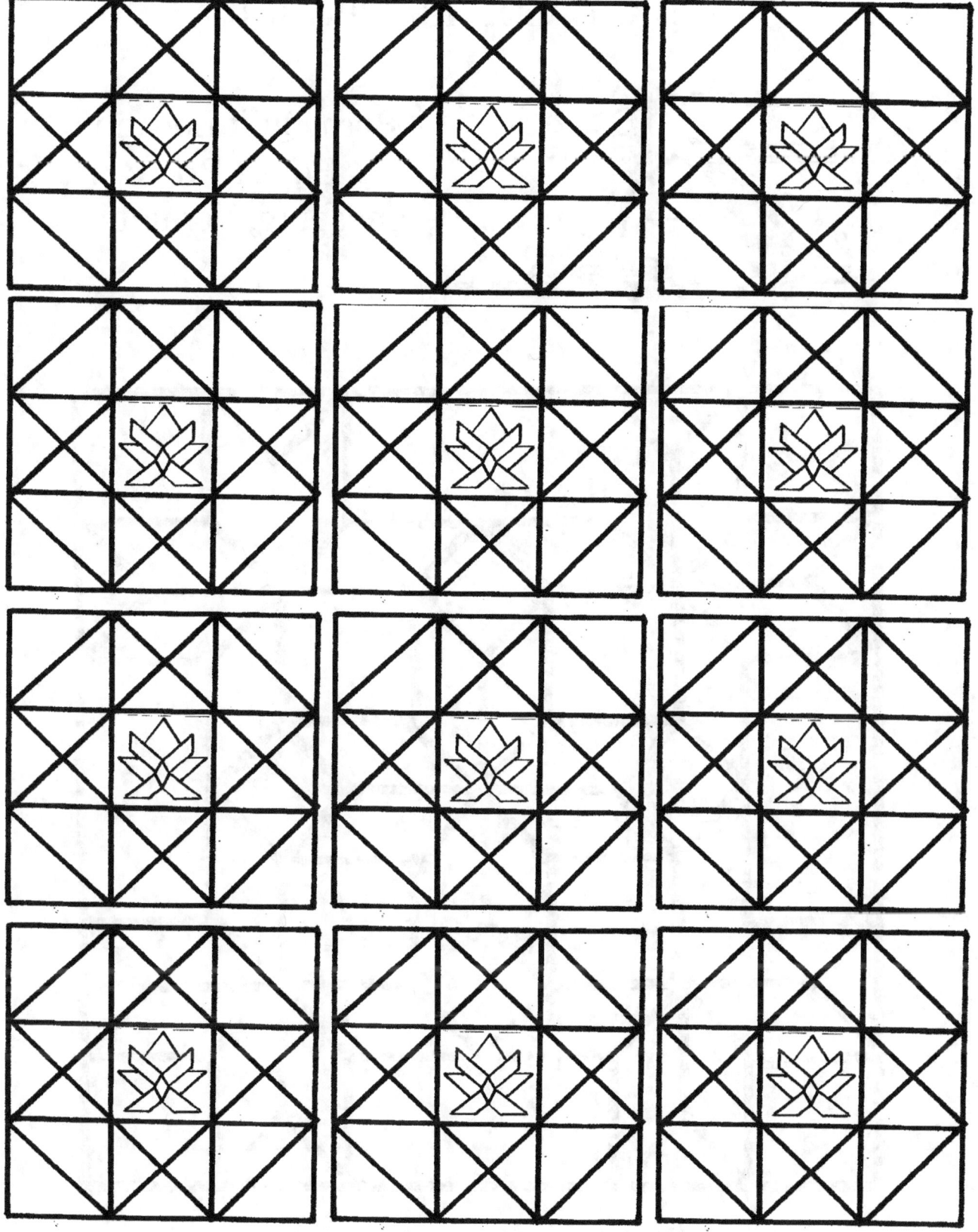

Barn Quilt Carpenter Wheel
Franklin County Vermont

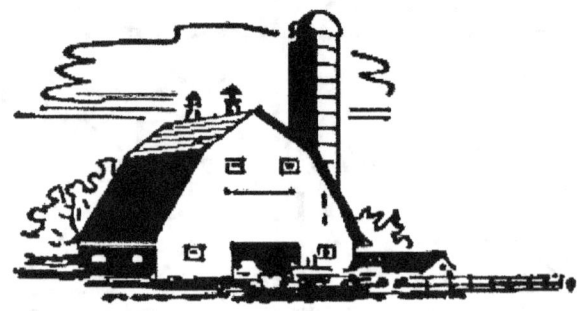

Barn Quilt Location
Bogue Rd
Enosburg, Vermont

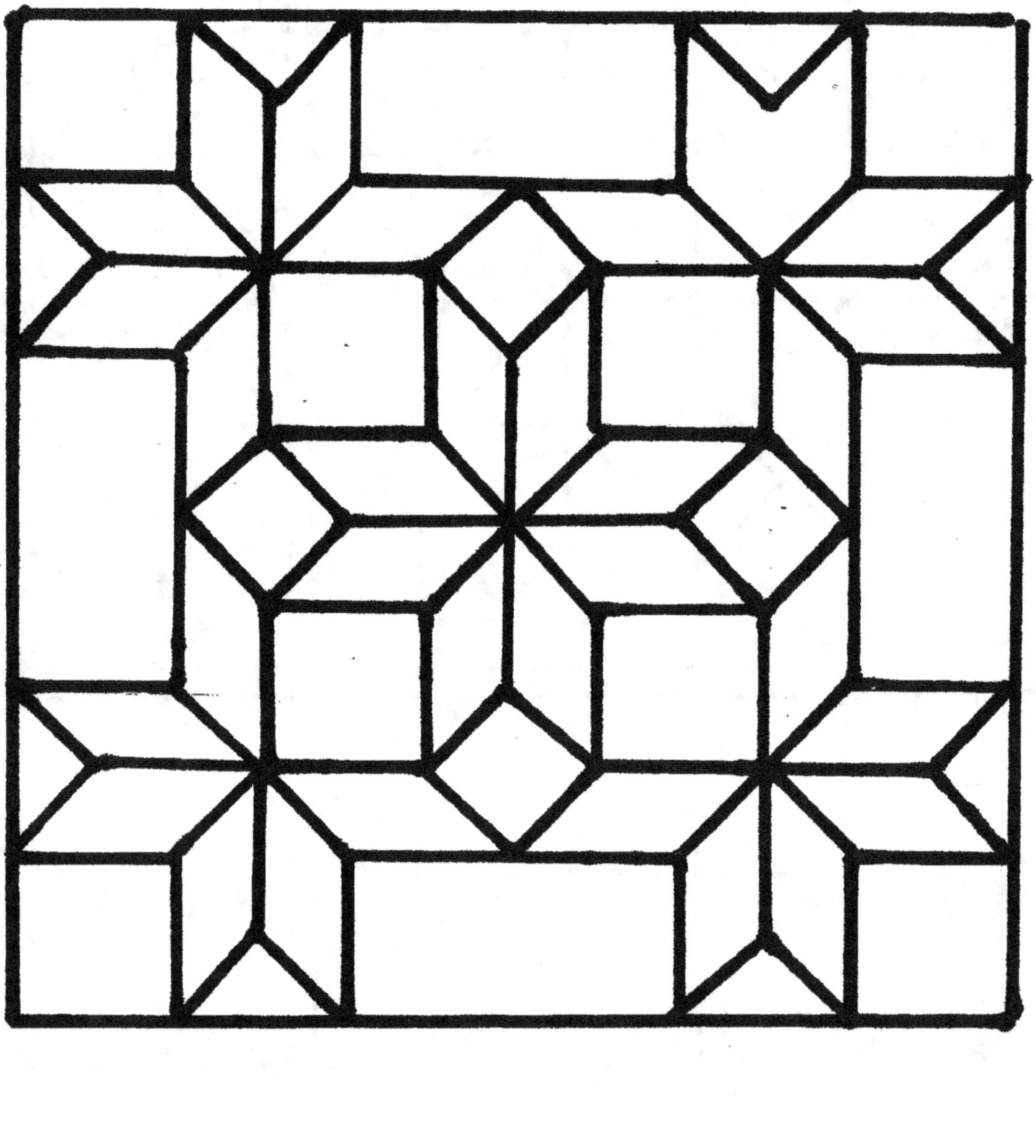

Franklin County Barn Quilt Carpenter Wheel

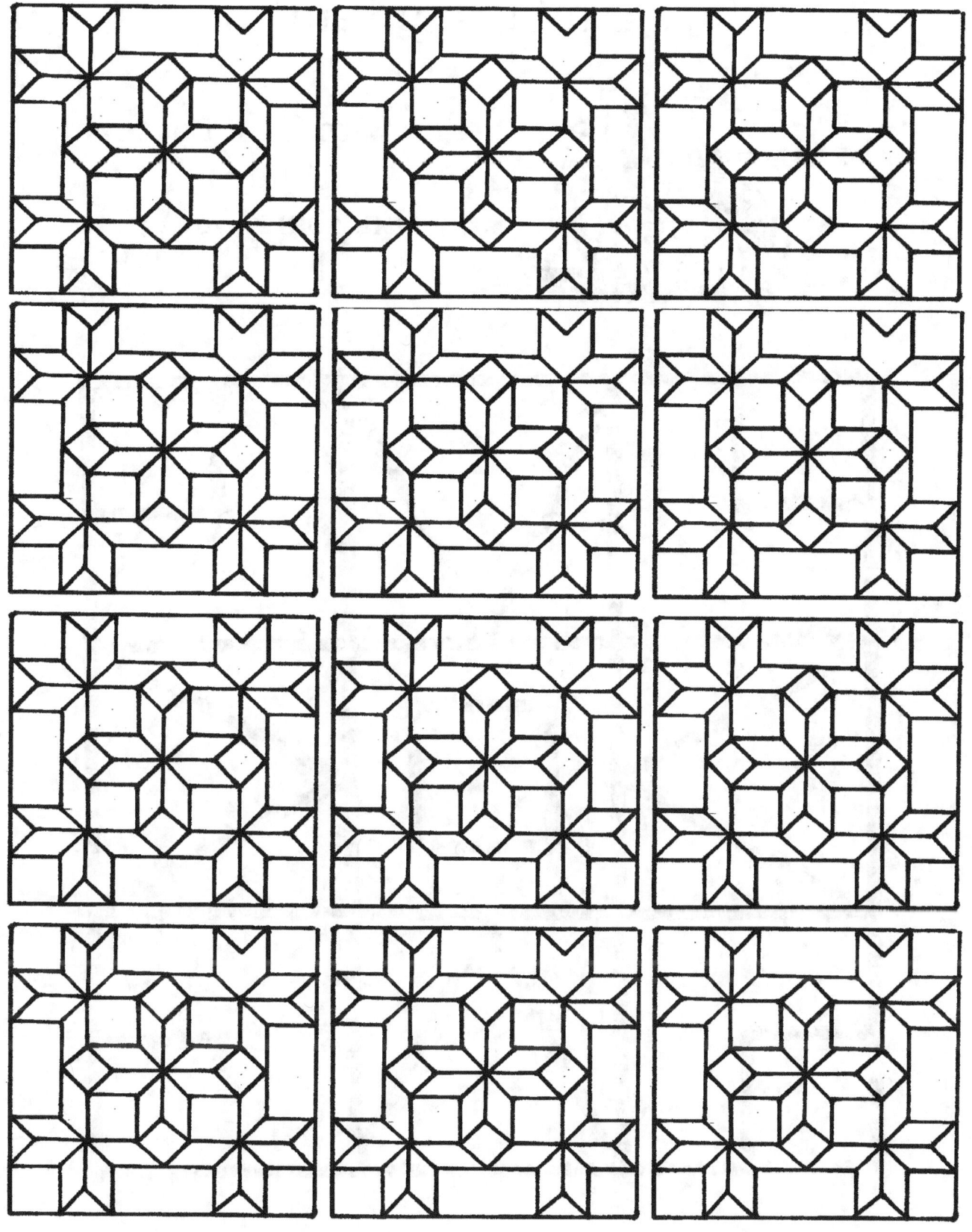

Barn Quilt Sun
Franklin County Vermont

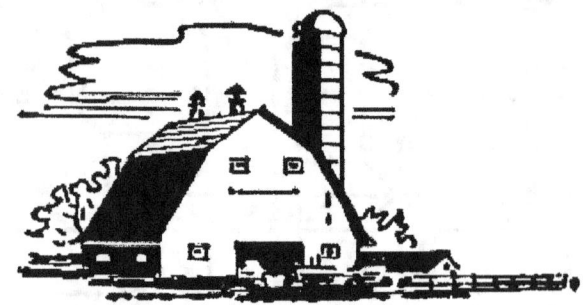

Barn Quilt Location
Elm St
Enosburg, Vermont

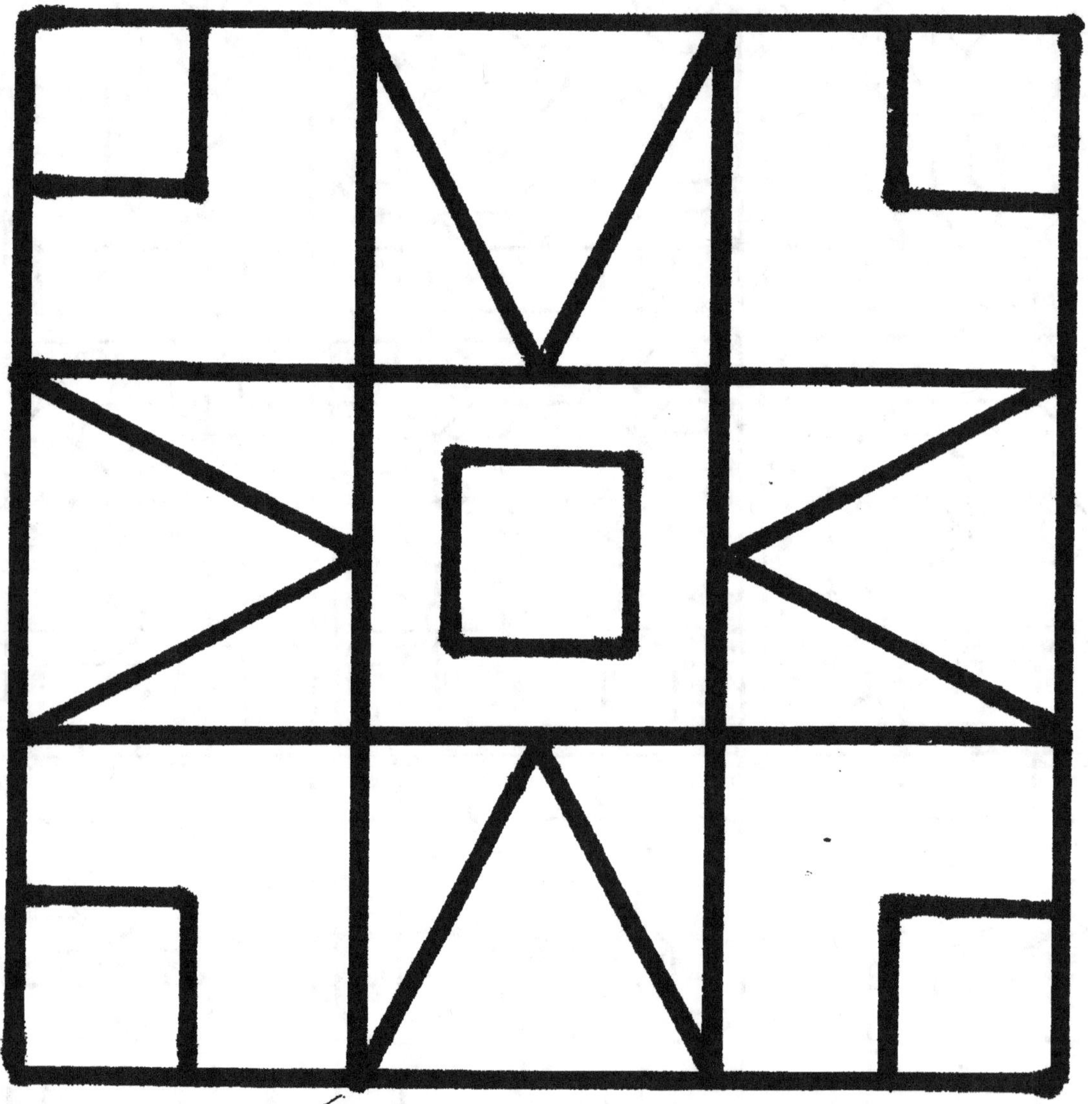

Franklin County Barn Quilt Sun

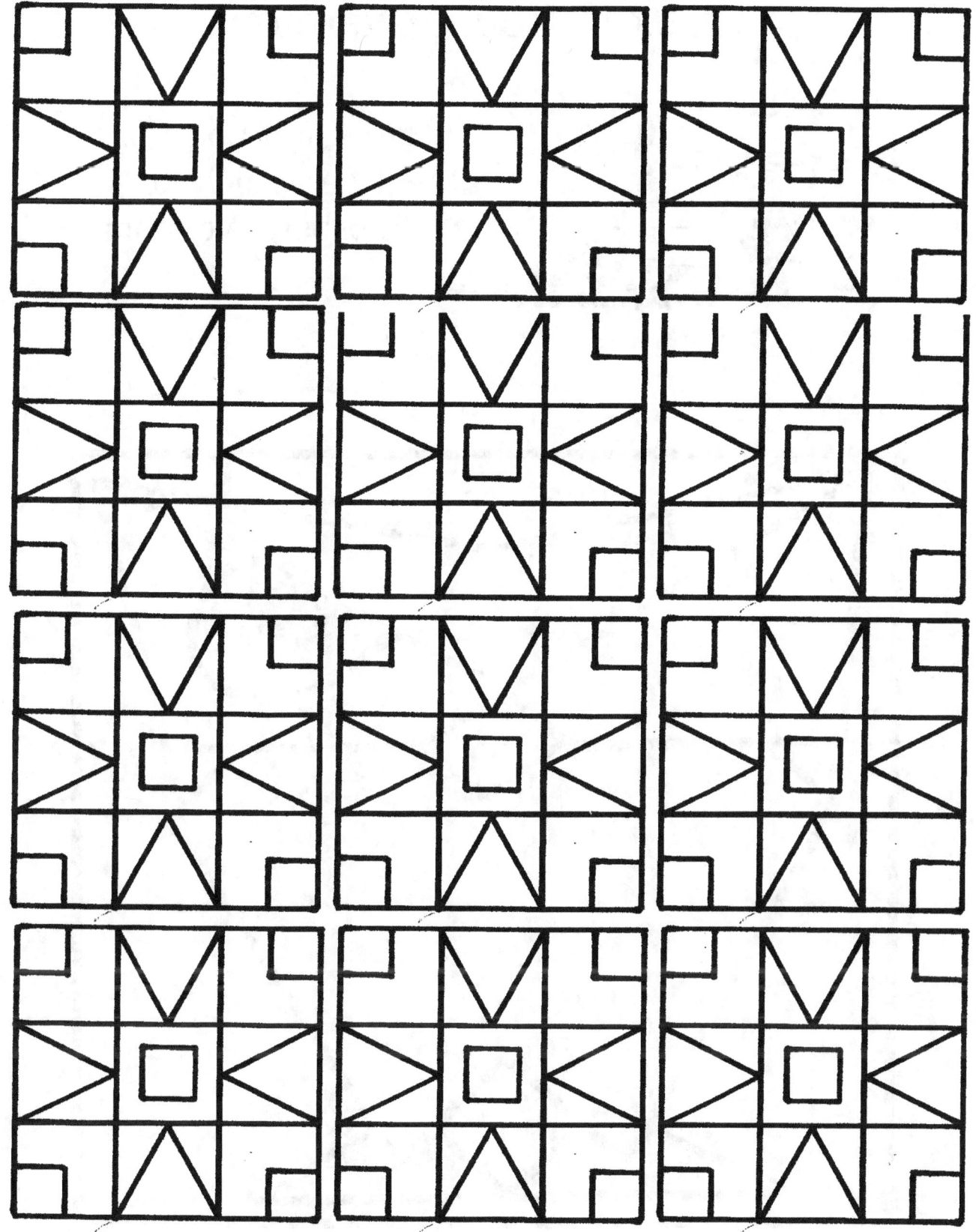

Barn Quilt Maya the Owl
Franklin County Vermont

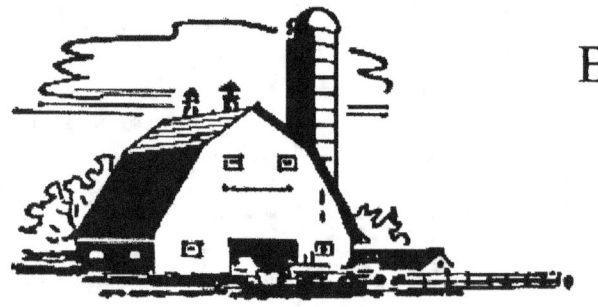

Barn Quilt Location
Tyler Ranch Rd
Enosburg, Vermont

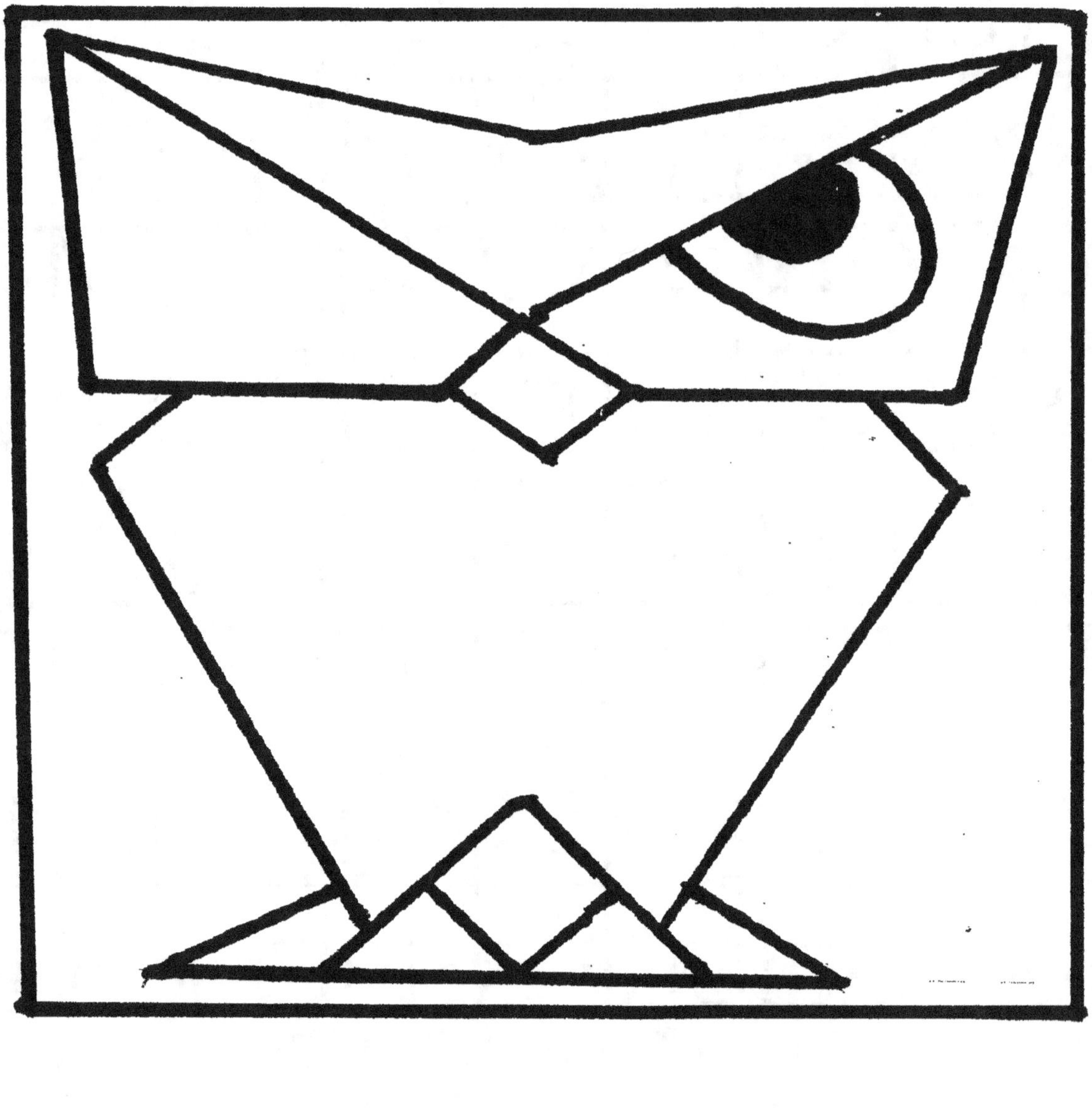

Franklin County Barn Quilt Maya the Owl

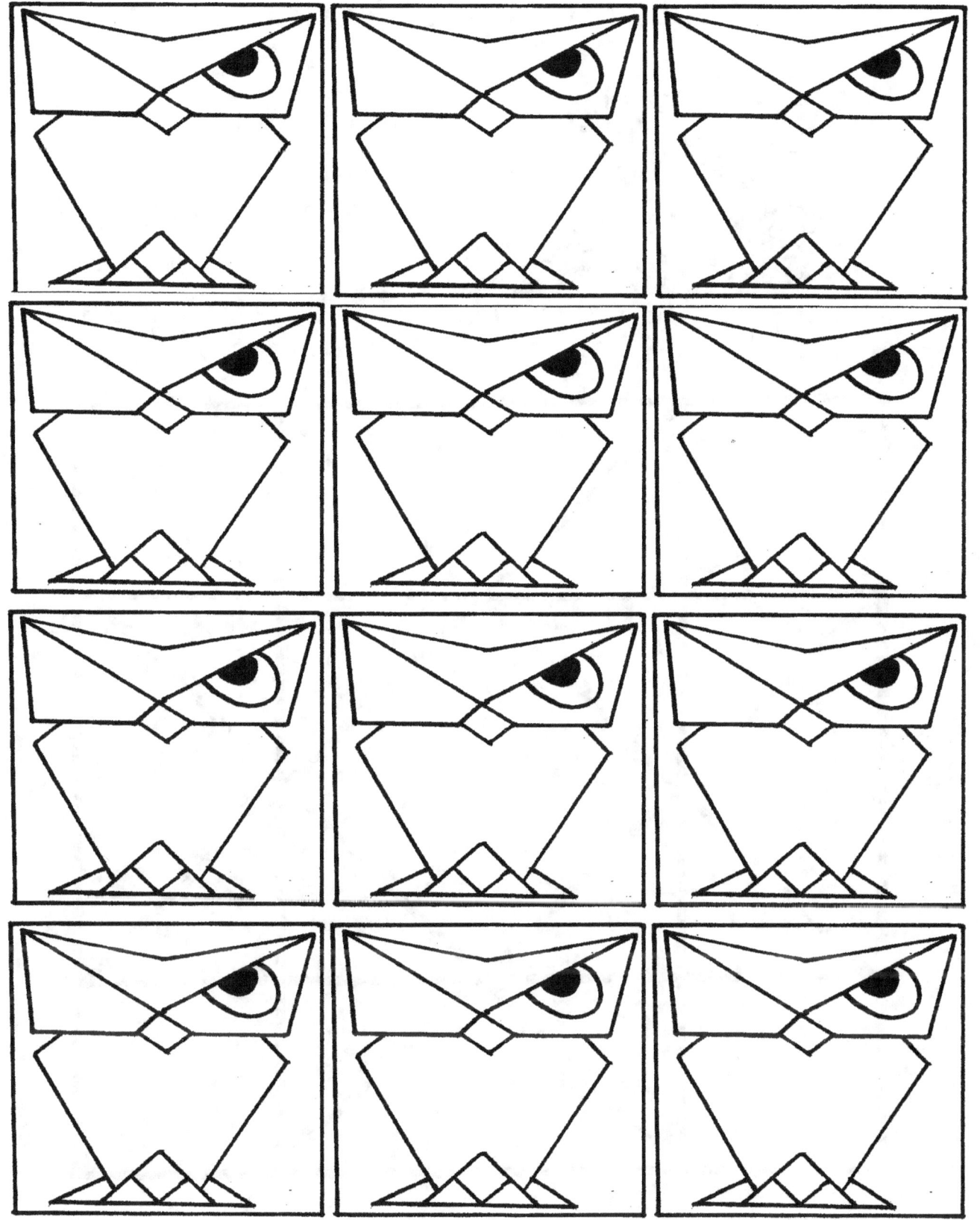

Barn Quilt Eight Pointed Star
Franklin County Vermont

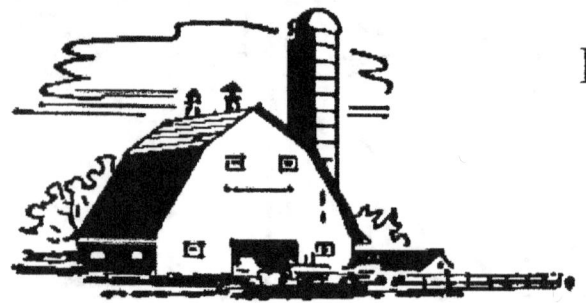

Barn Quilt Location
VT Rte 105
Sheldon, Vermont

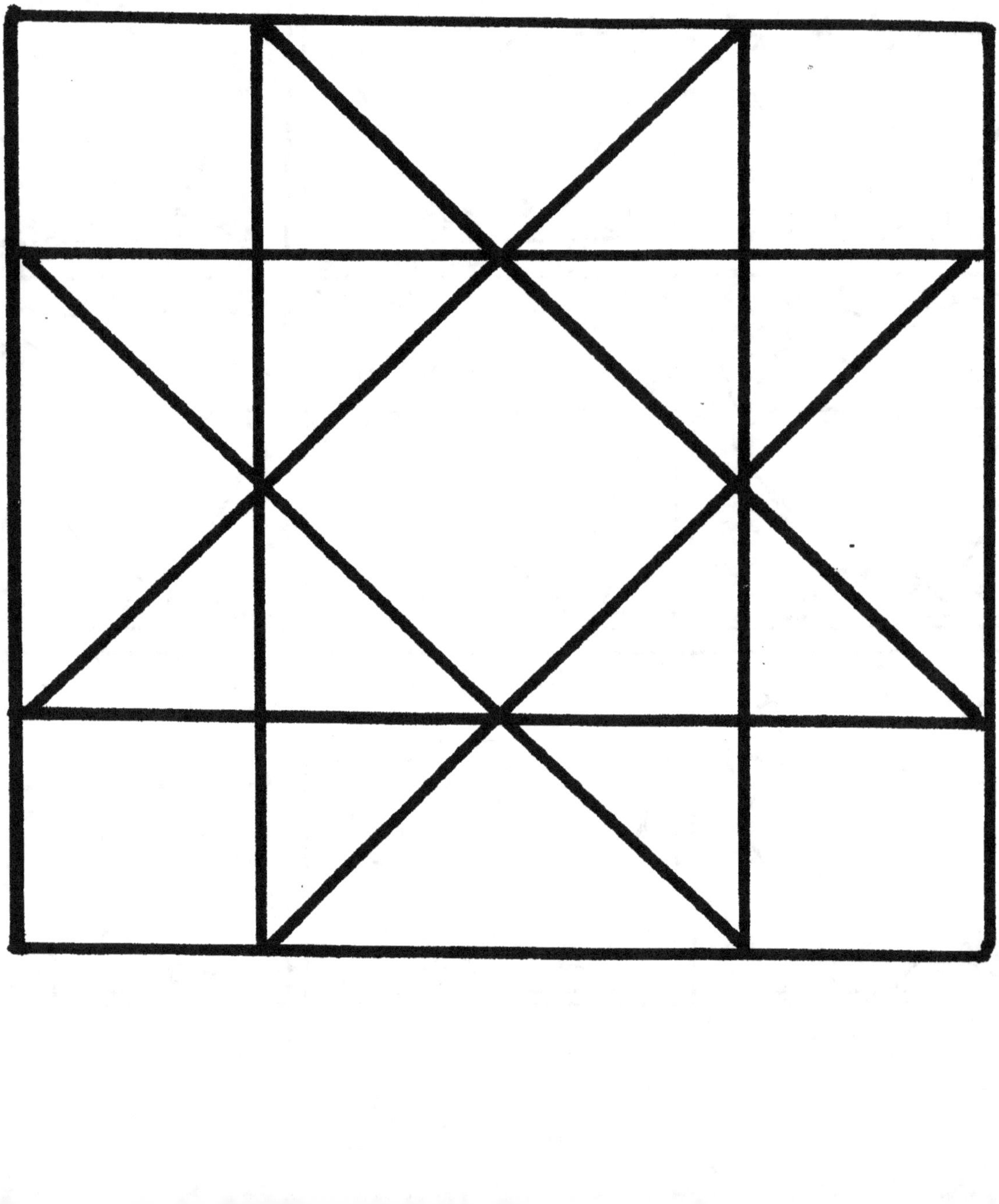

Franklin County Barn Quilt Eight Pointed Star

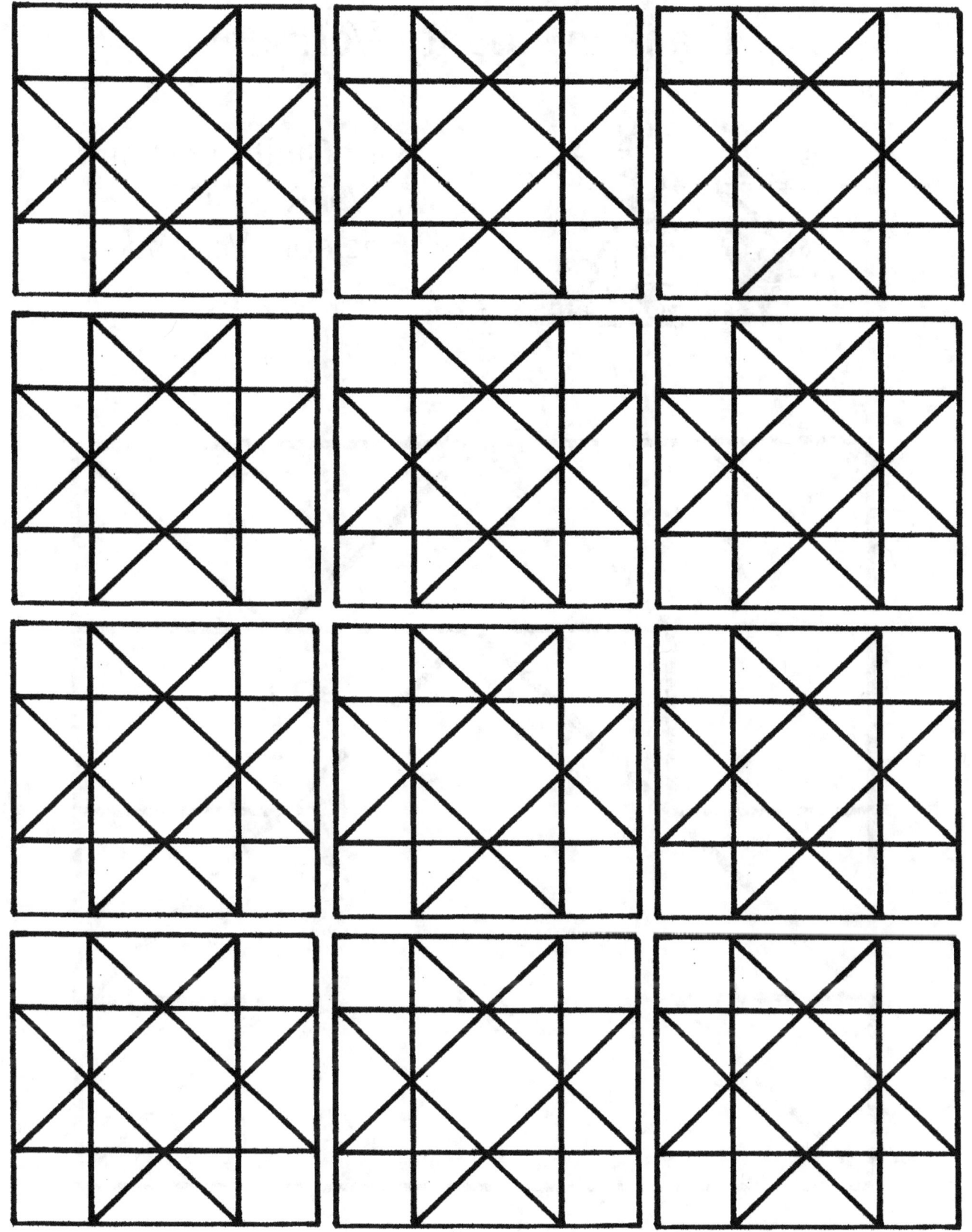

Barn Quilt The Green Mountains
Franklin County Vermont

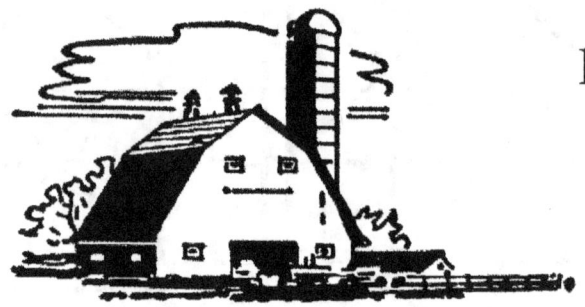

Barn Quilt Location
VT Rte 105
Sheldon, Vermont

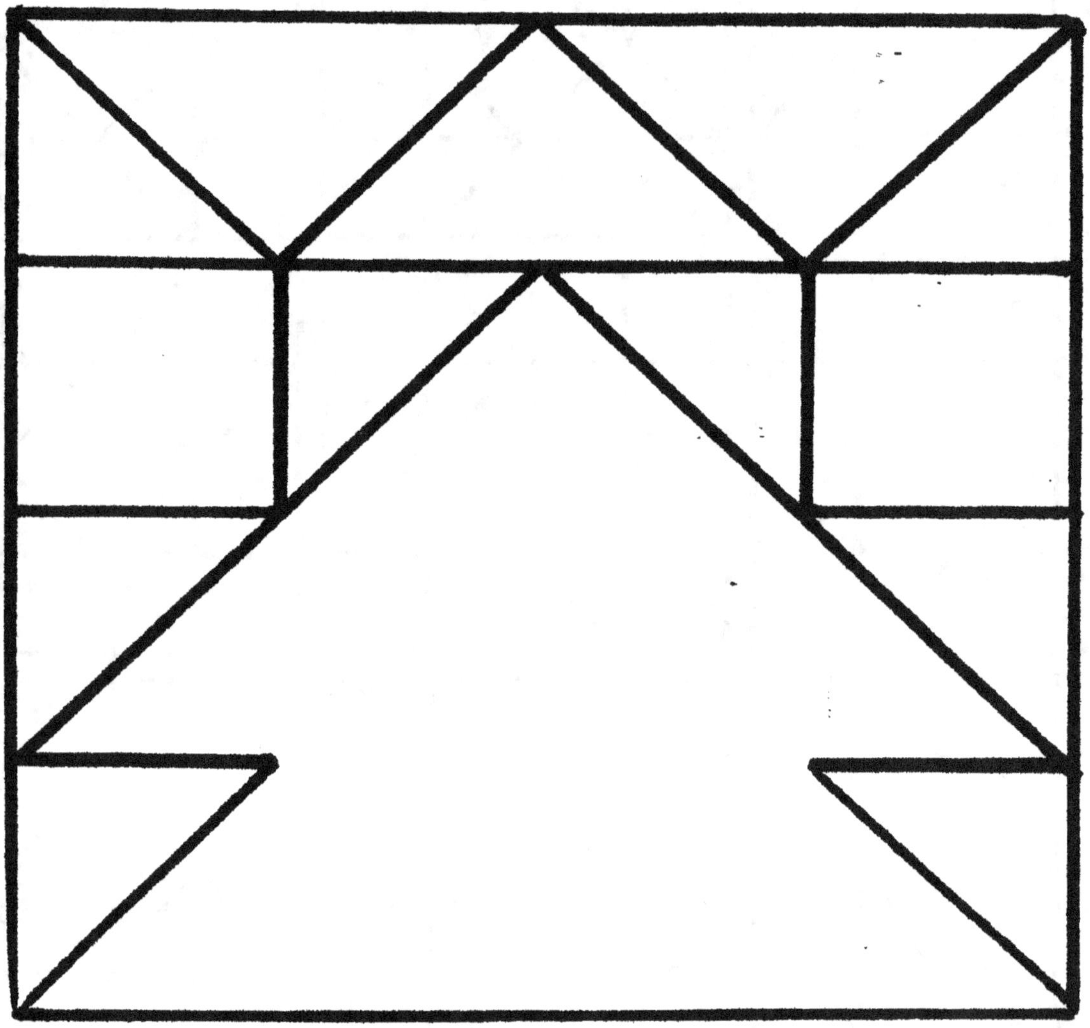

Franklin County Barn Quilt The Green Mountains

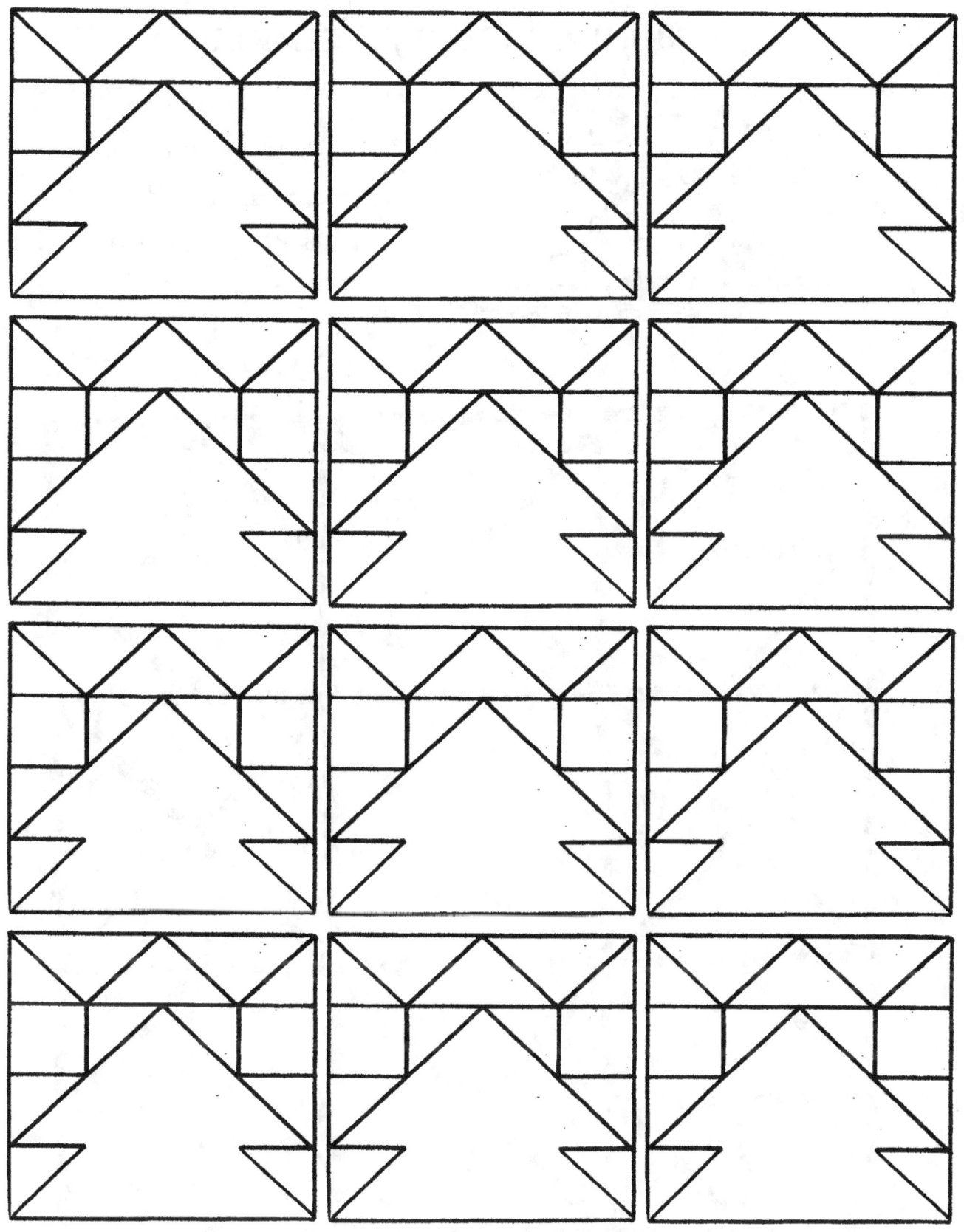

Barn Quilt Star Burst
Franklin County Vermont

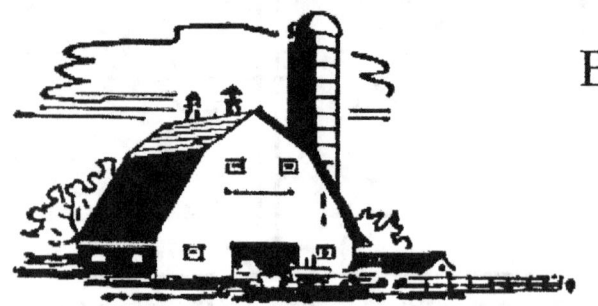

Barn Quilt Location
E. Sheldon Rd
Sheldon, Vermont

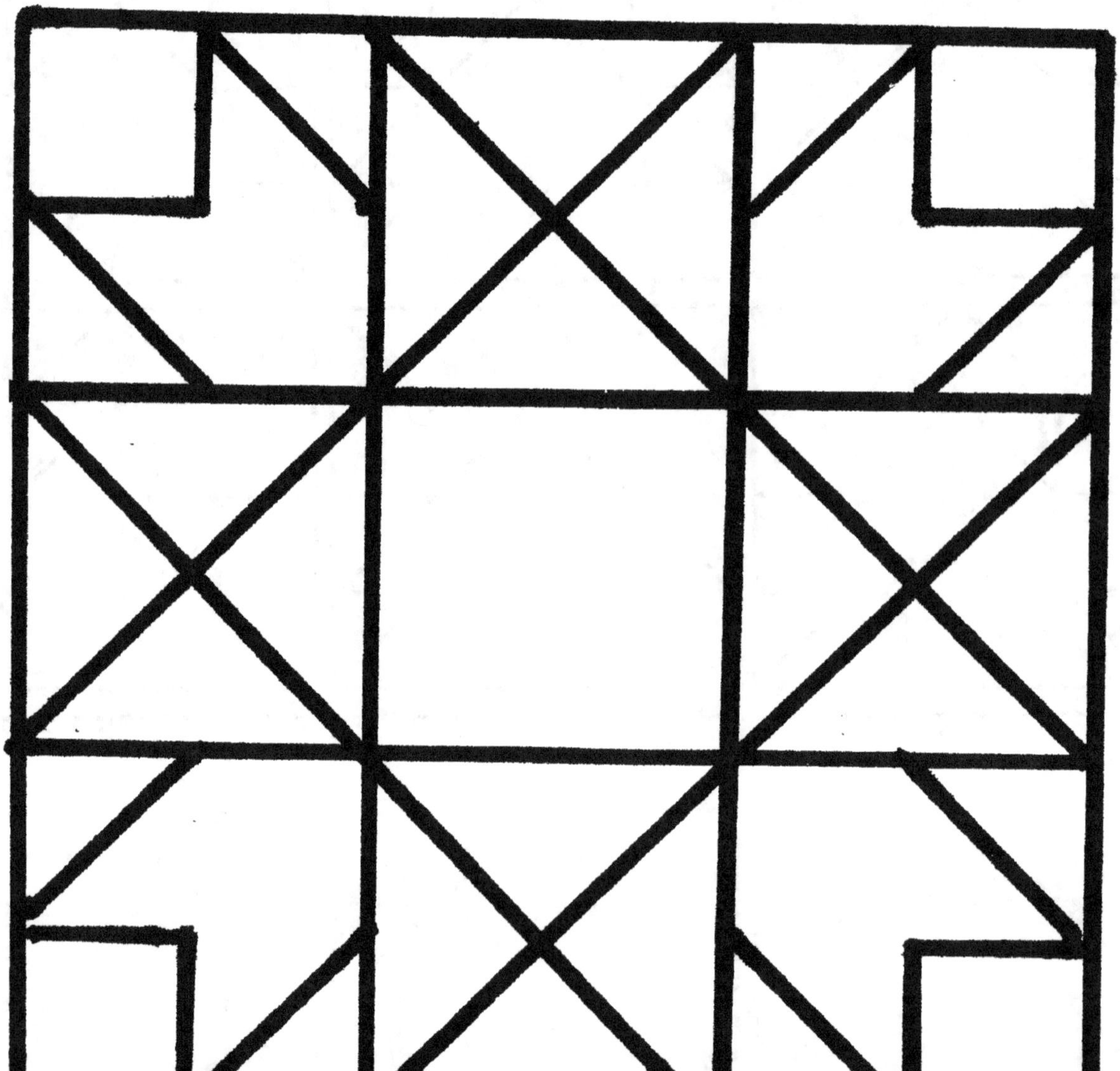

Franklin County Barn Quilt Star Burst

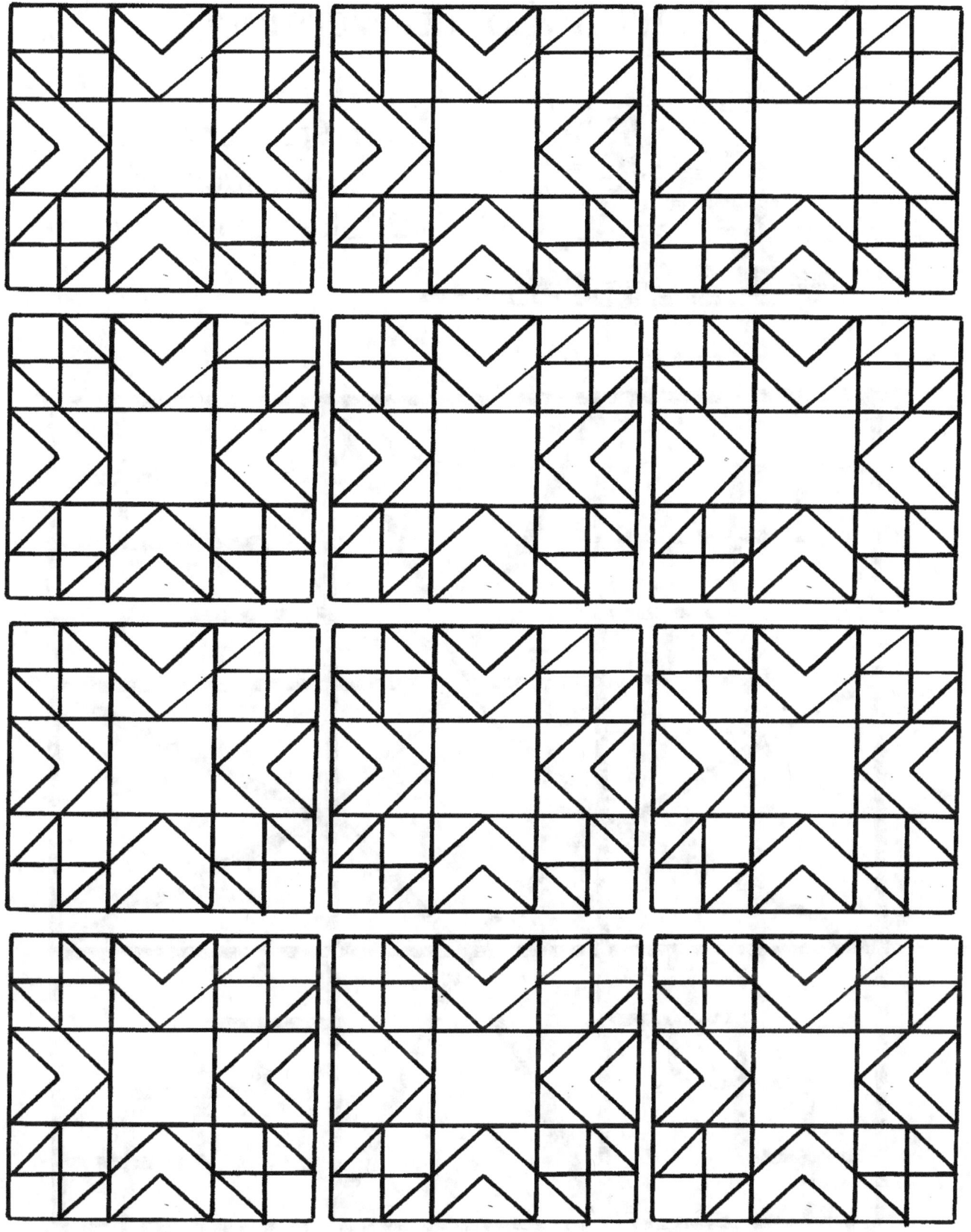

Barn Quilt Friendship Star Variation
Franklin County Vermont

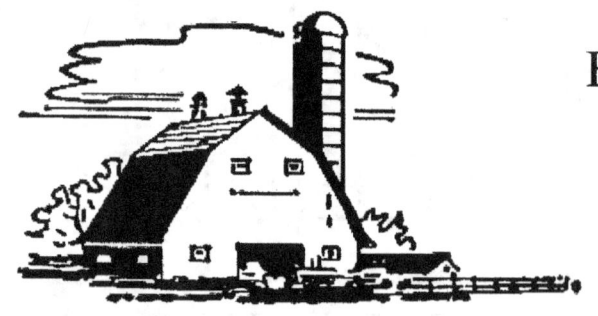

Barn Quilt Location
E. Sheldon Rd
Sheldon, Vermont

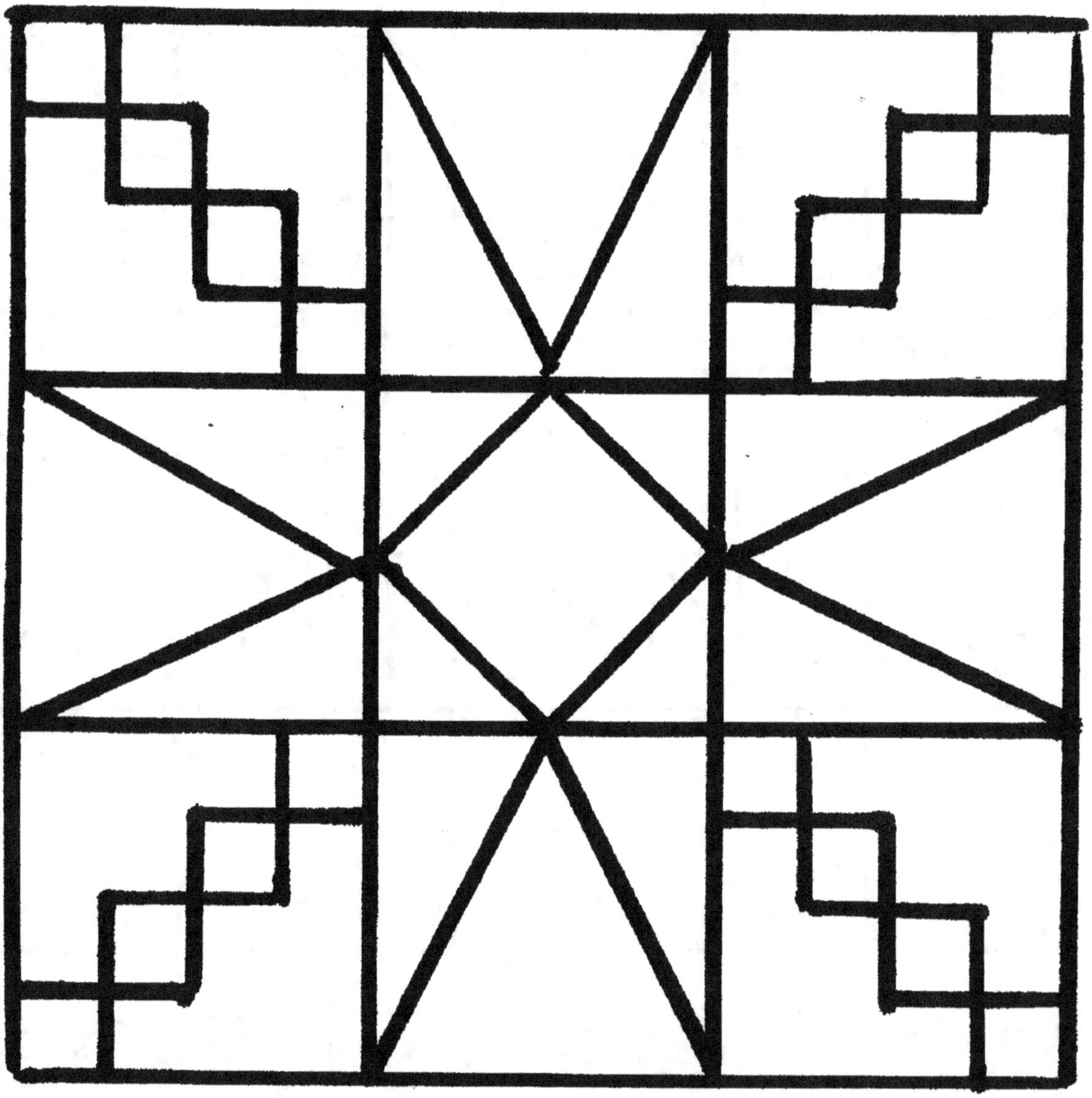

Franklin County Barn Quilt Friendship Star Variation

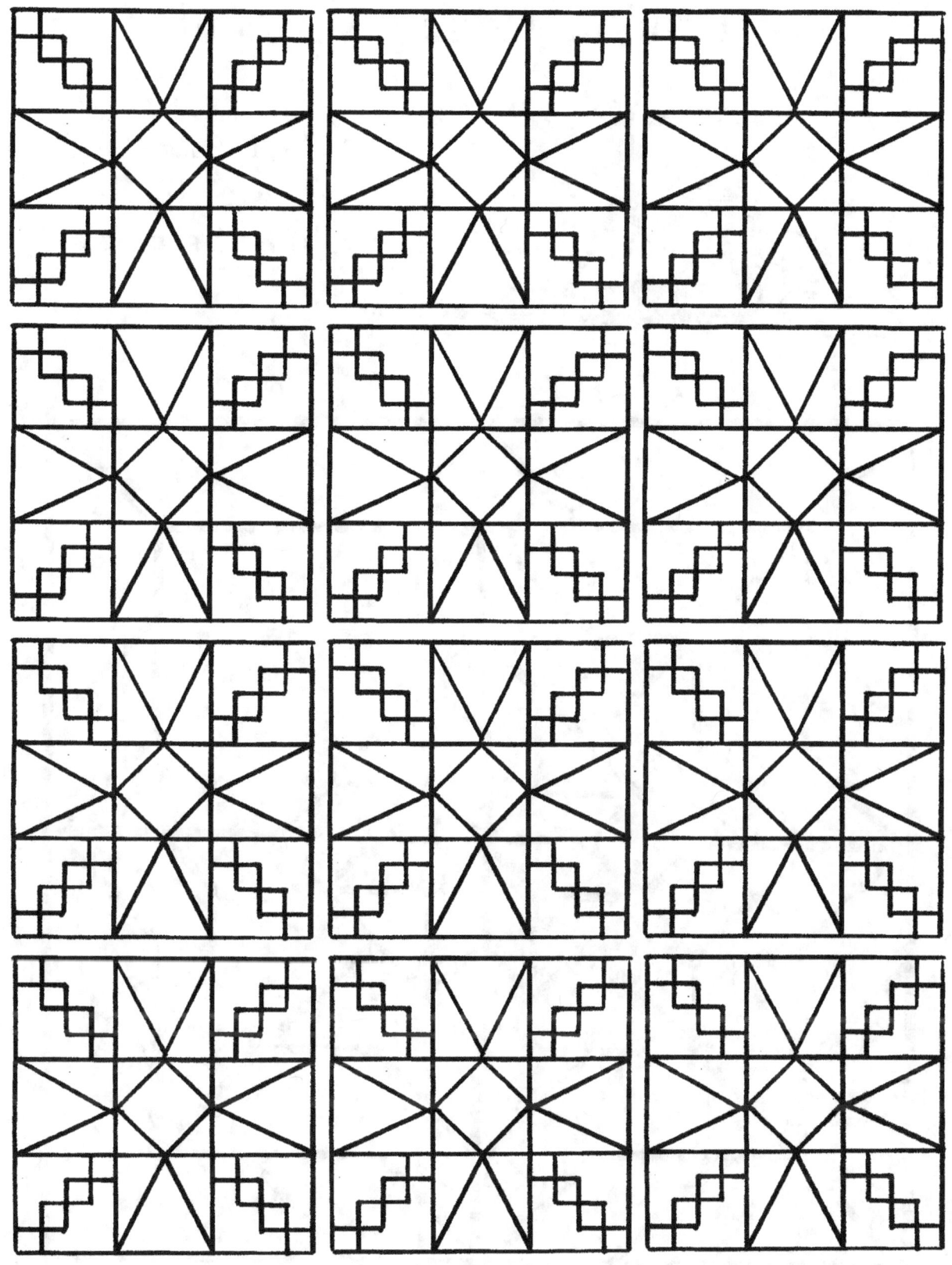

Barn Quilt Chained Star Variation
Franklin County Vermont

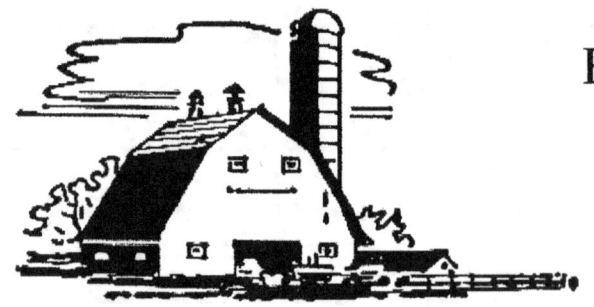

Barn Quilt Location
VT Rte 105
Sheldon, Vermont

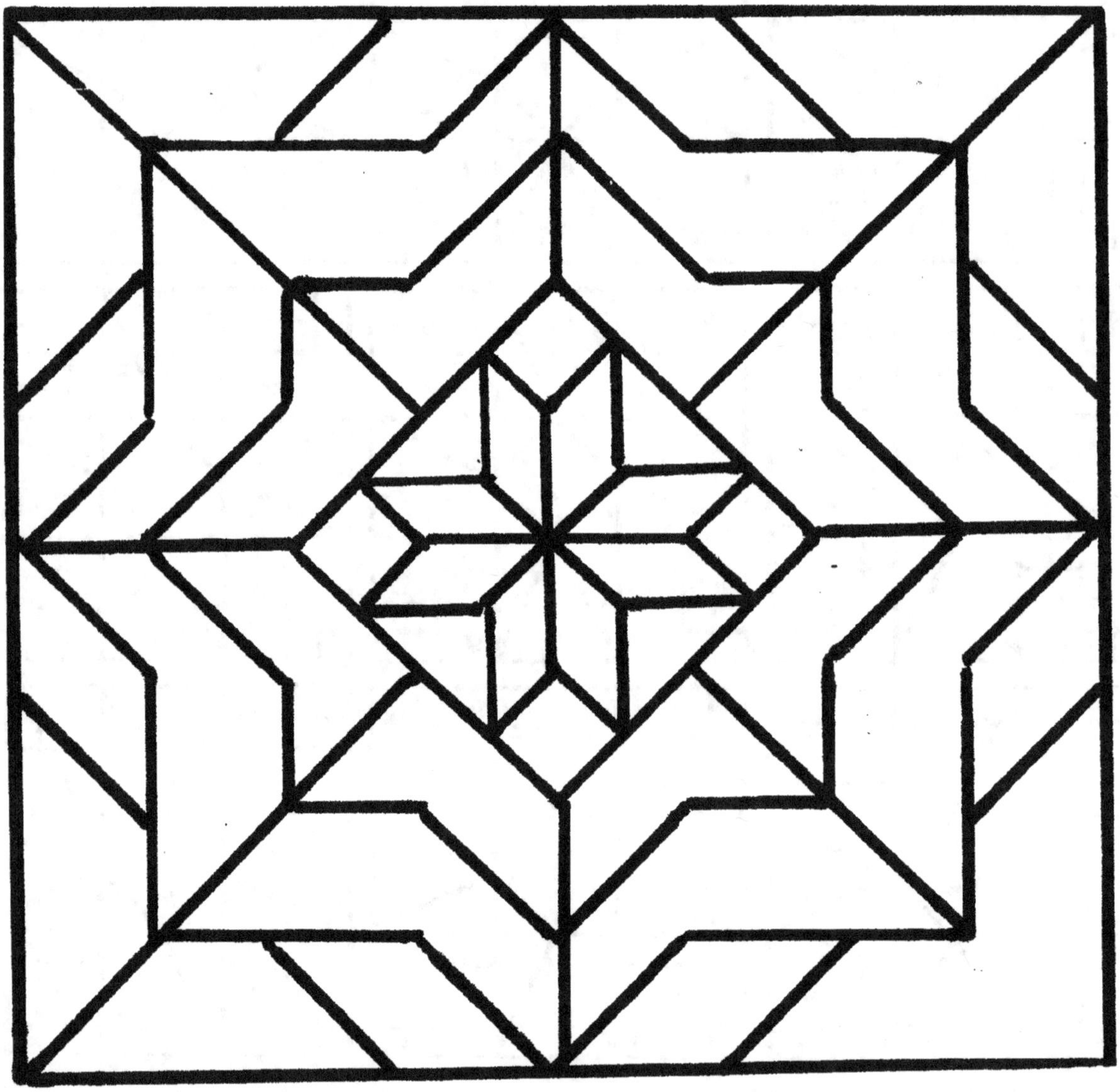

Franklin County Barn Quilt Chained Star Variation

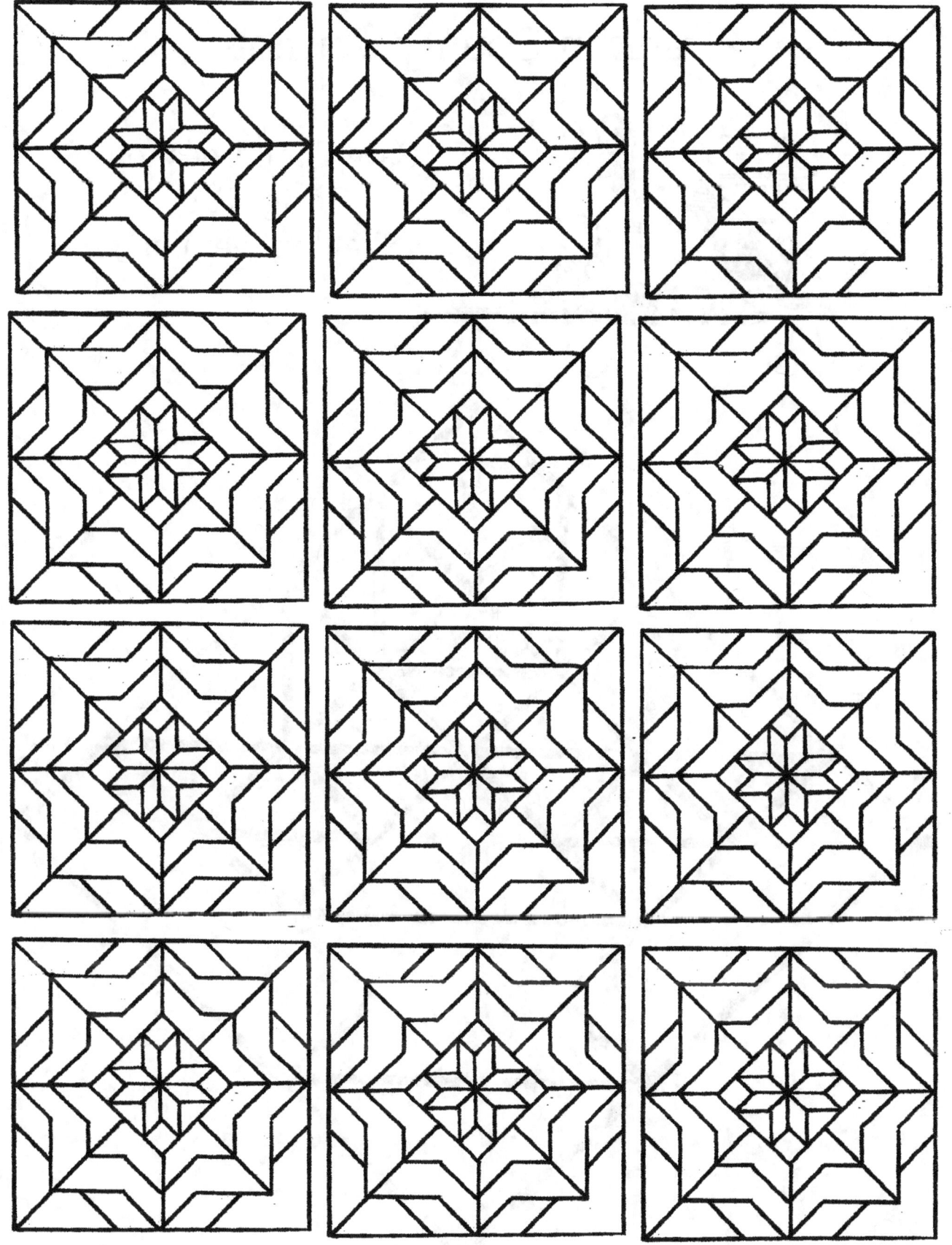

Barn Quilt Basket of Flowers
Franklin County Vermont

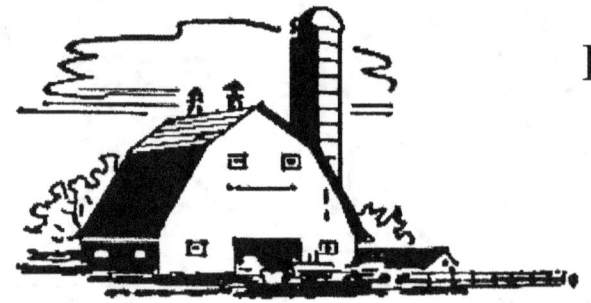

Barn Quilt Location
Bridge Rd
Sheldon, Vermont

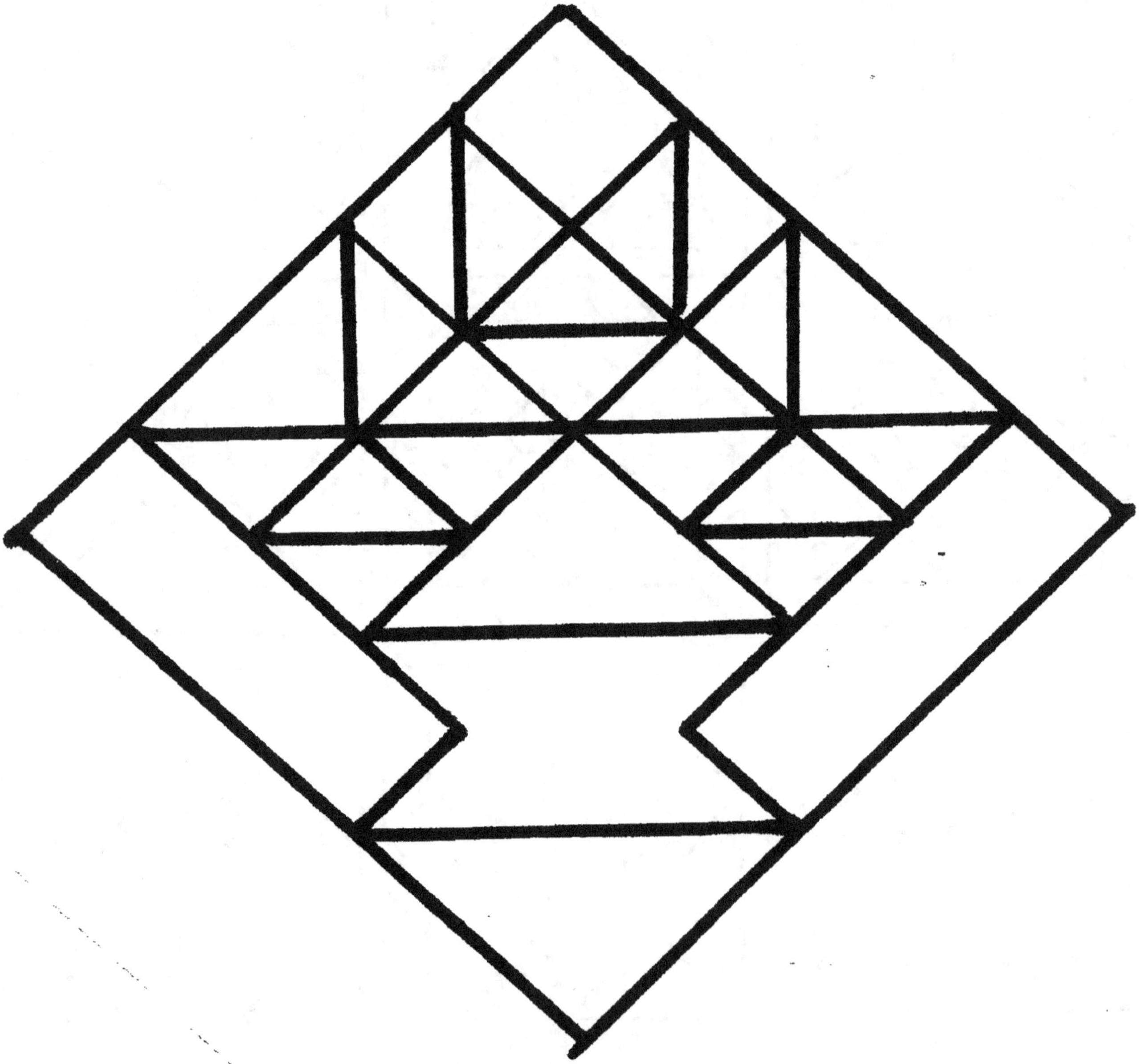

Franklin County Barn Basket of Flowers

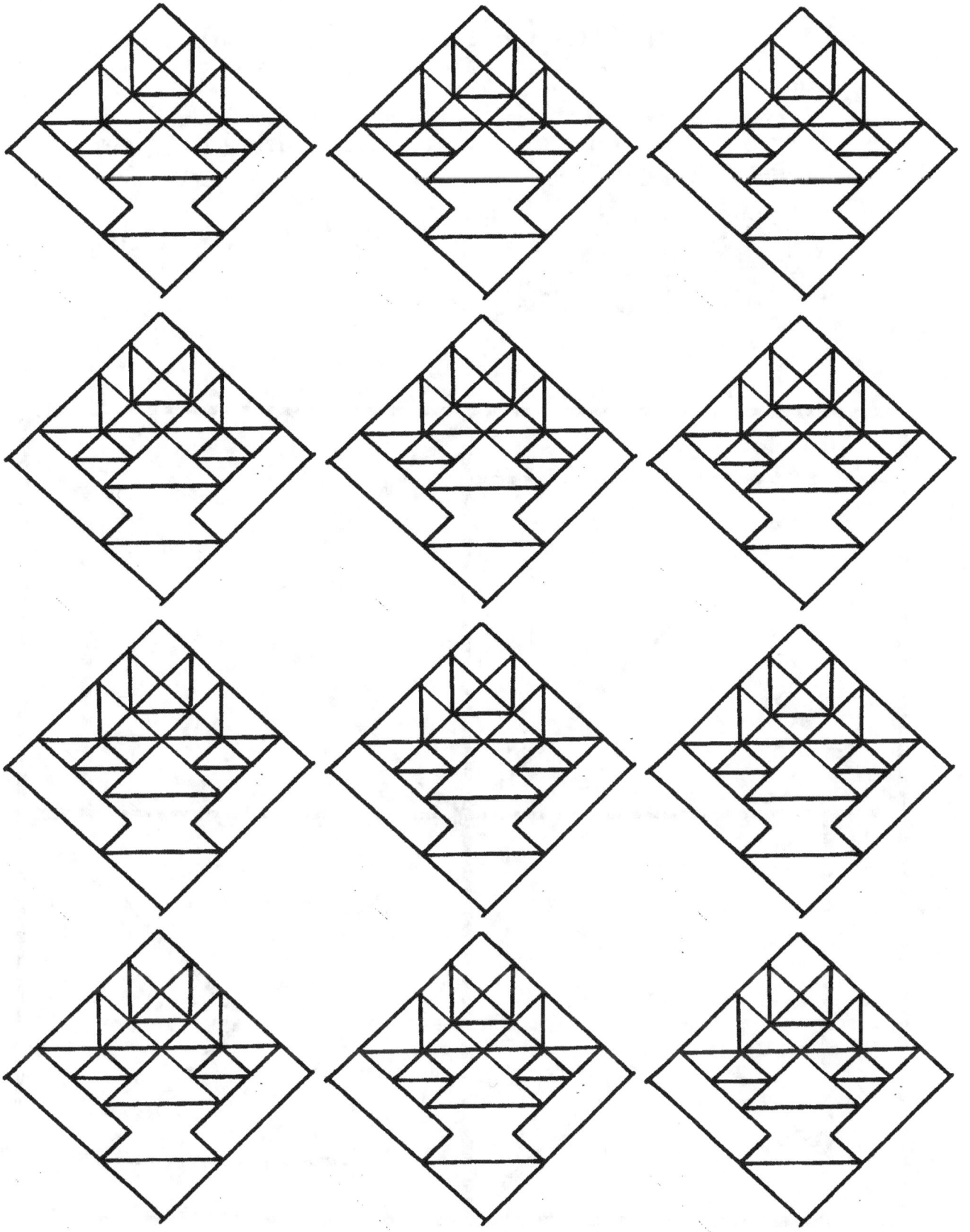

Barn Quilt Blazing Star
Franklin County Vermont

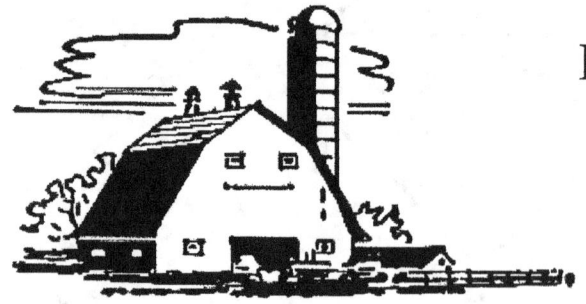

Barn Quilt Location
Kane Rd
Sheldon, Vermont

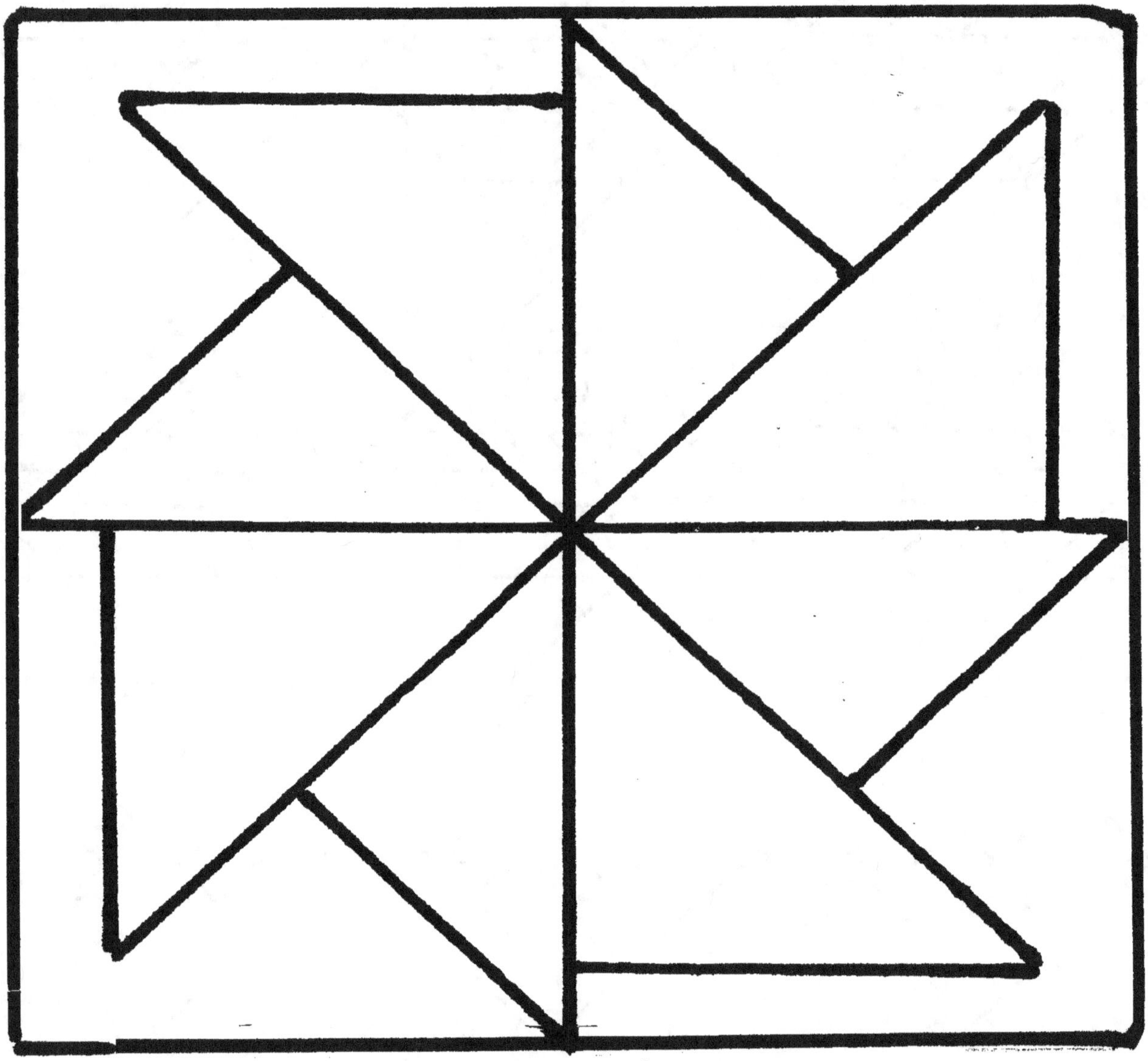

Franklin County Barn Quilt Blazing Star

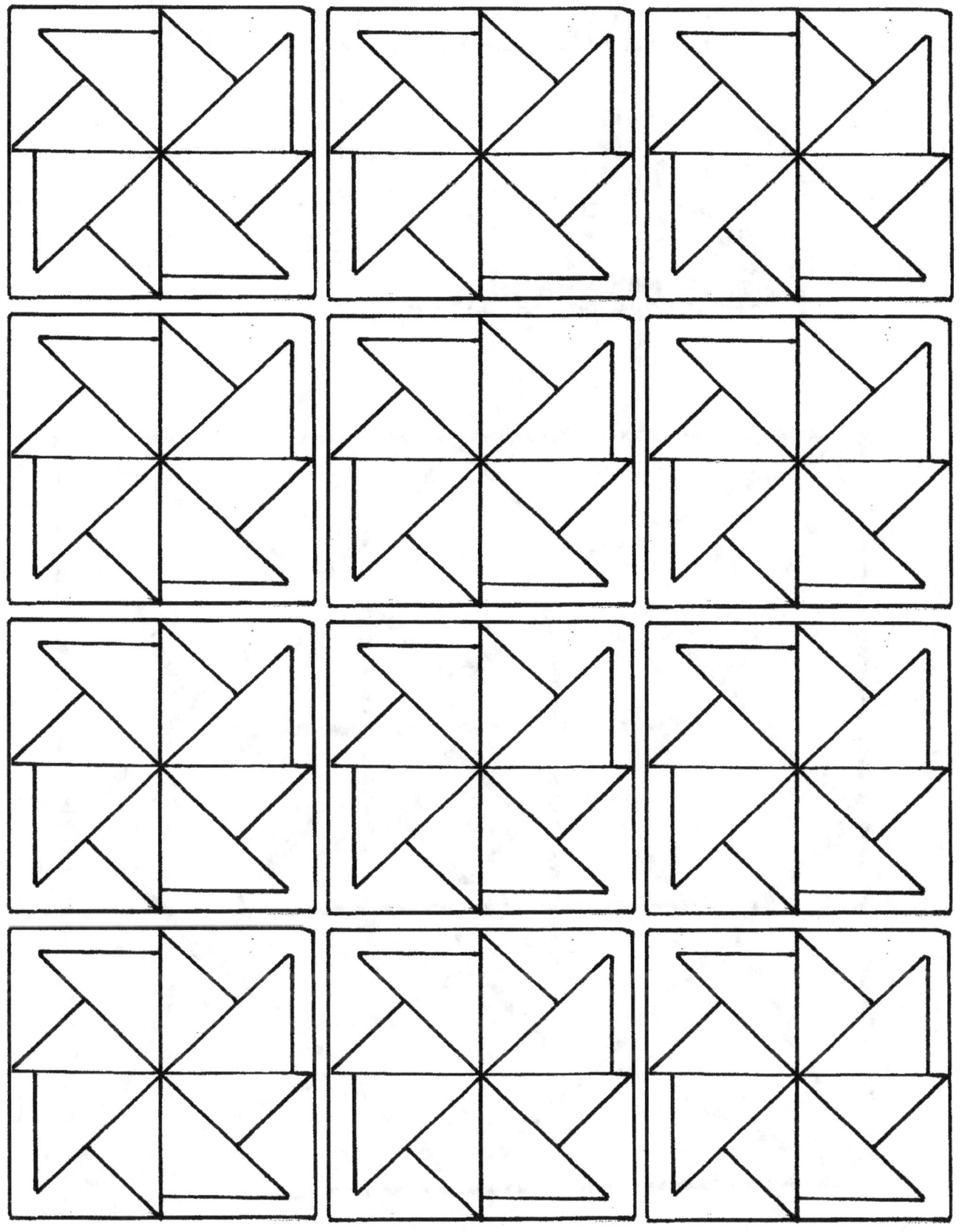

Barn Quilt Pinwheel
Franklin County Vermont

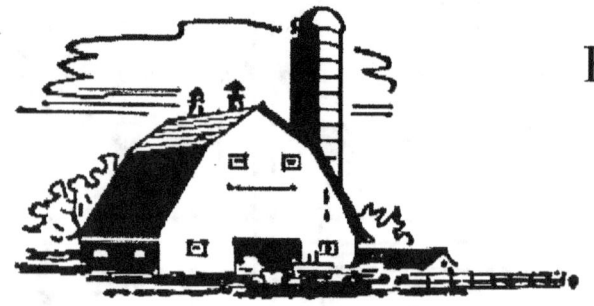

Barn Quilt Location
Kane Rd
Sheldon, Vermont

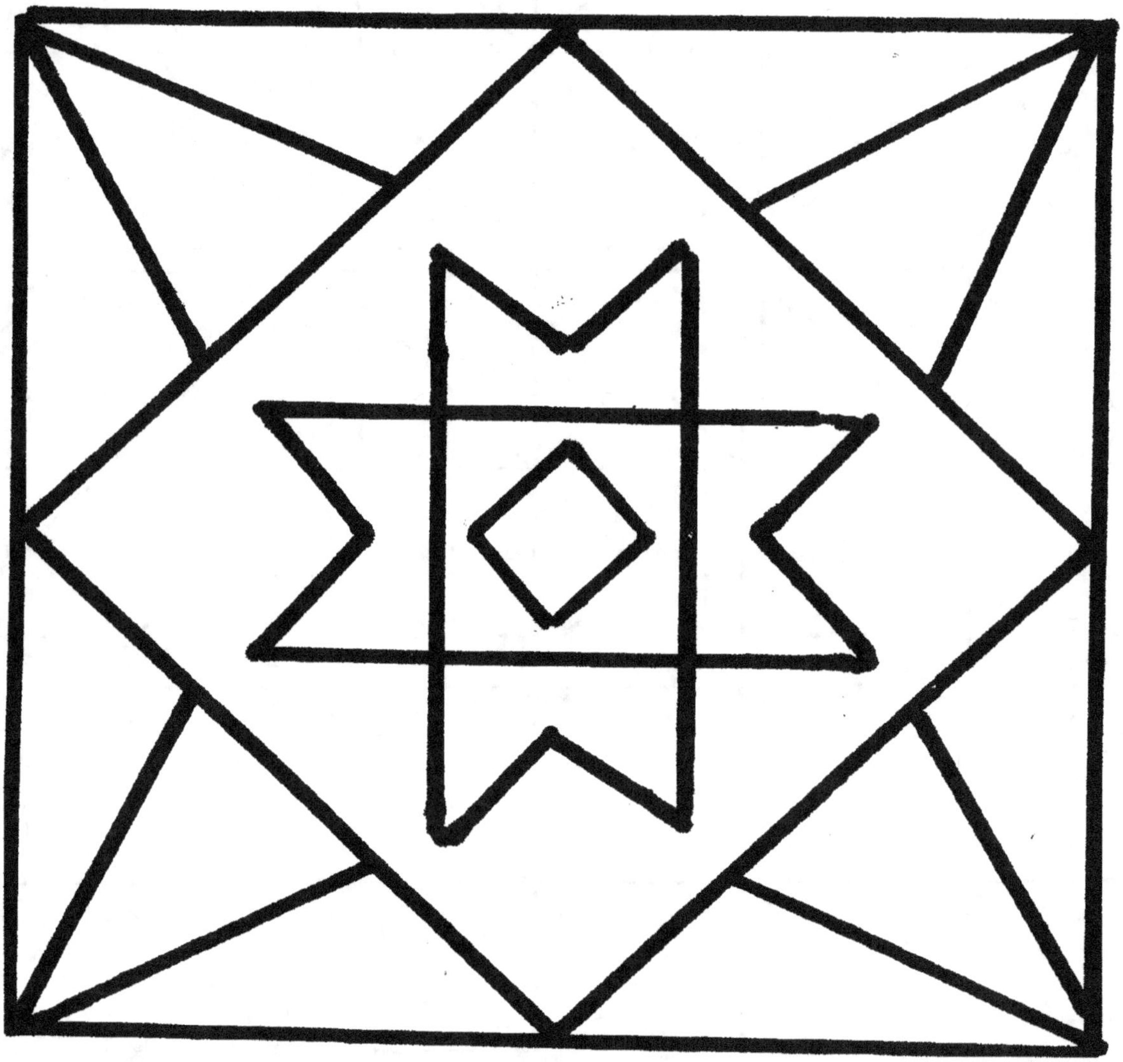

Franklin County Barn Quilt Pinwheel

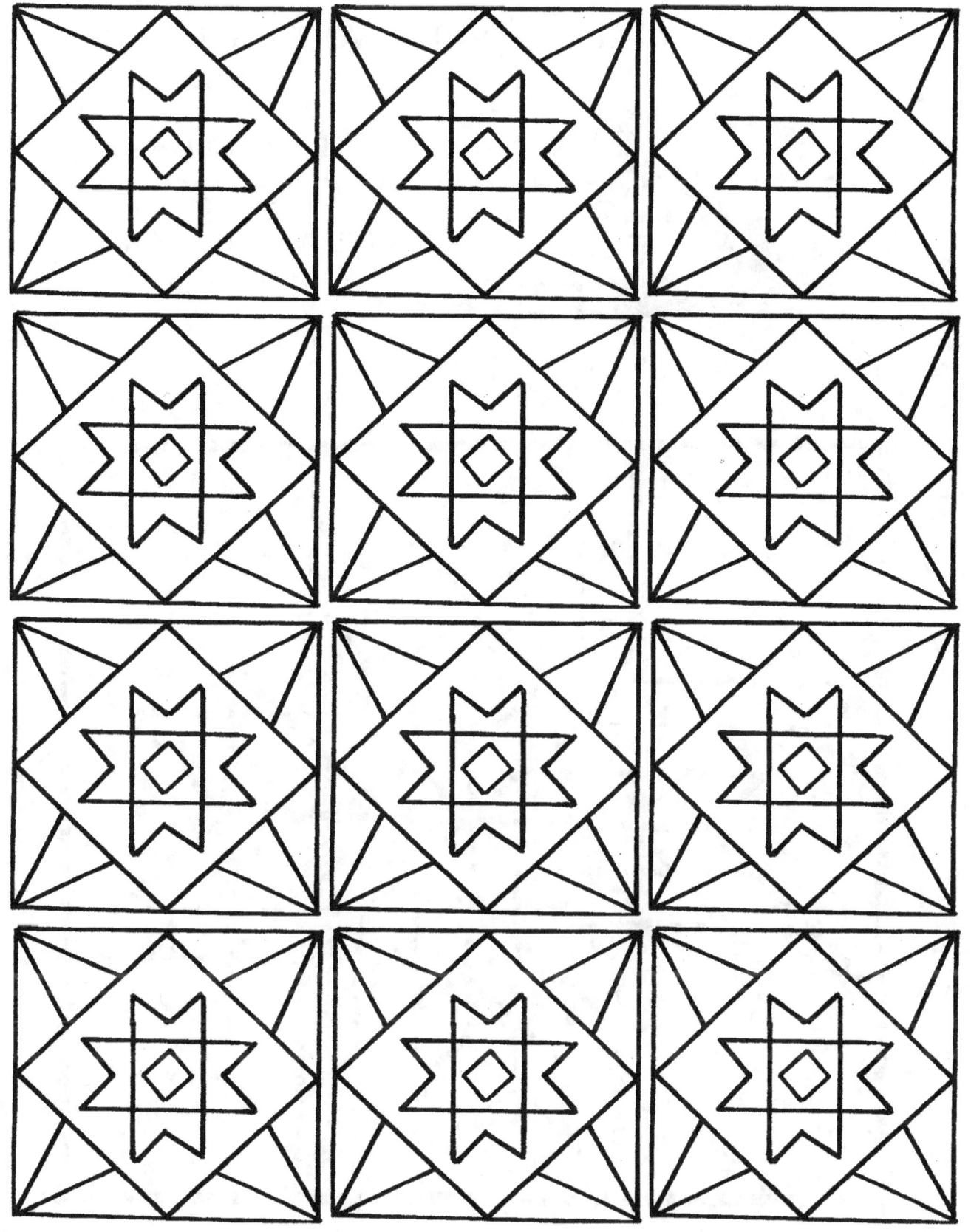

Barn Quilt Radiant Star
Franklin County Vermont

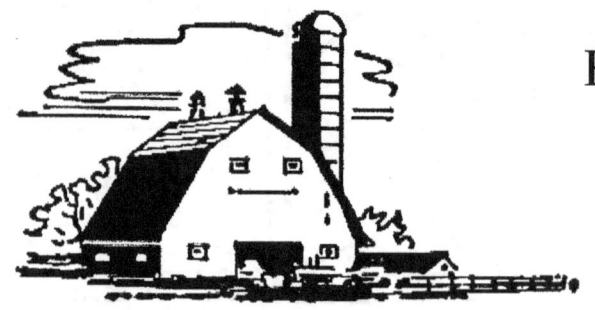

Barn Quilt Location
VT Rte 105
Sheldon, Vermont

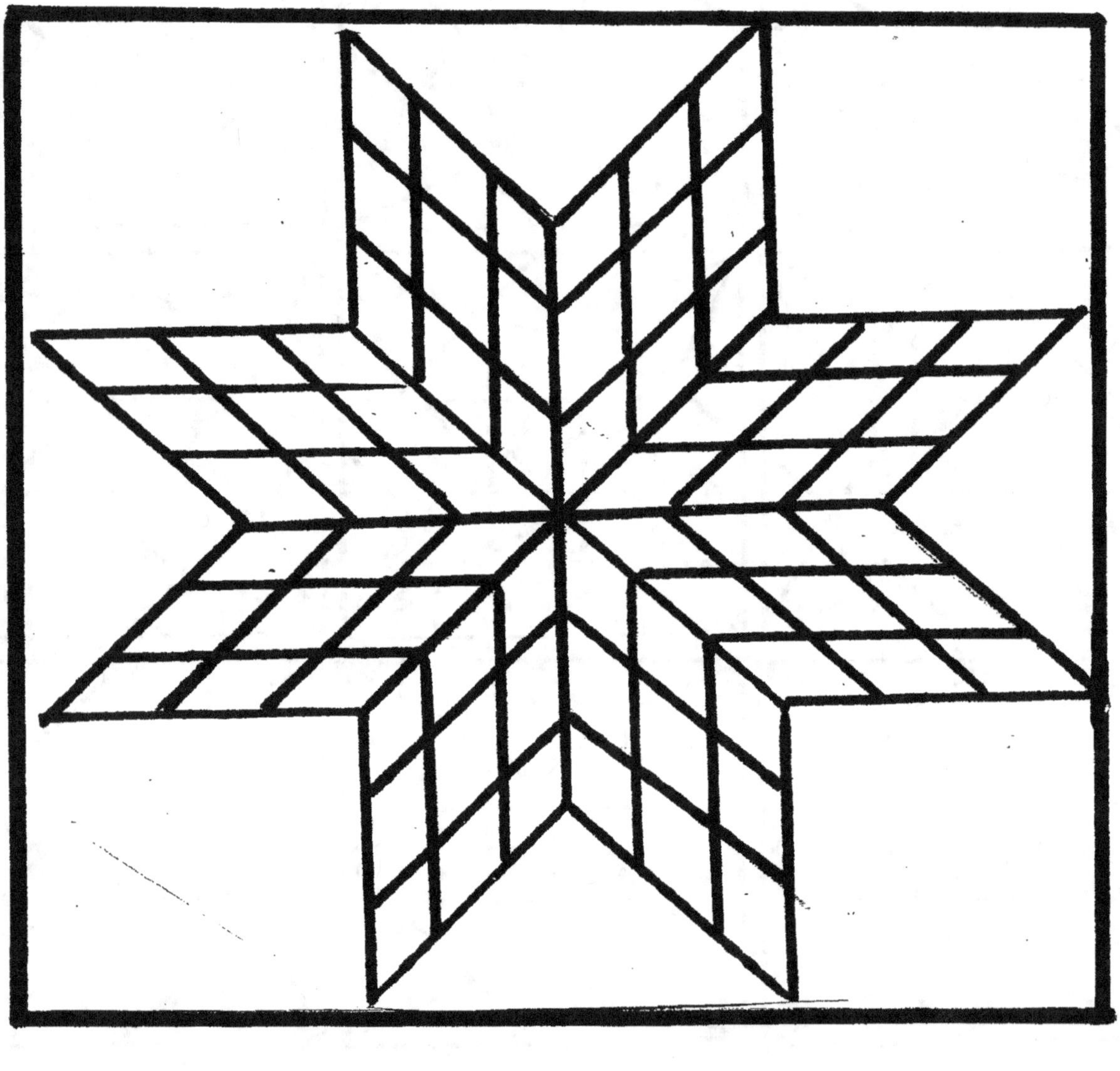

Franklin County Barn Quilt Radiant Star

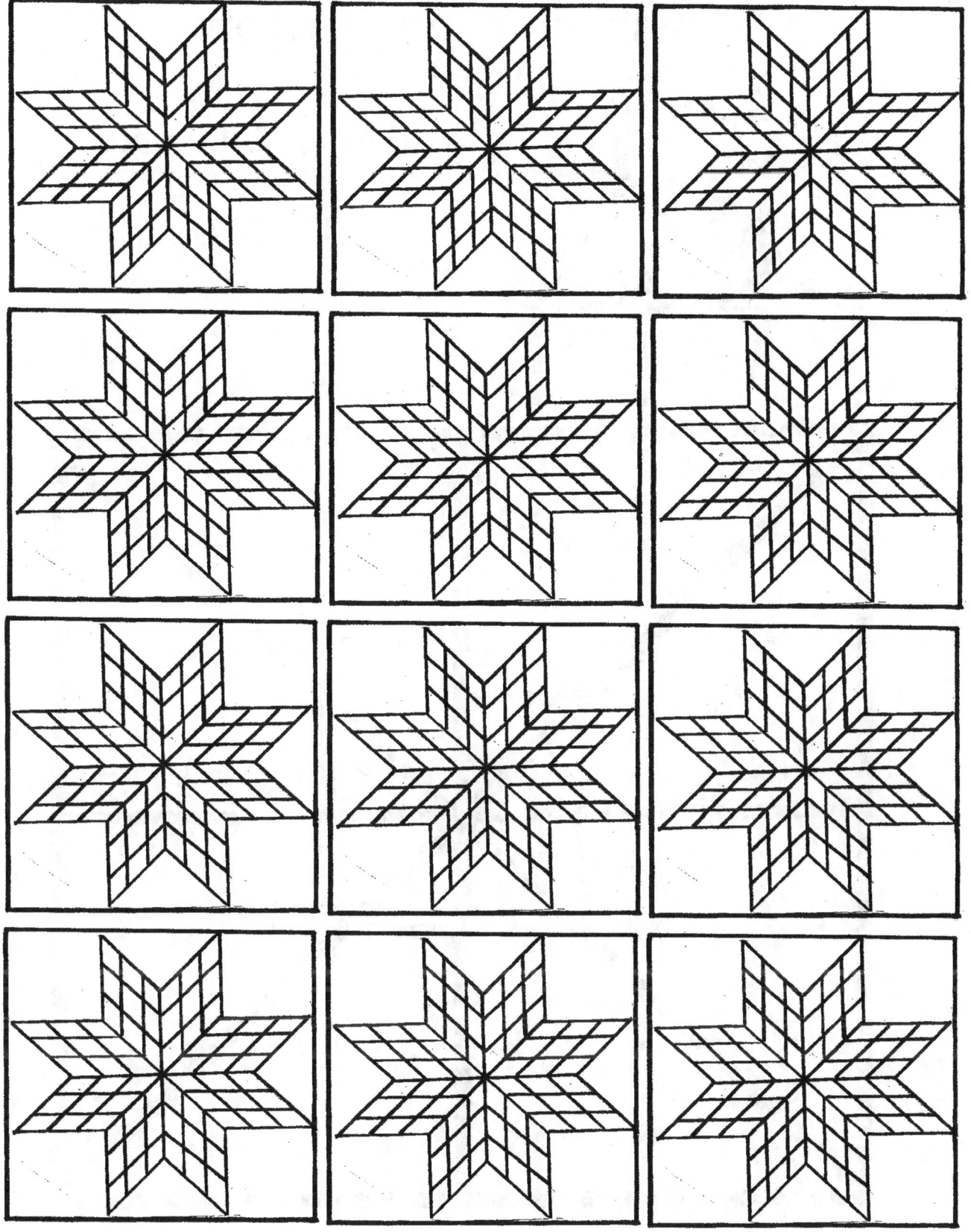

Barn Quilt Pinwheel
Franklin County Vermont

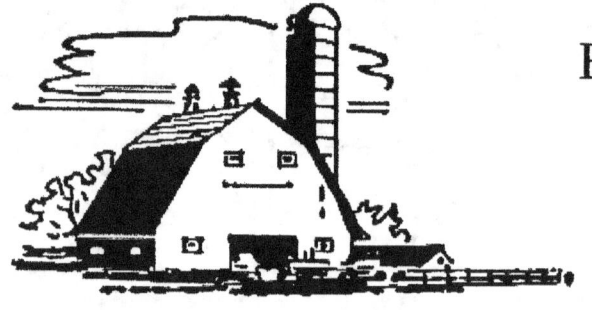

Barn Quilt Location
VT Rte 105
Sheldon, Vermont

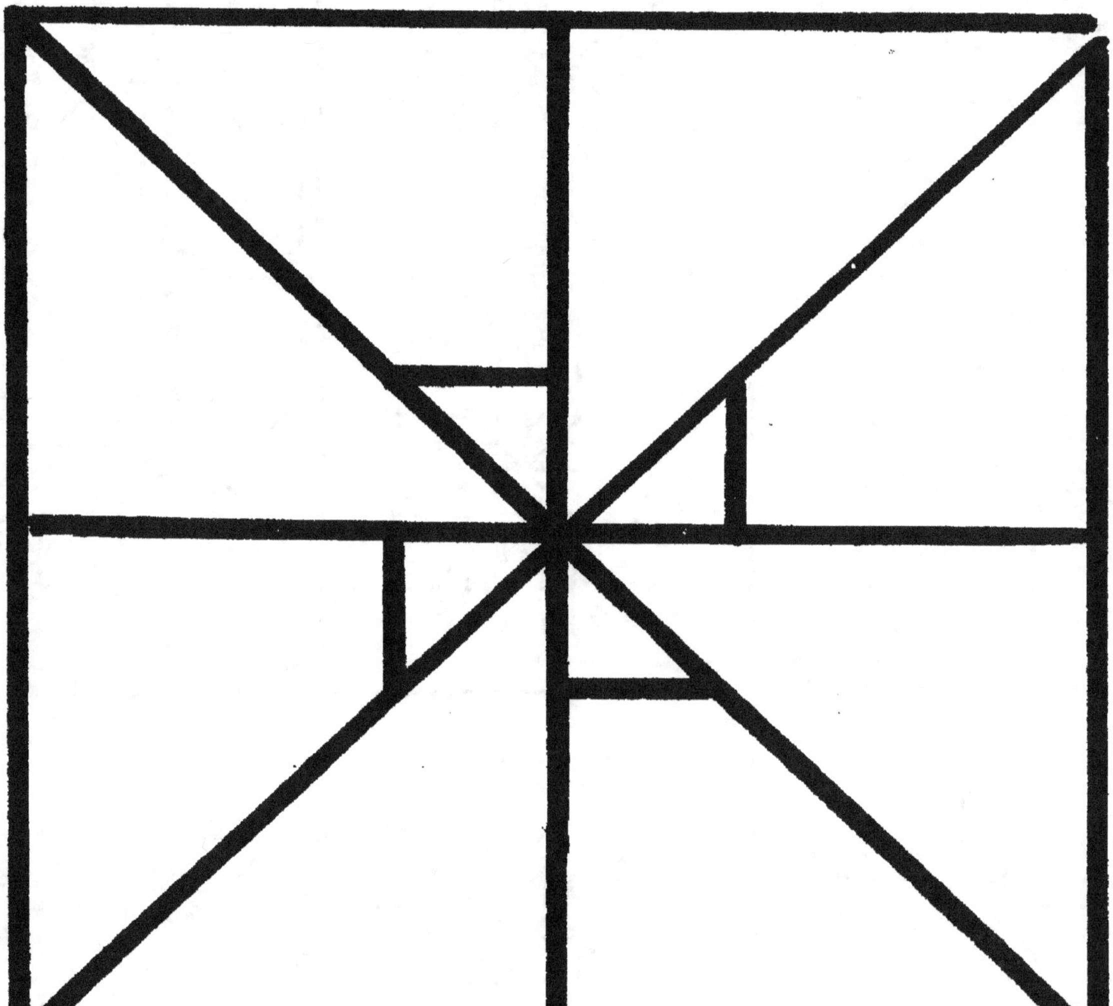

Franklin County Barn Quilt Pinwheel

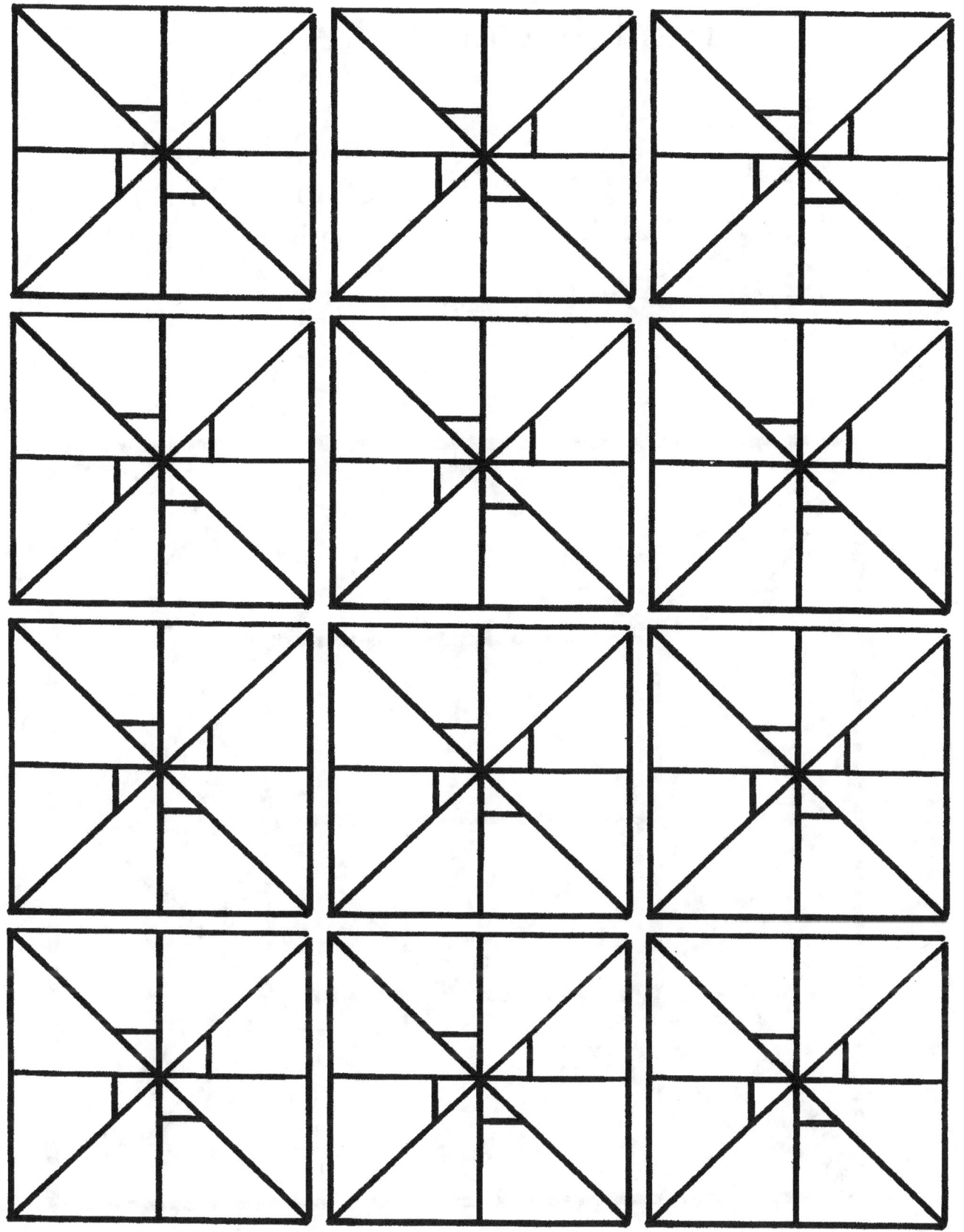

Barn Quilt Children Take Wing
Franklin County Vermont

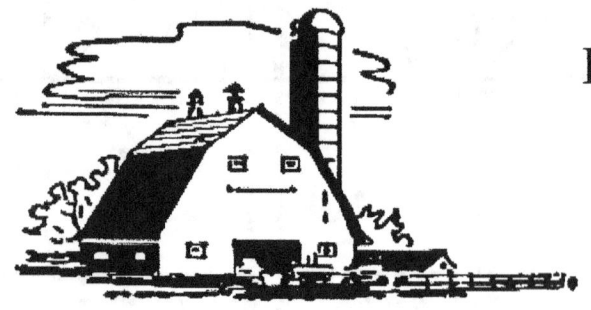

Barn Quilt Location
Poor Farm Rd
Sheldon, Vermont

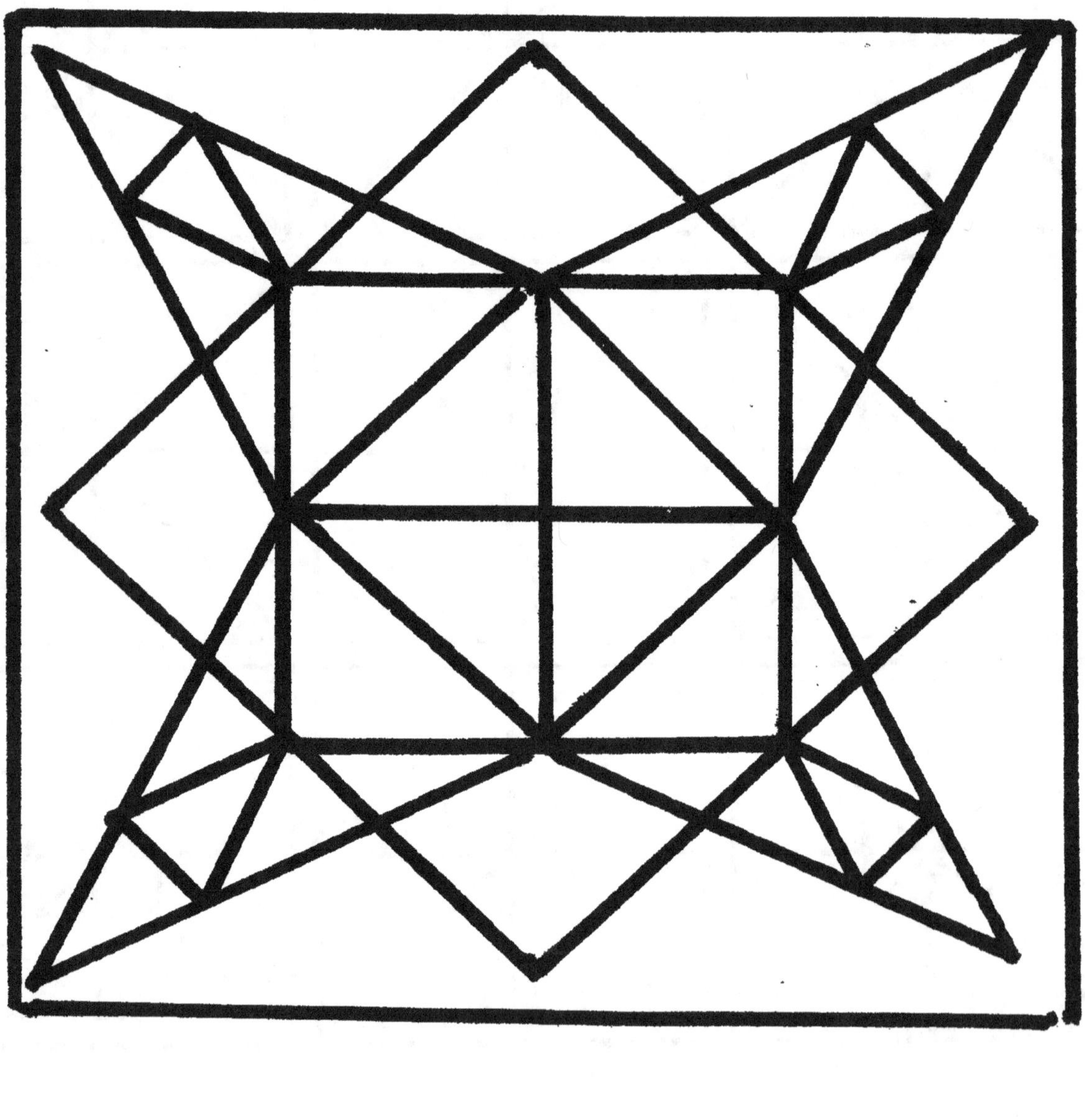

Franklin County Barn Quilt Children Take Wing

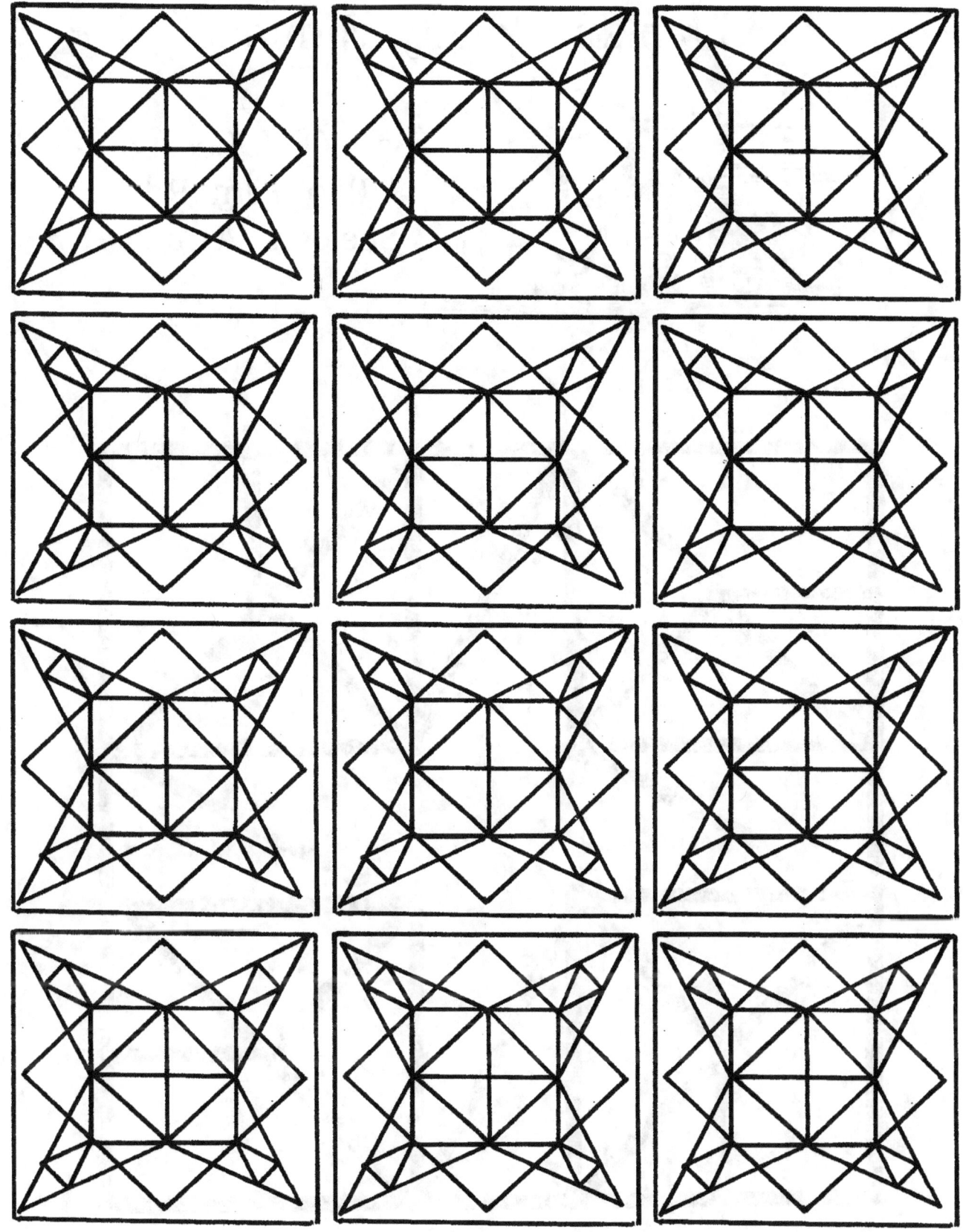

Barn Quilt Follow the Leader
Franklin County Vermont

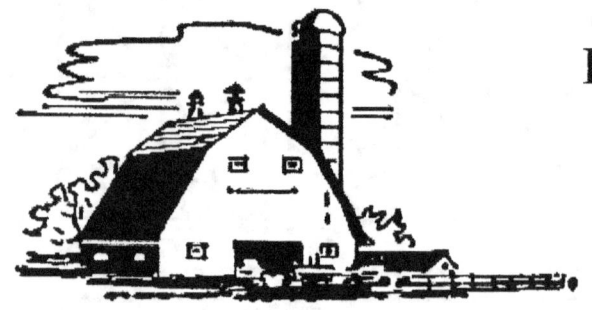

Barn Quilt Location
Poor Farm Rd
Sheldon, Vermont

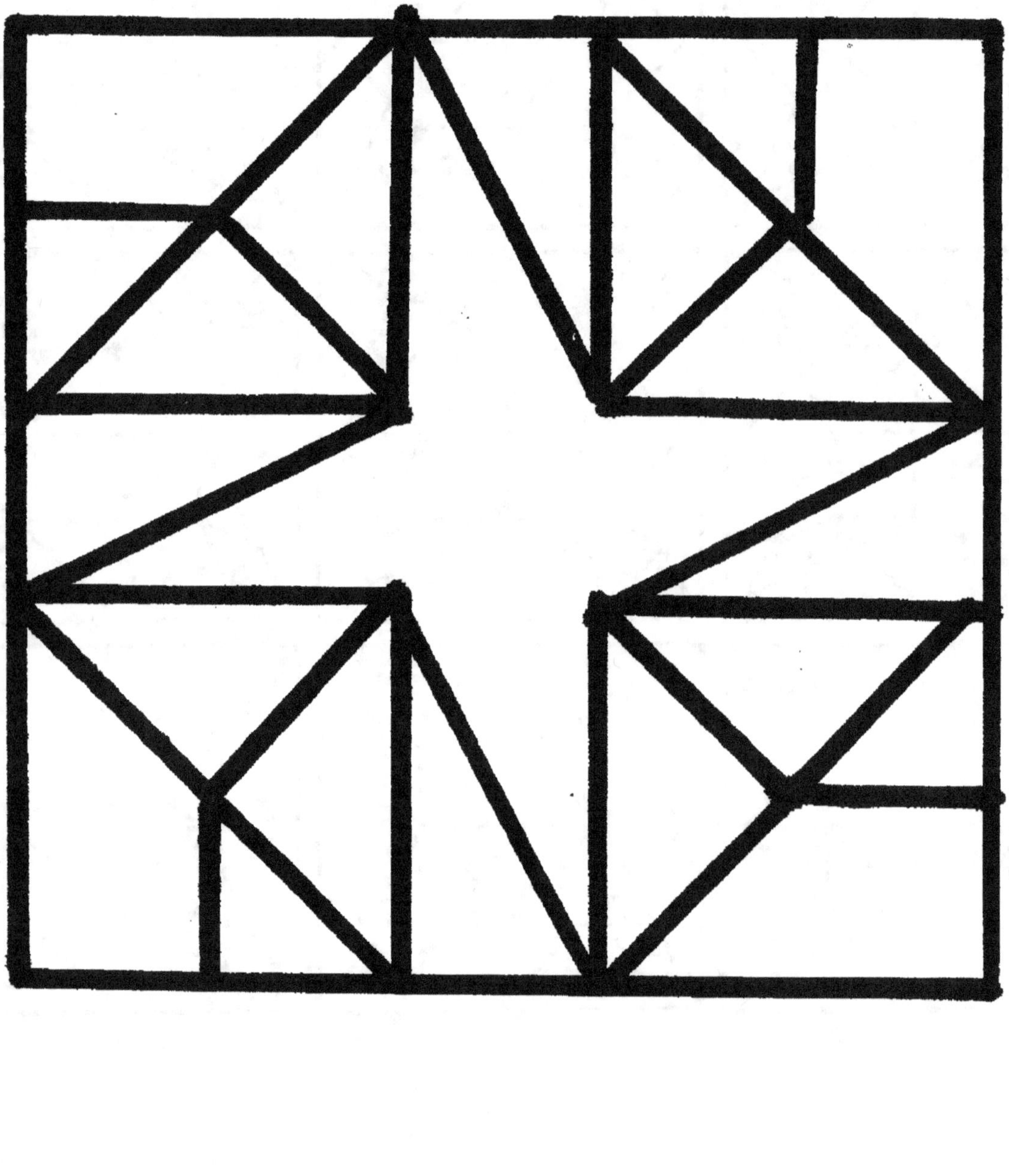

Franklin County Barn Quilt Follow the Leader

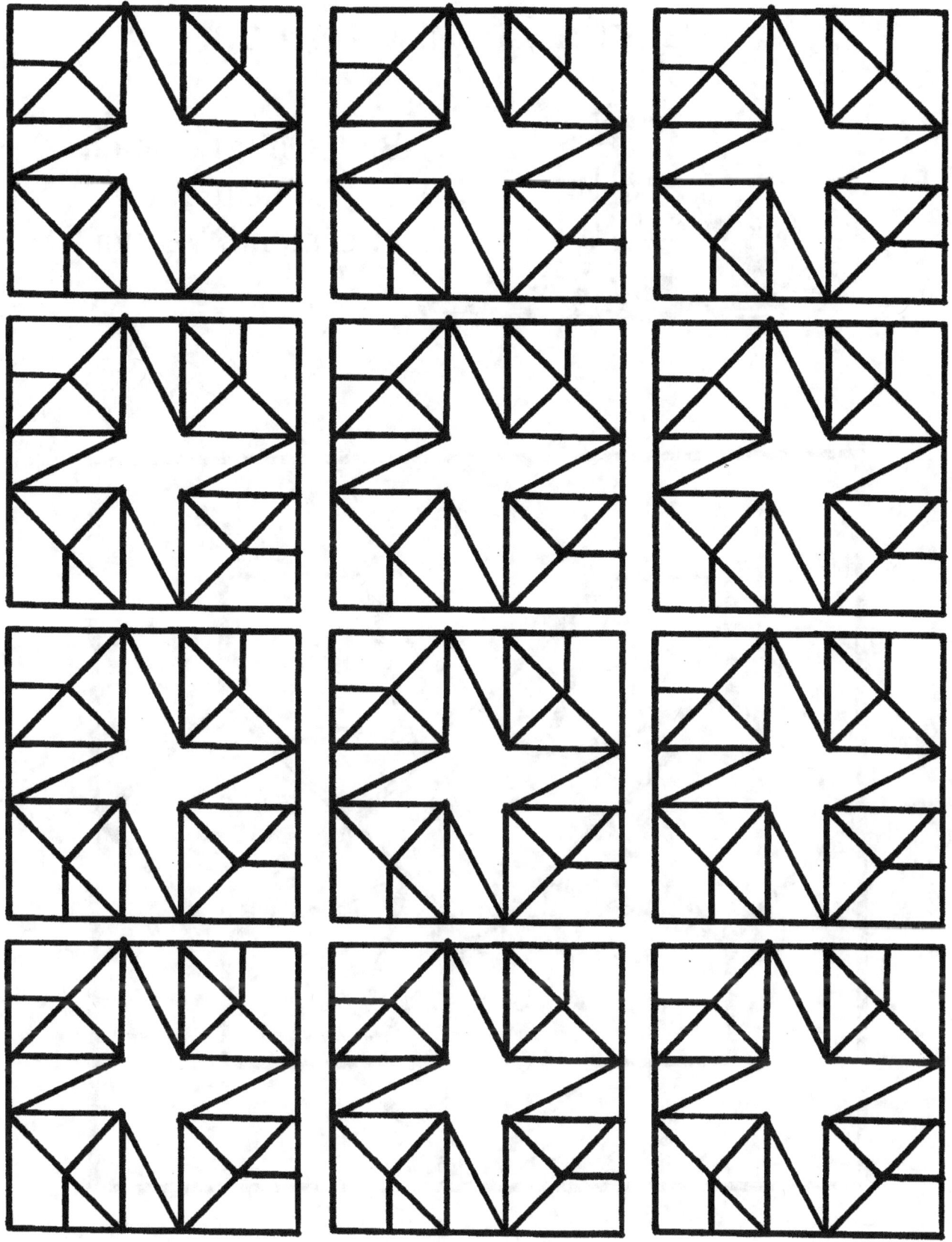

Barn Quilt Grandmother's Garden
Franklin County Vermont

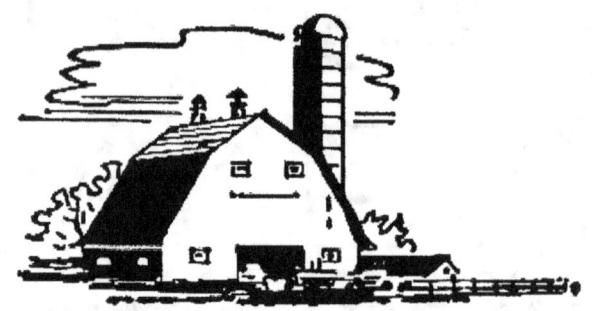

Barn Quilt Location
Guilnette Rd
Richmond, Vermont

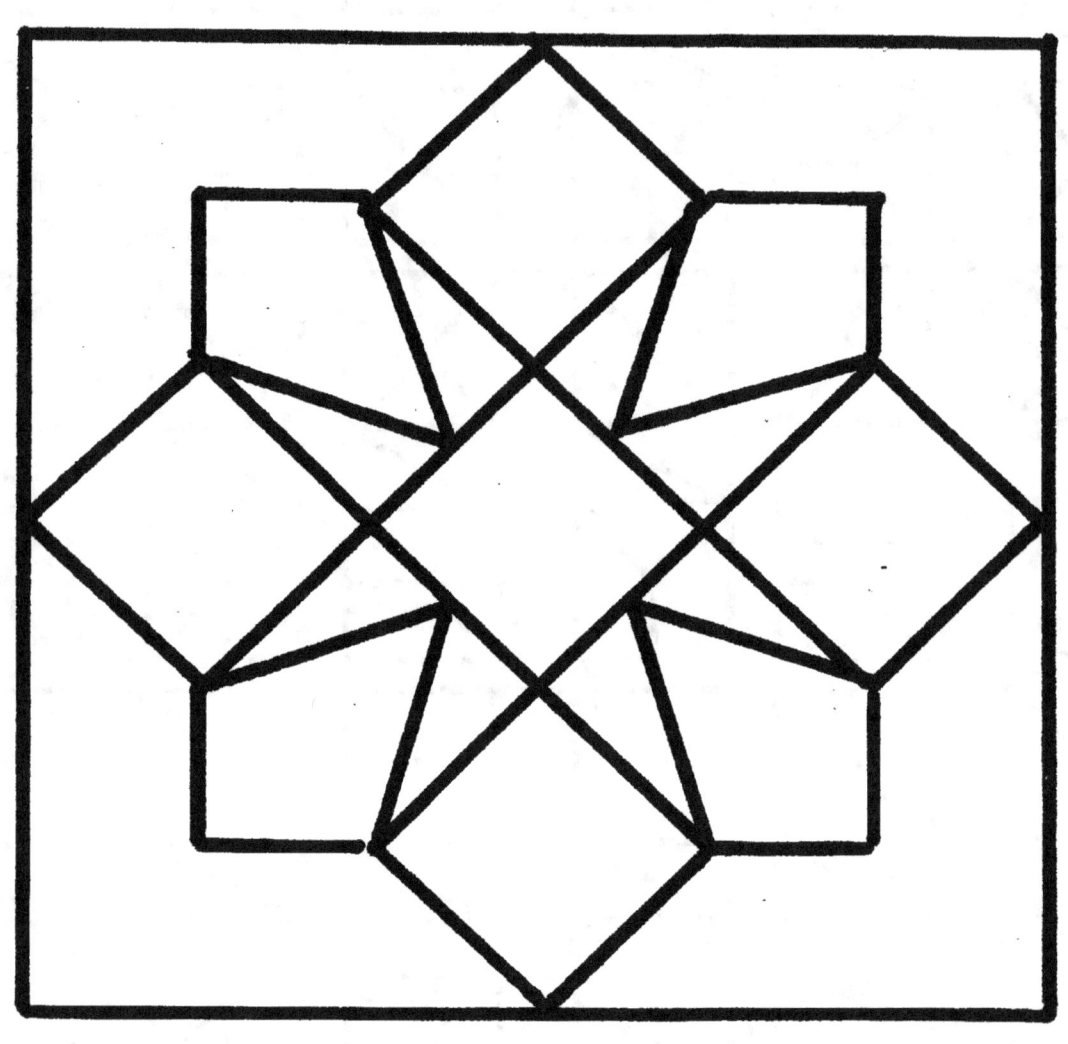

Franklin County Barn Quilt Grandmother's Garden

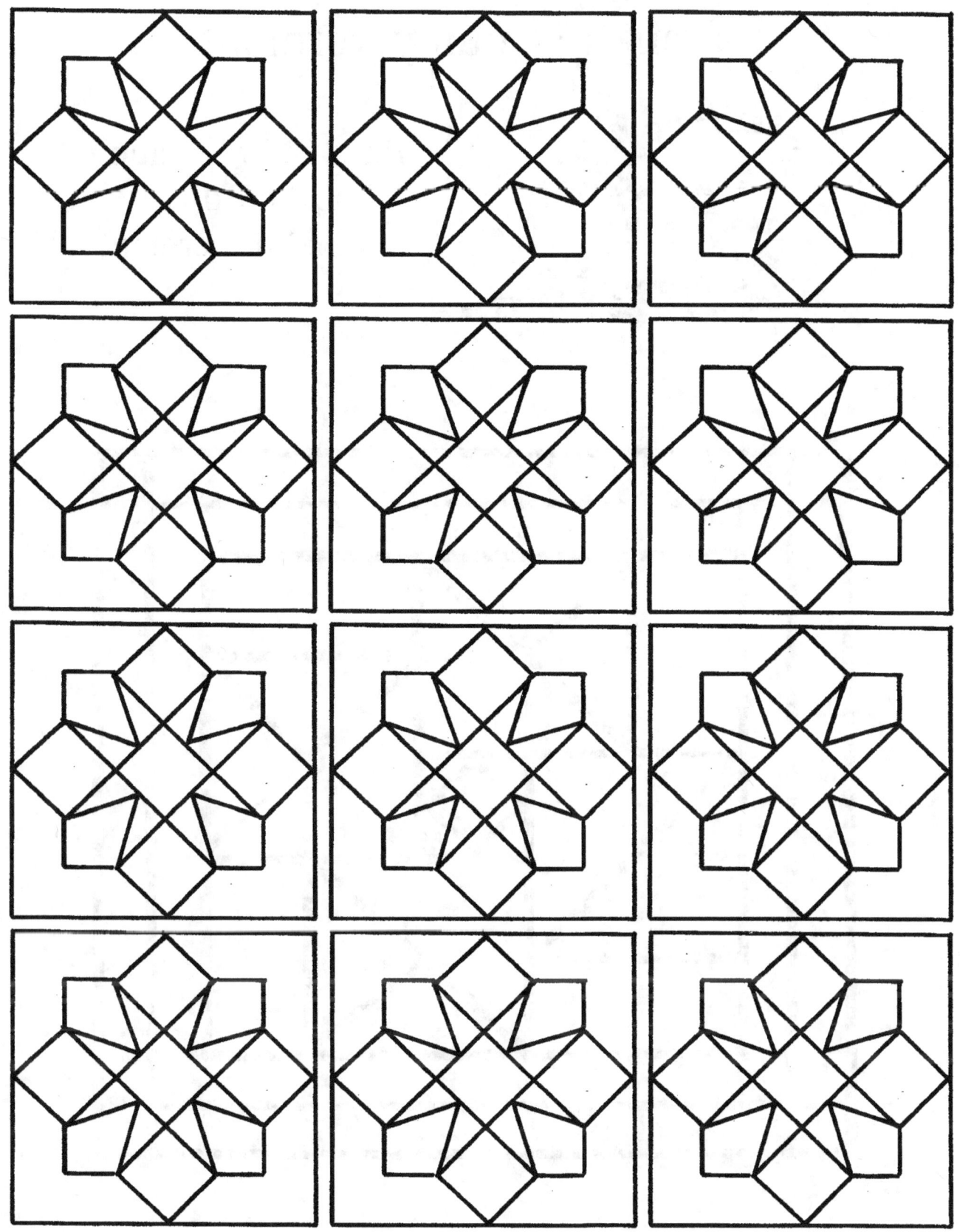

Barn Quilt Double Stars
Franklin County Vermont

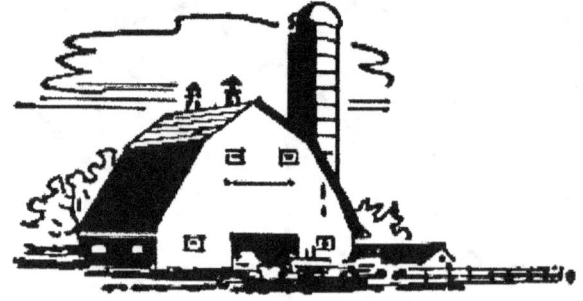

Barn Quilt Location
Lake Rd
Franklin, Vermont

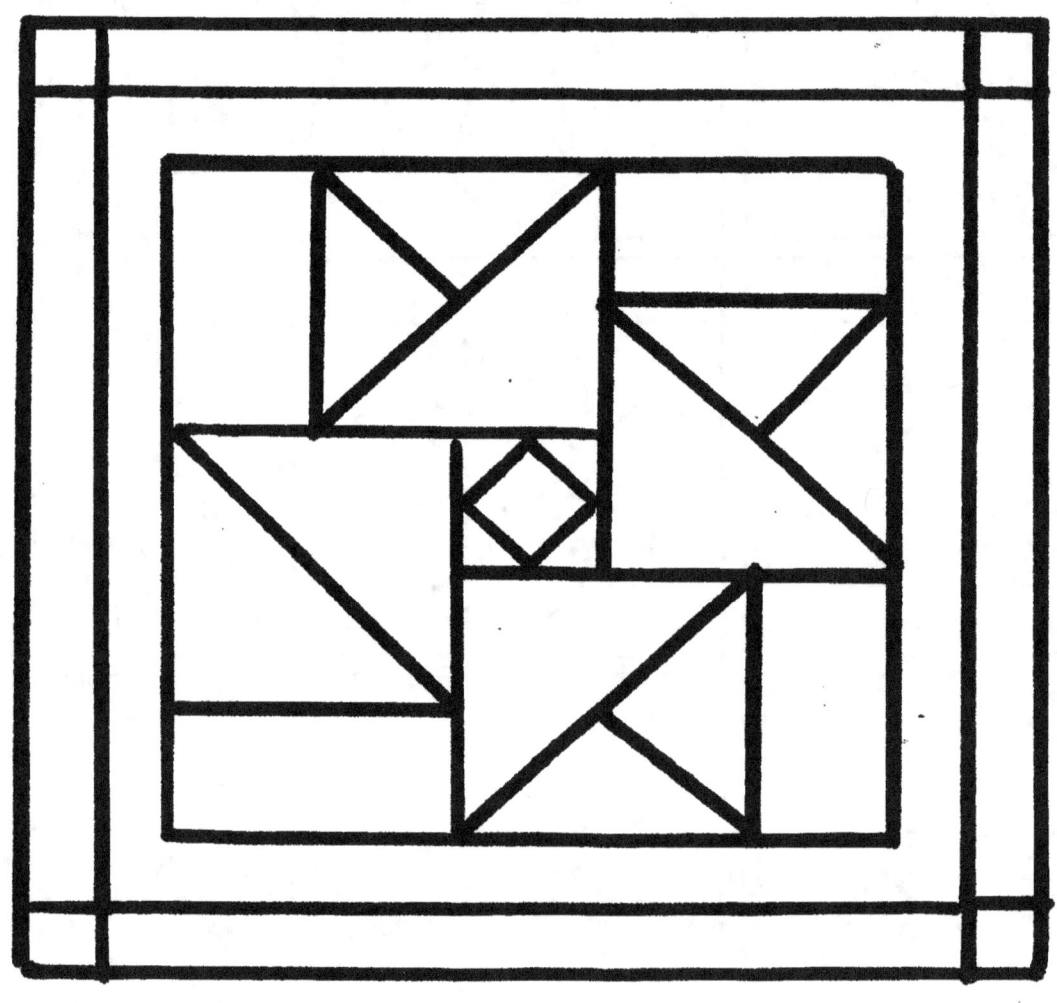

Franklin County Barn Quilt Double Stars

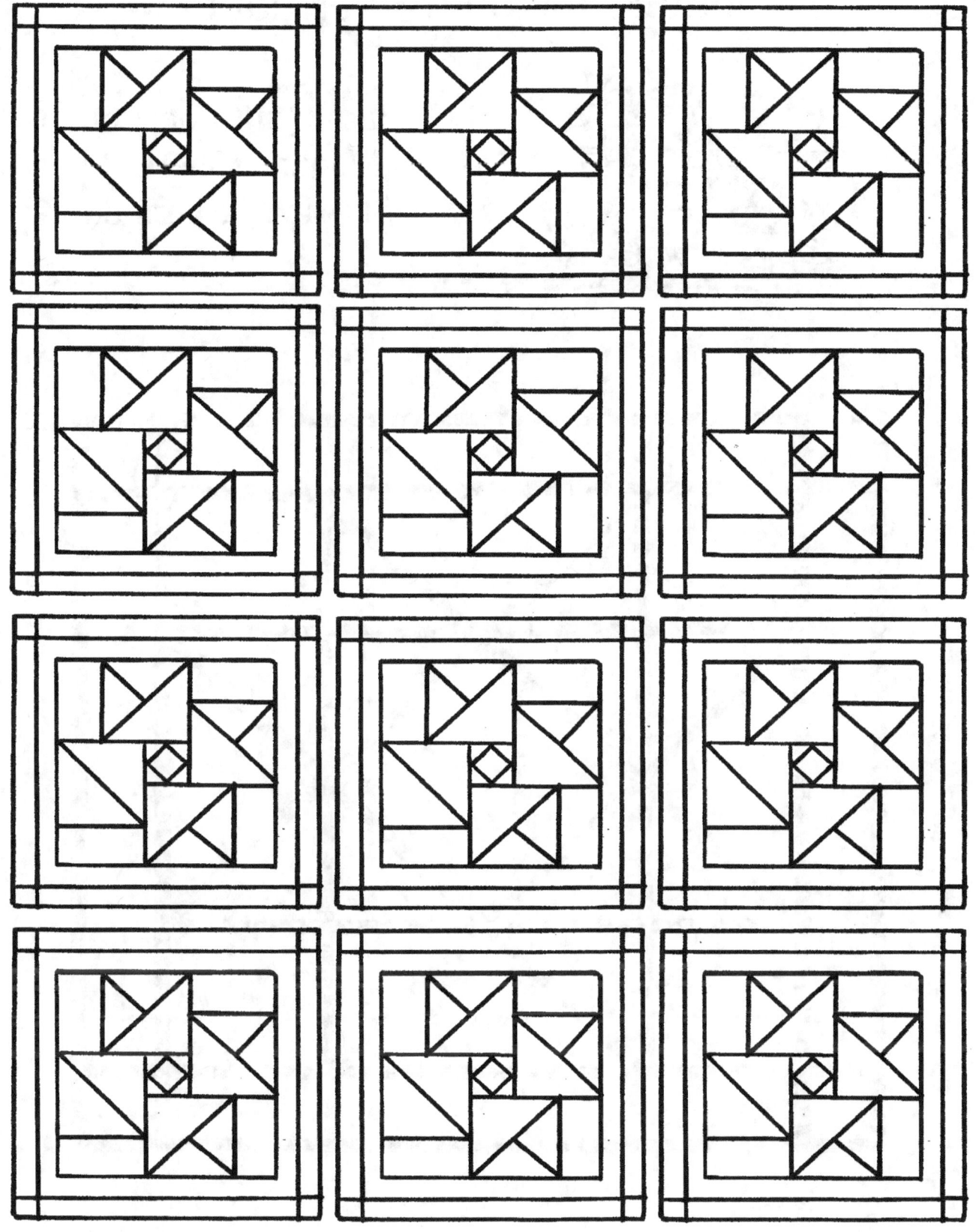

Barn Quilt Sawtooth Star Variation
Franklin County Vermont

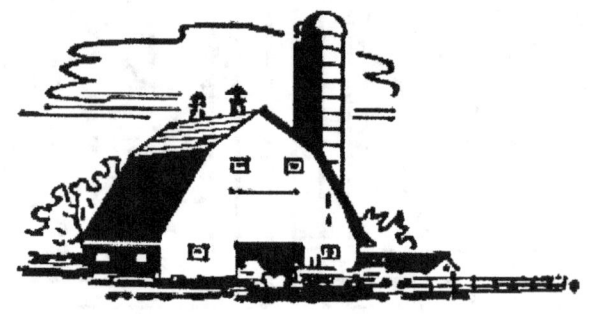

Barn Quilt Location
Maquam Shore Rd
St. Albans, Vermont

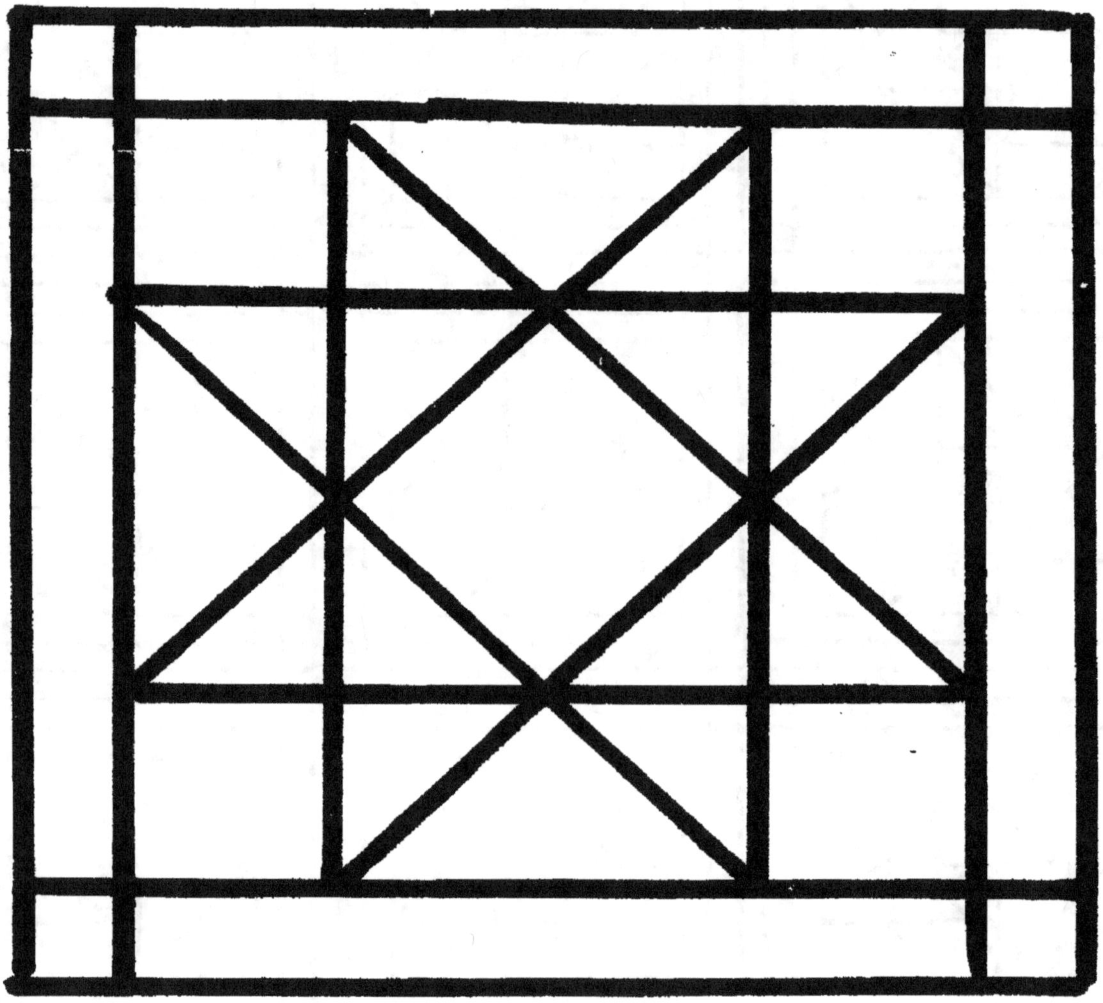

Franklin County Barn Quilt Sawtooth Star Variation

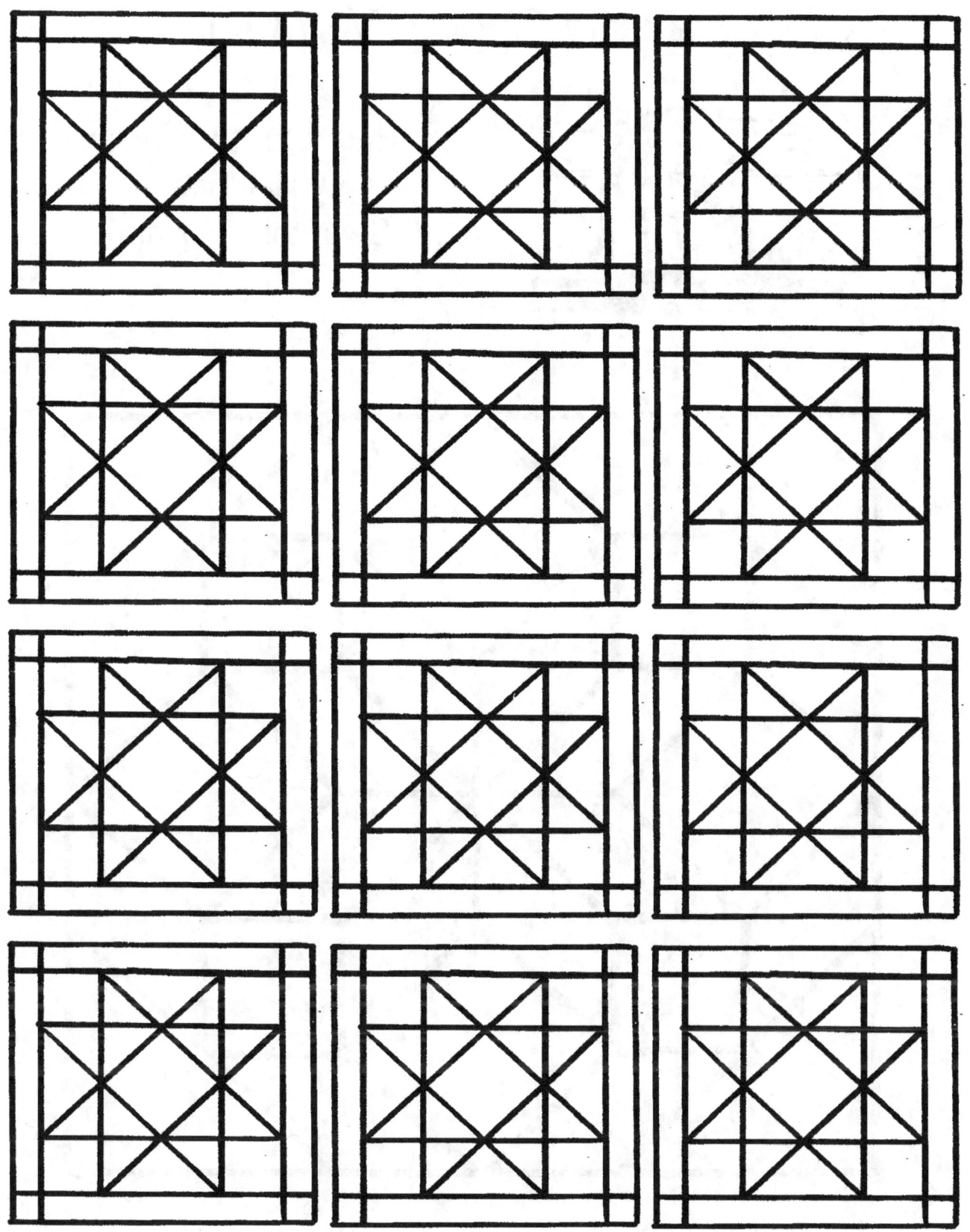

Barn Quilt Rolling Star
Franklin County Vermont

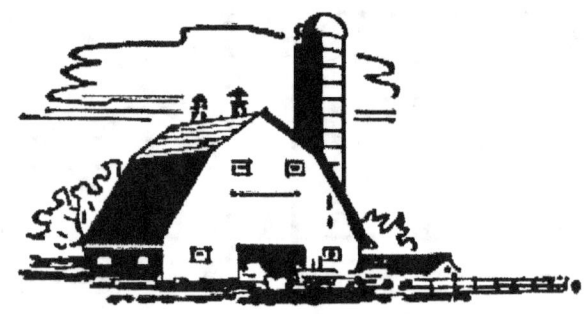

Barn Quilt Location
Fourier Lane
Swanton, Vermont

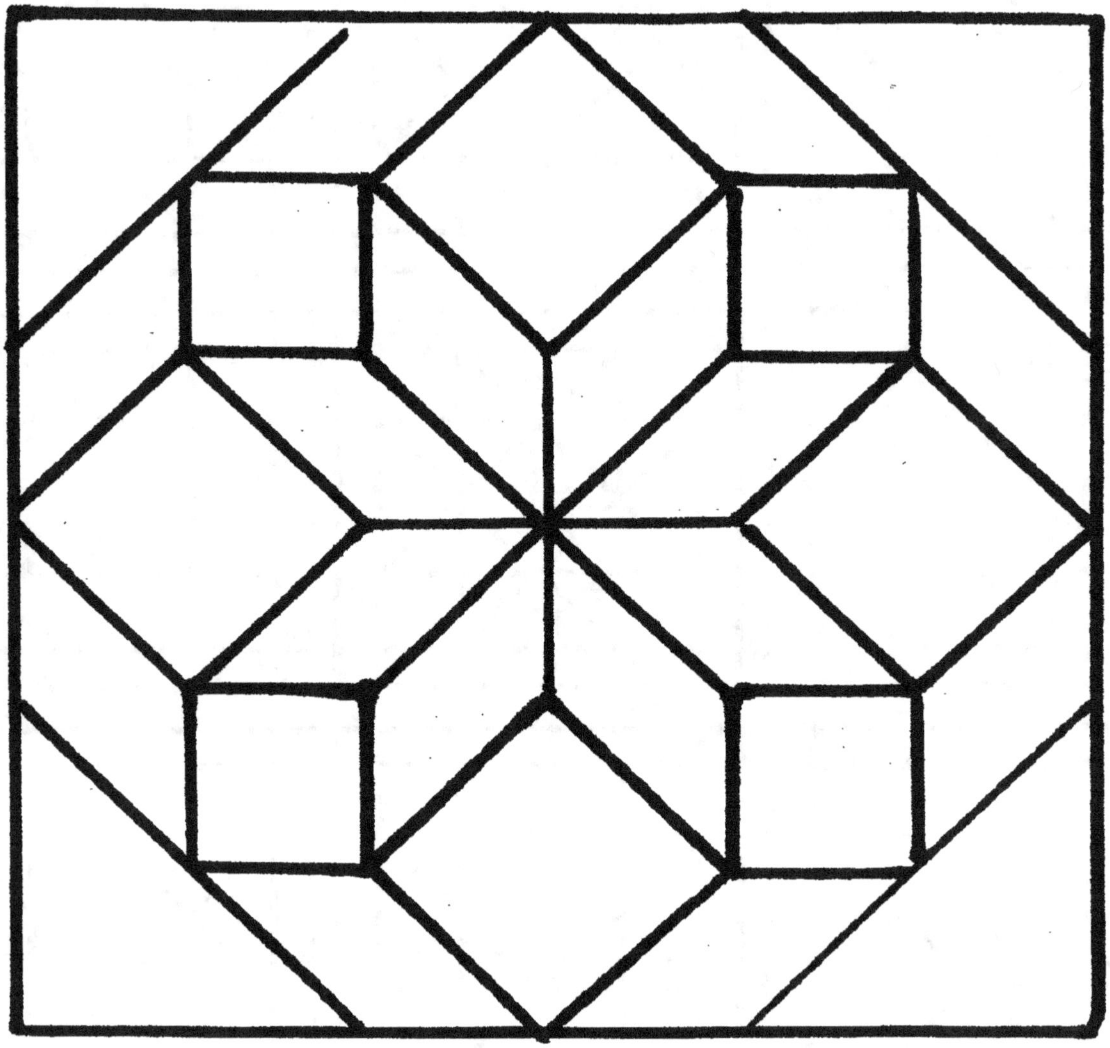

Franklin County Barn Quilt Rolling Star

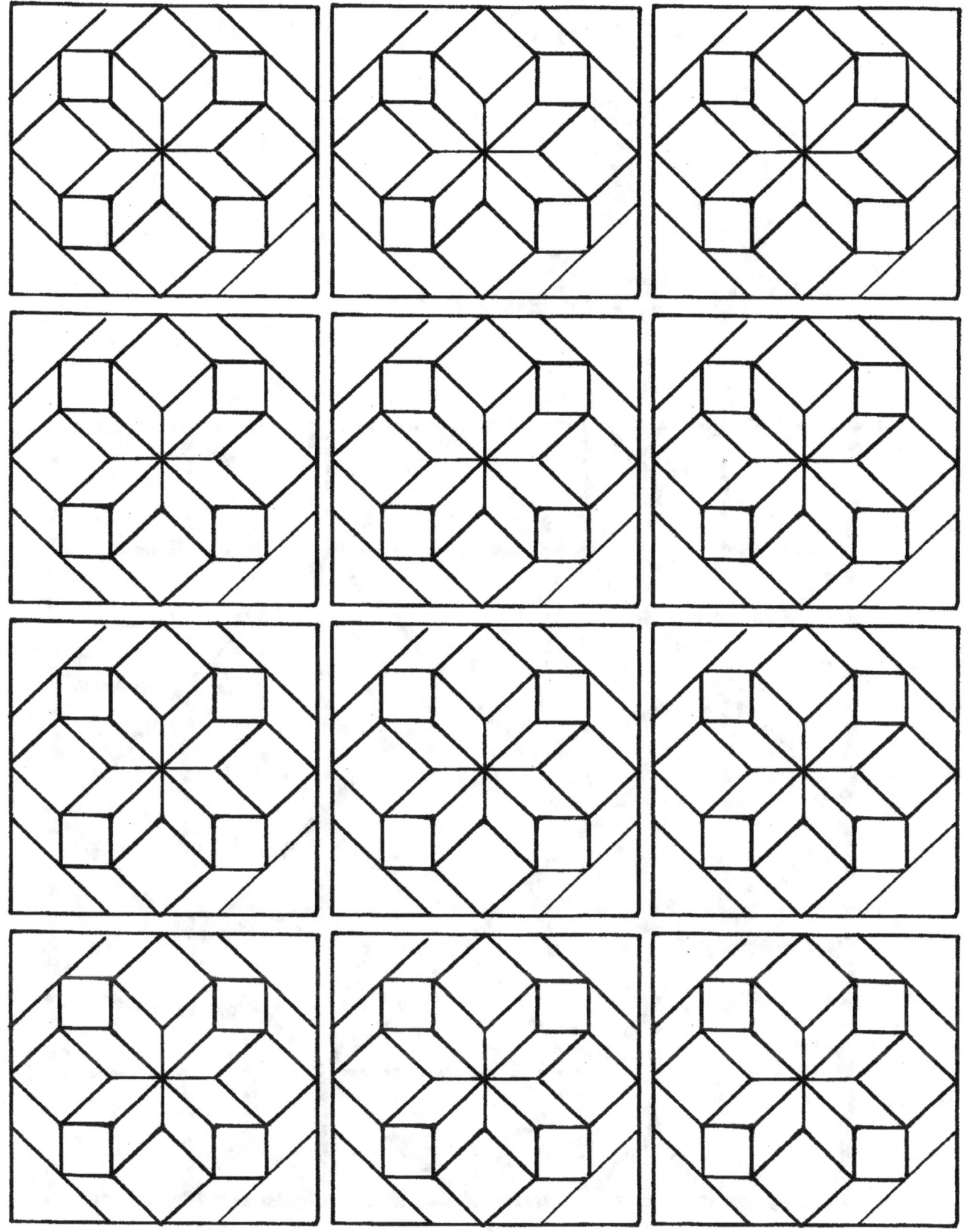

Barn Quilt Star & Lilies
Franklin County Vermont

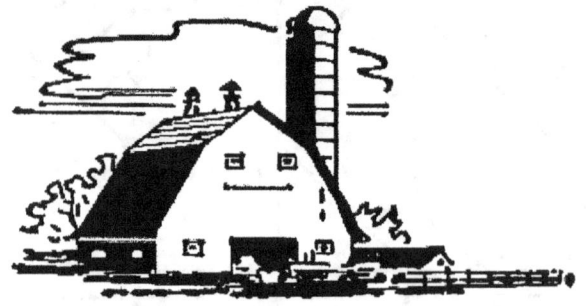

Barn Quilt Location
Sheldon Rd
Swanton, Vermont

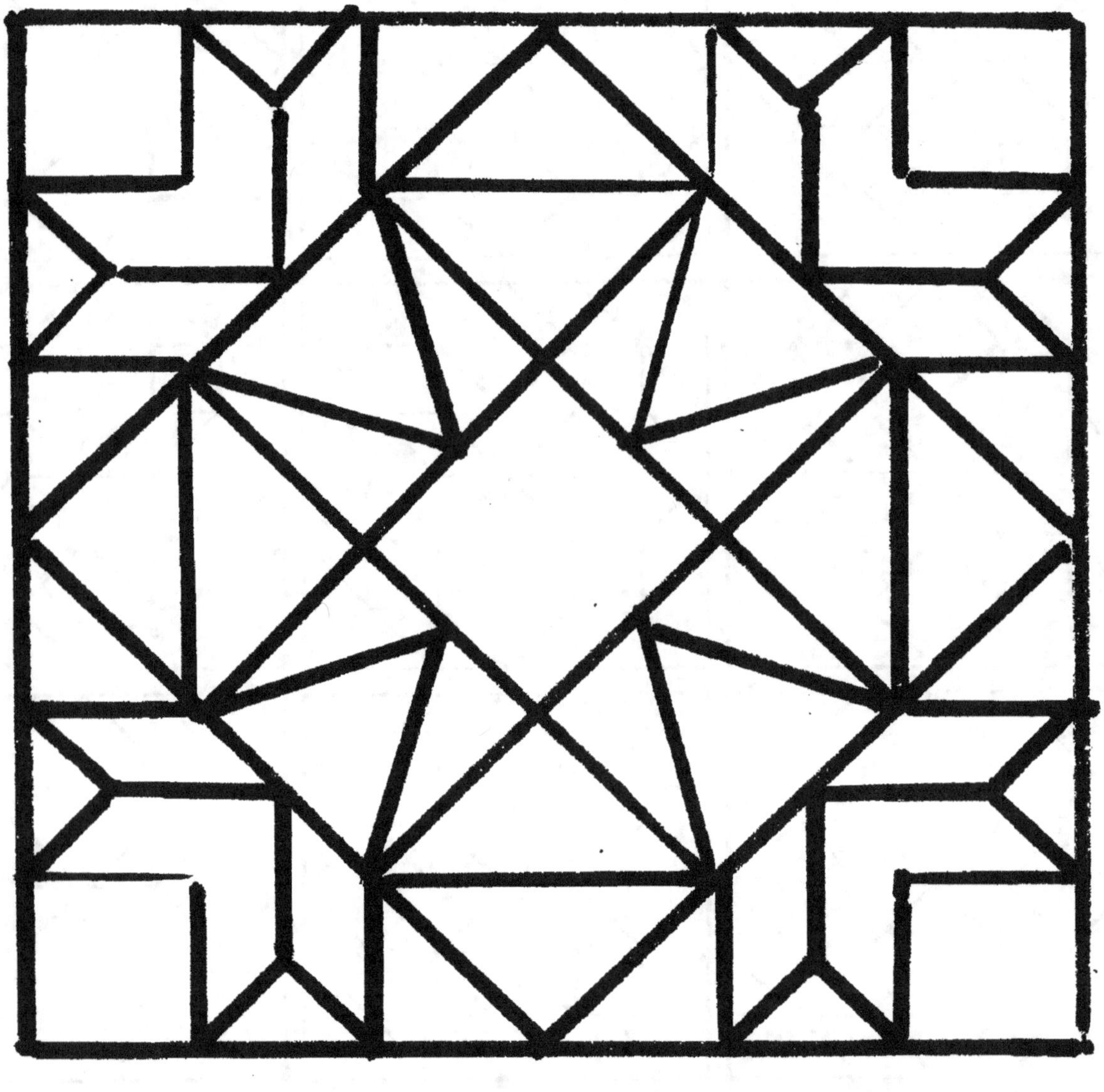

Franklin County Barn Quilt Star & Lilies

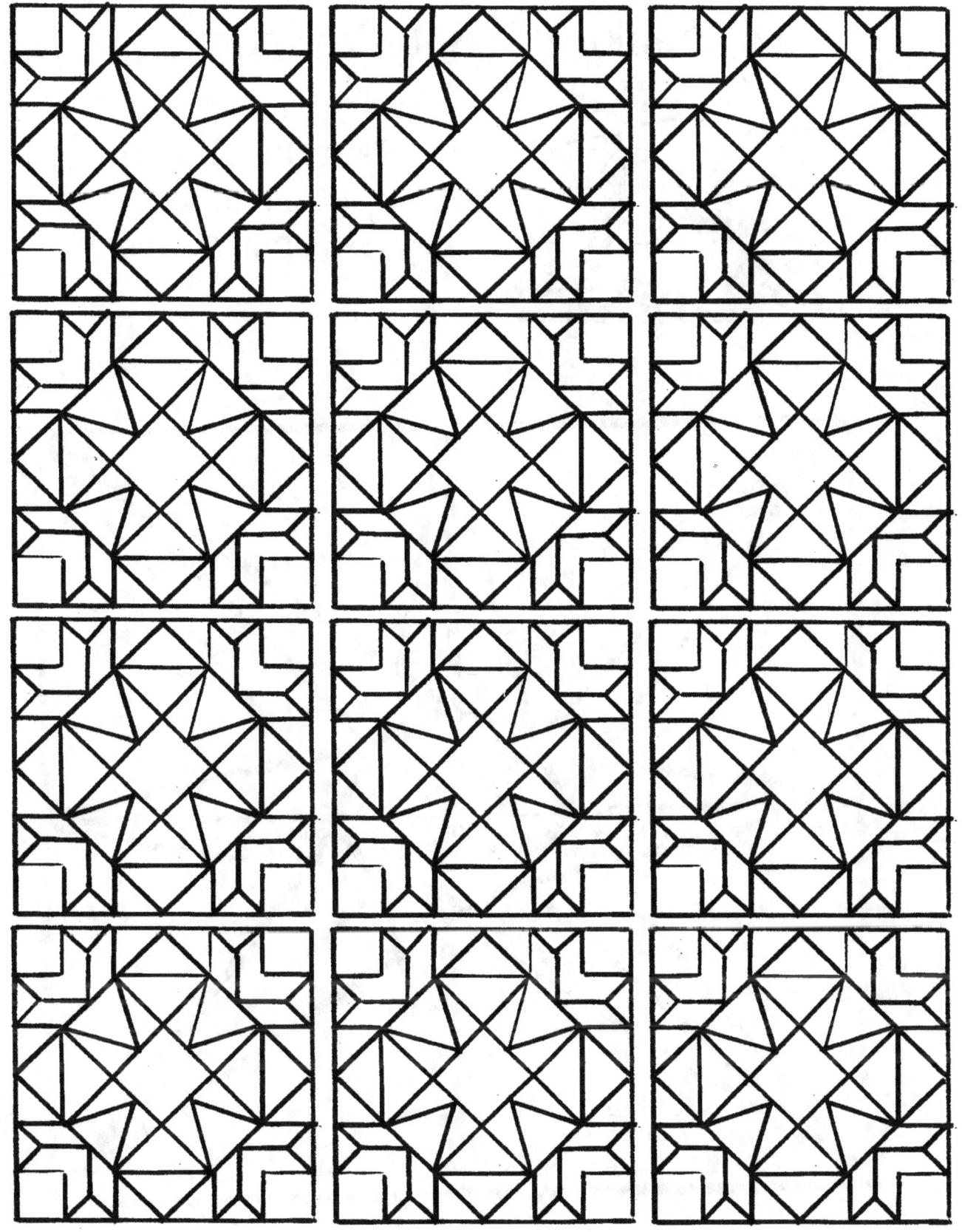

Barn Quilt Compass Star
Franklin County Vermont

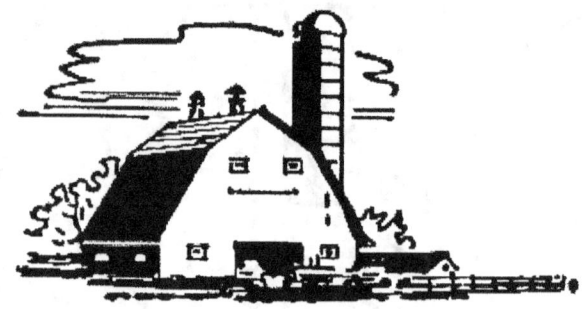

Barn Quilt Location
Church Rd
Swanton, Vermont

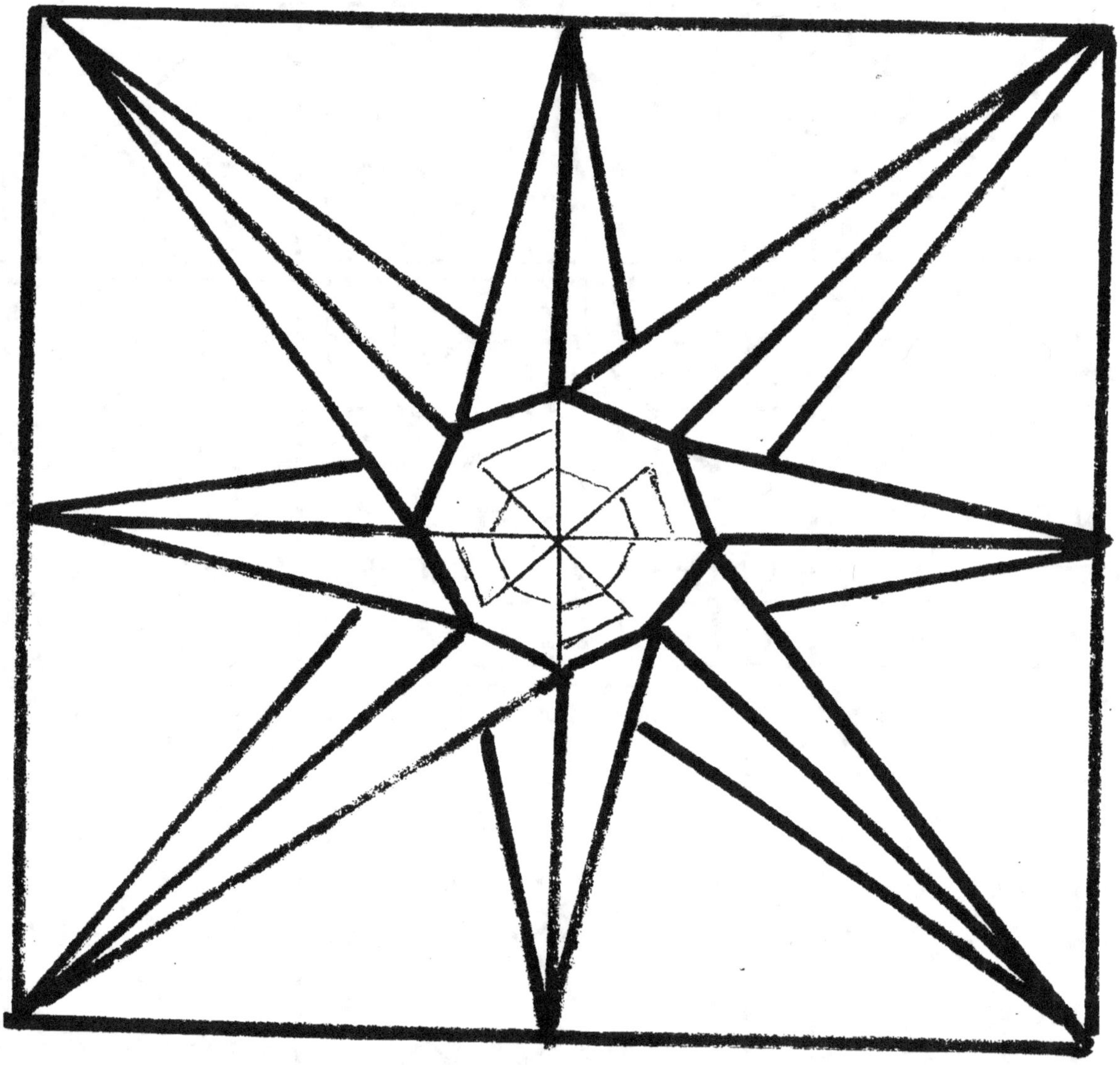

Franklin County Barn Quilt Compass Star

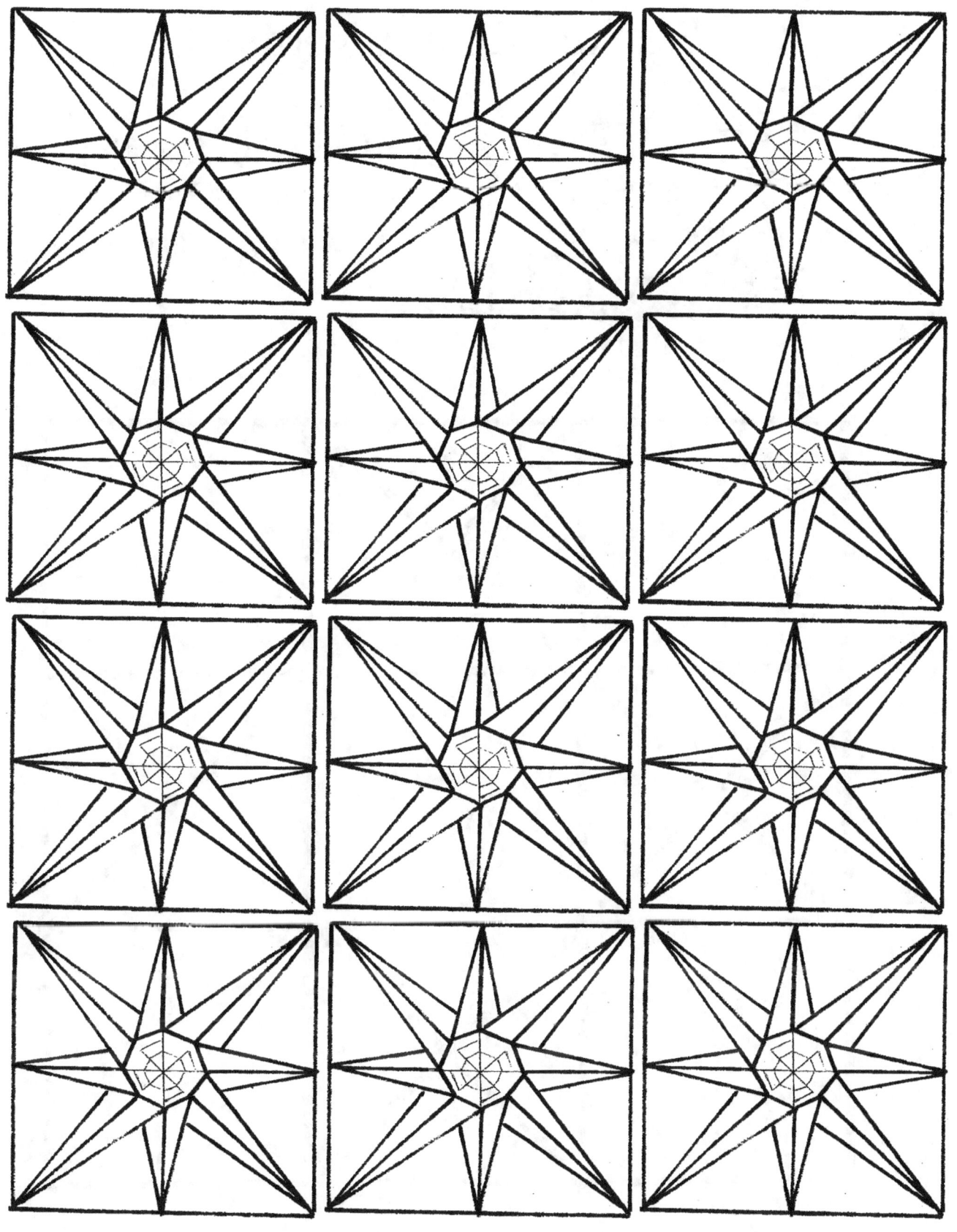

Barn Quilt Ohio Star
Franklin County Vermont

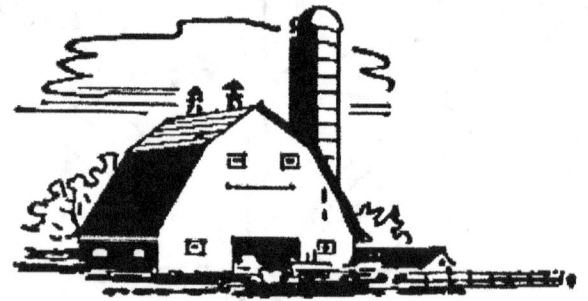

Barn Quilt Location
Albans Rd
Swanton, Vermont

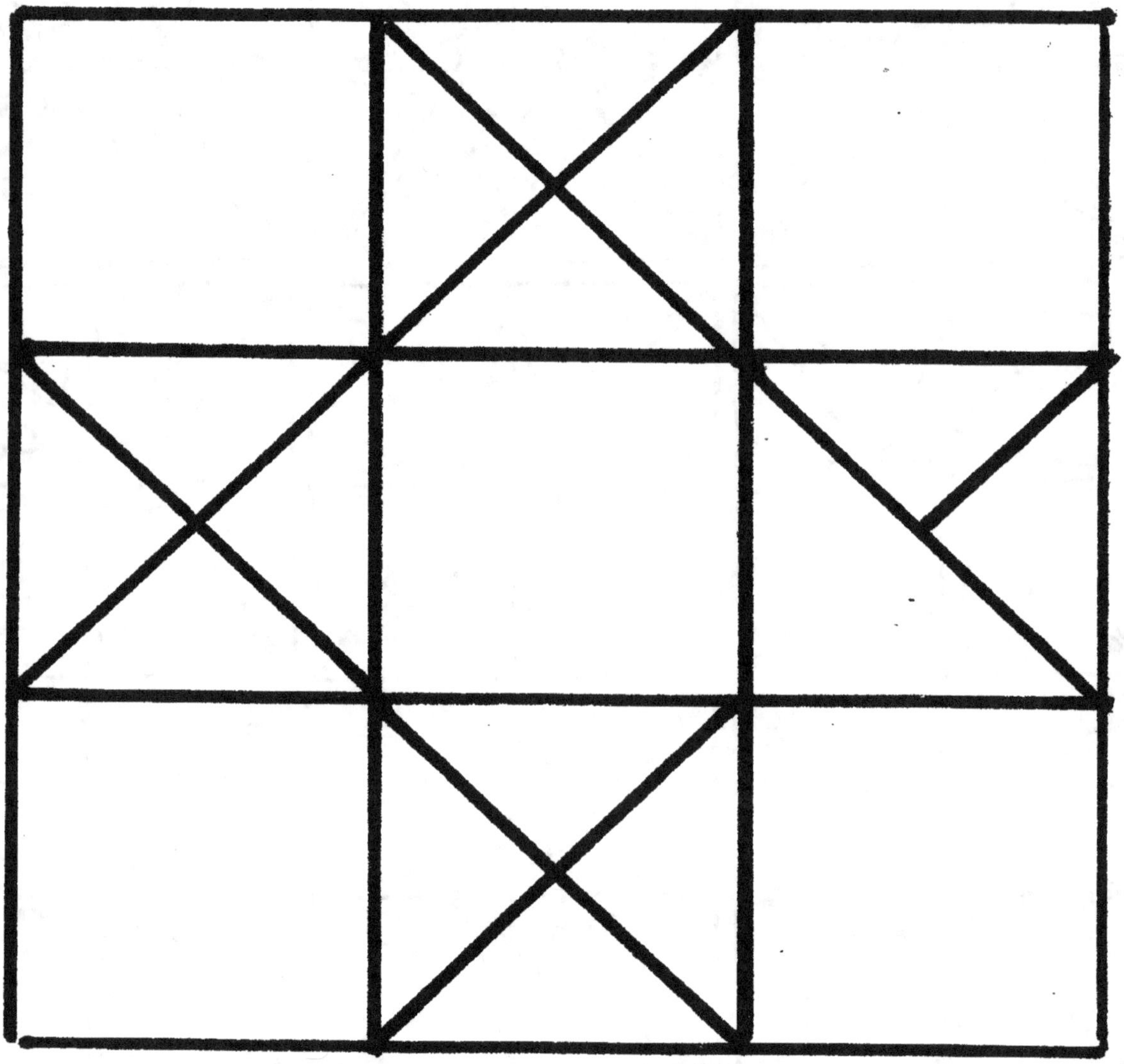

Franklin County Barn Quilt Ohio Star

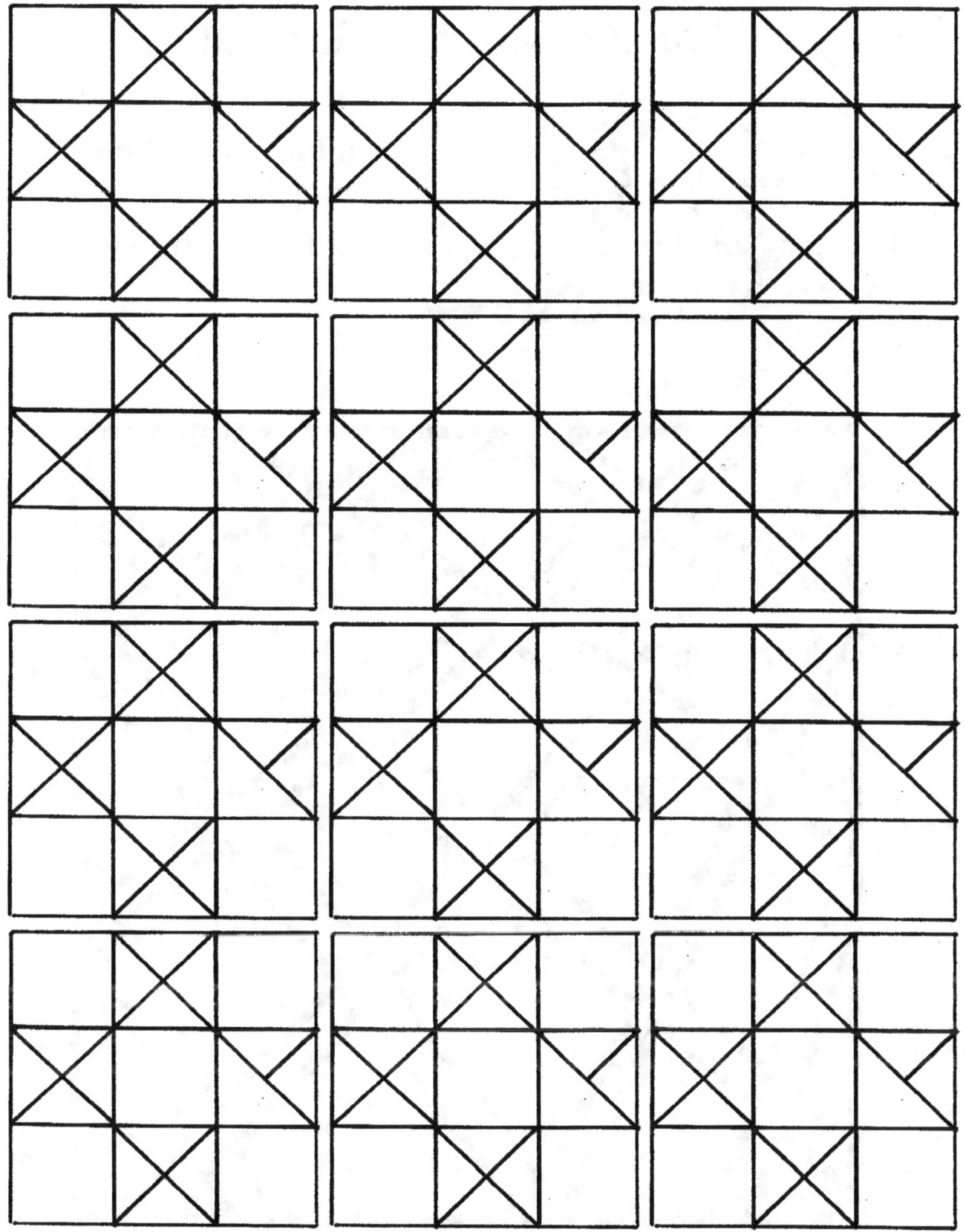

Barn Quilt Broken Glass
Franklin County Vermont

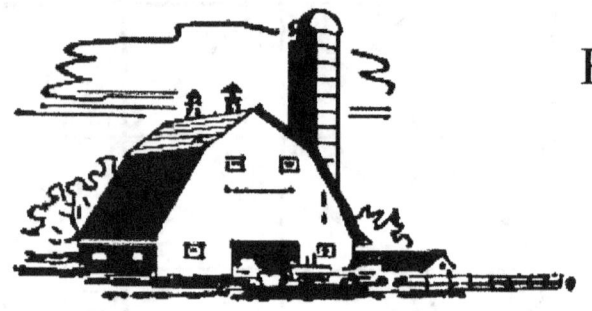

Barn Quilt Location
Spring St
Swanton, Vermont

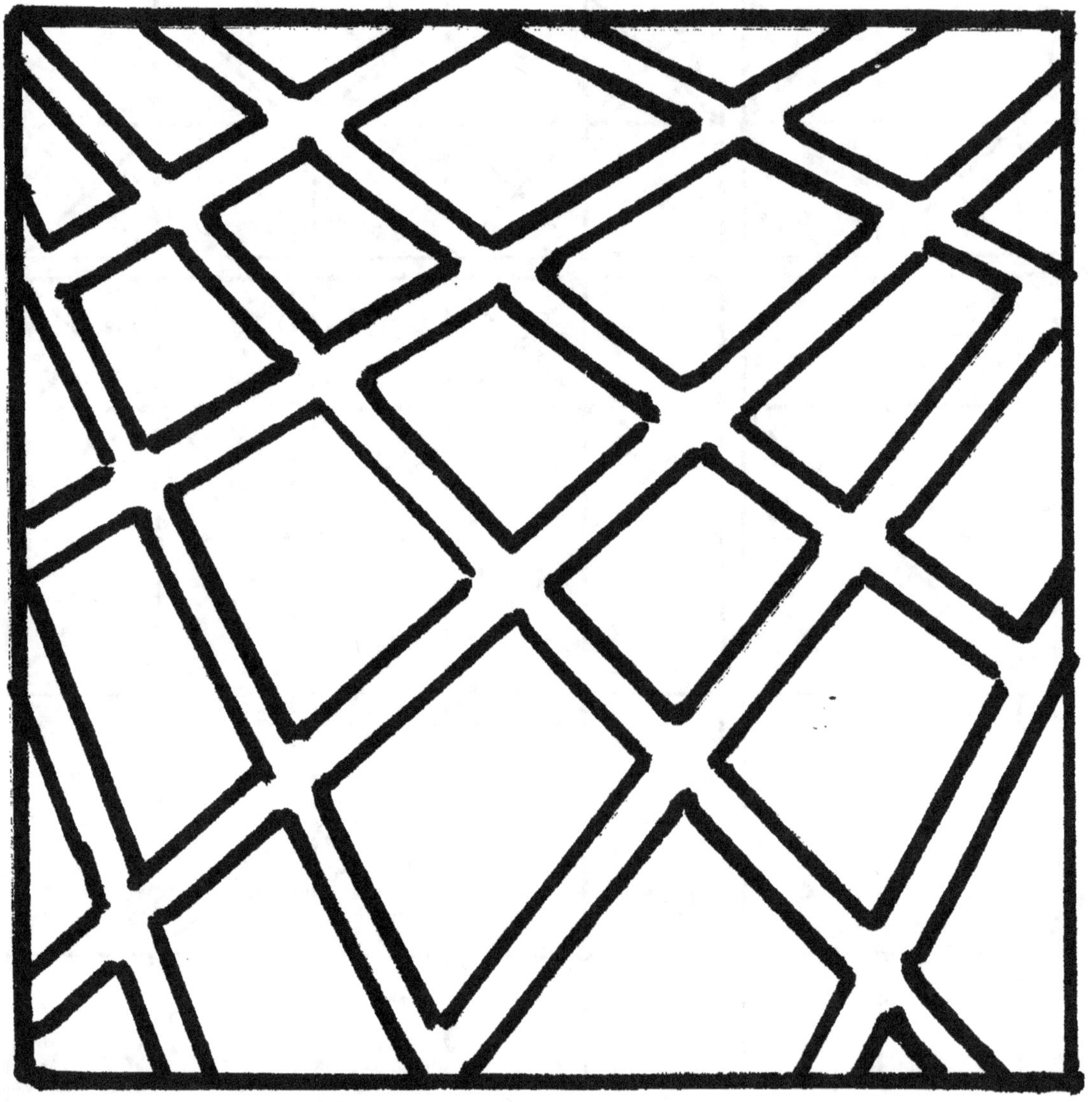

Franklin County Barn Quilt Broken Glass

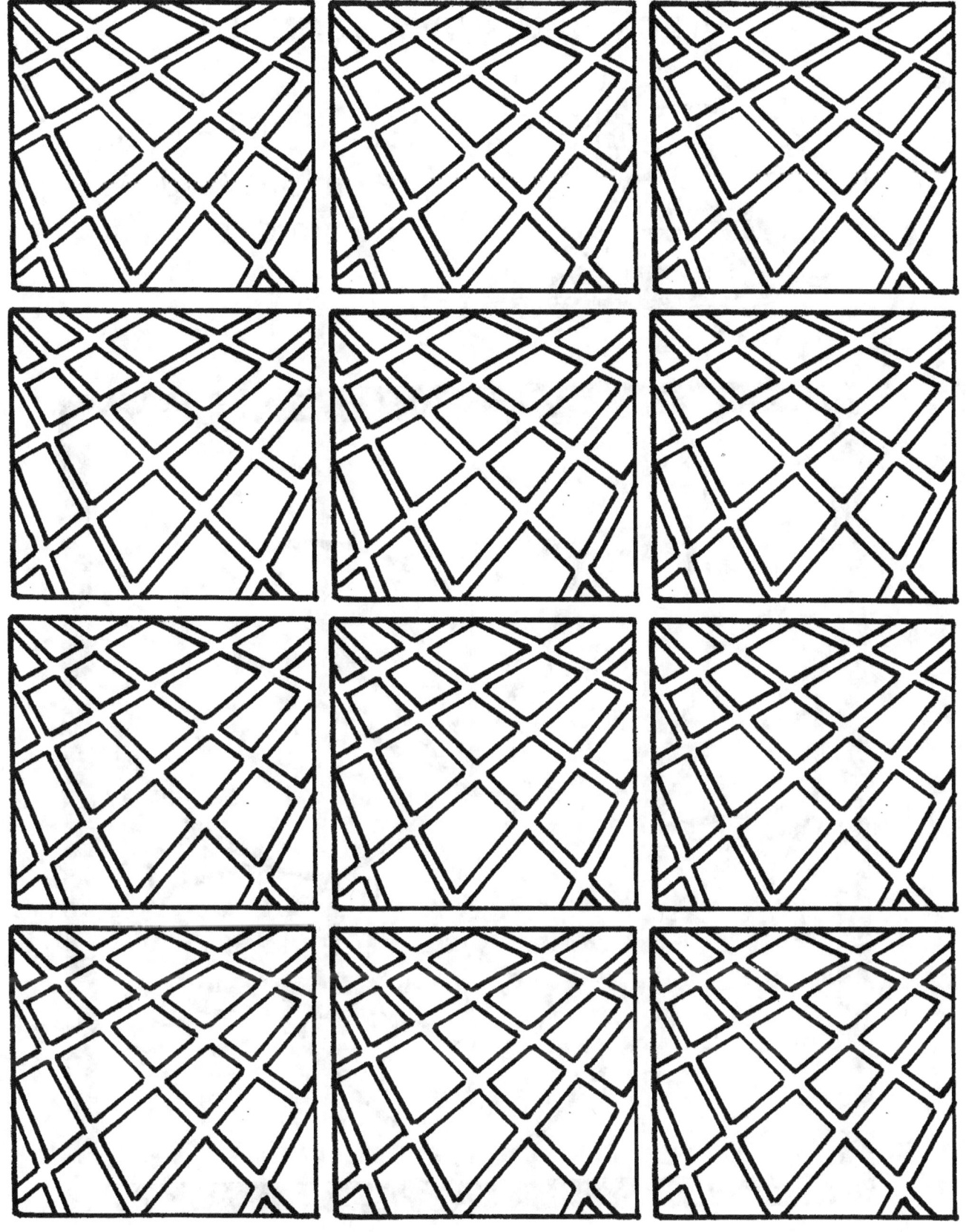

Barn Quilt Dove Inside Heart
Franklin County Vermont

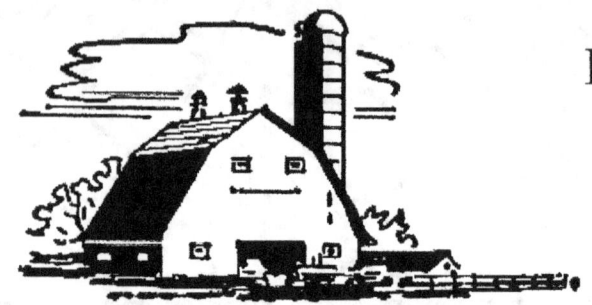

Barn Quilt Location
Pinnacle Meadows
Richford, Vermont

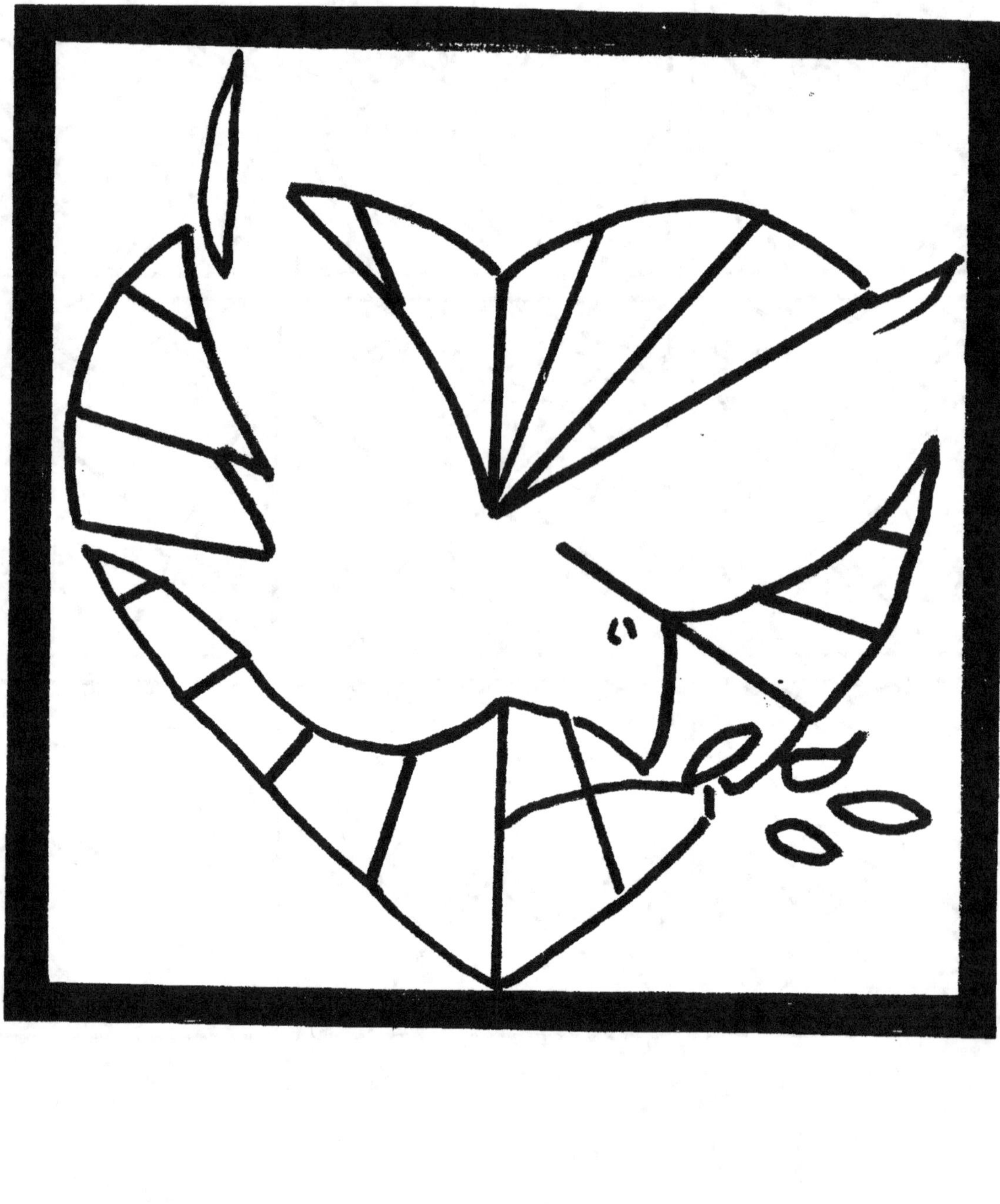

Franklin County Barn Quilt Dove Inside Heart

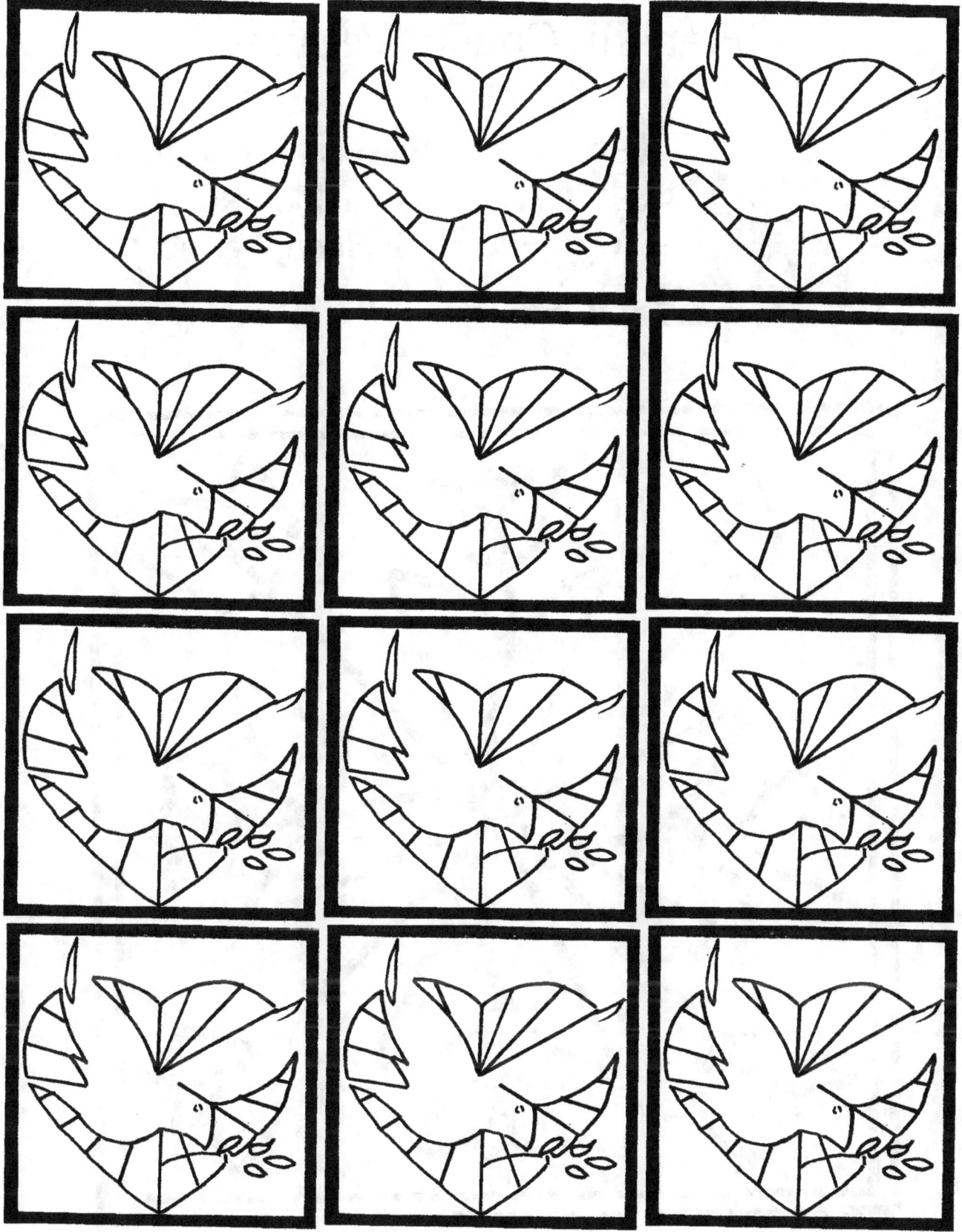

Barn Quilt Tulips in Bloom
Franklin County Vermont

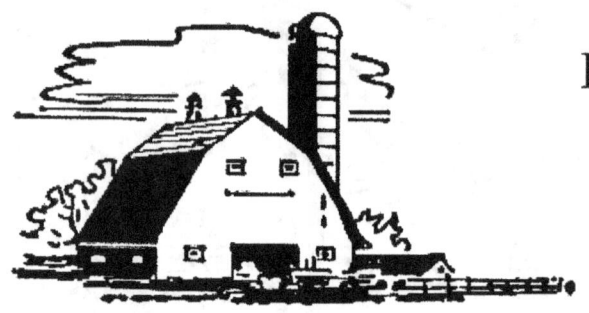

Barn Quilt Location
Sheldon Rd
Sheldon, Vermont

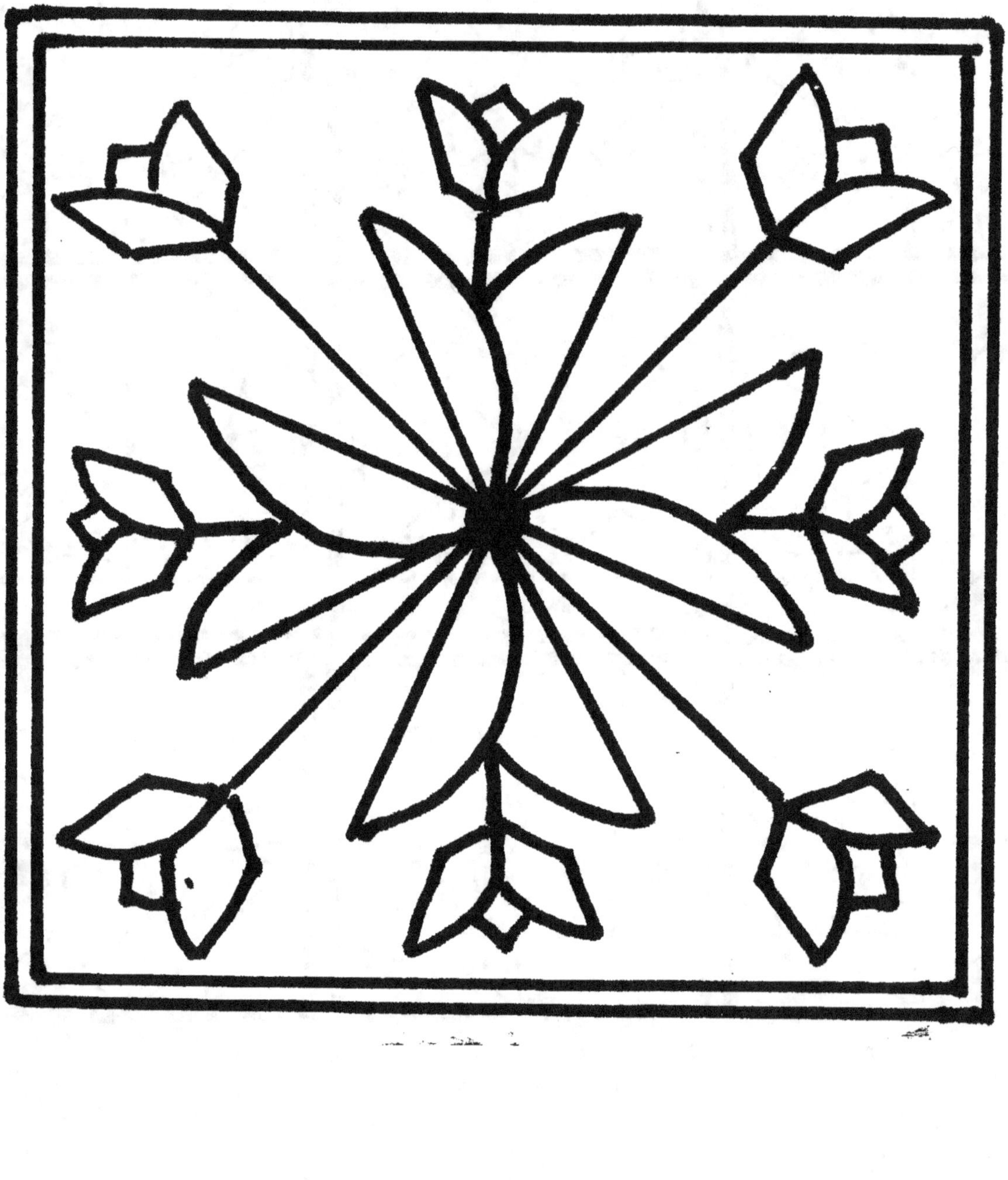

Franklin County Barn Quilt Tulips in Bloom

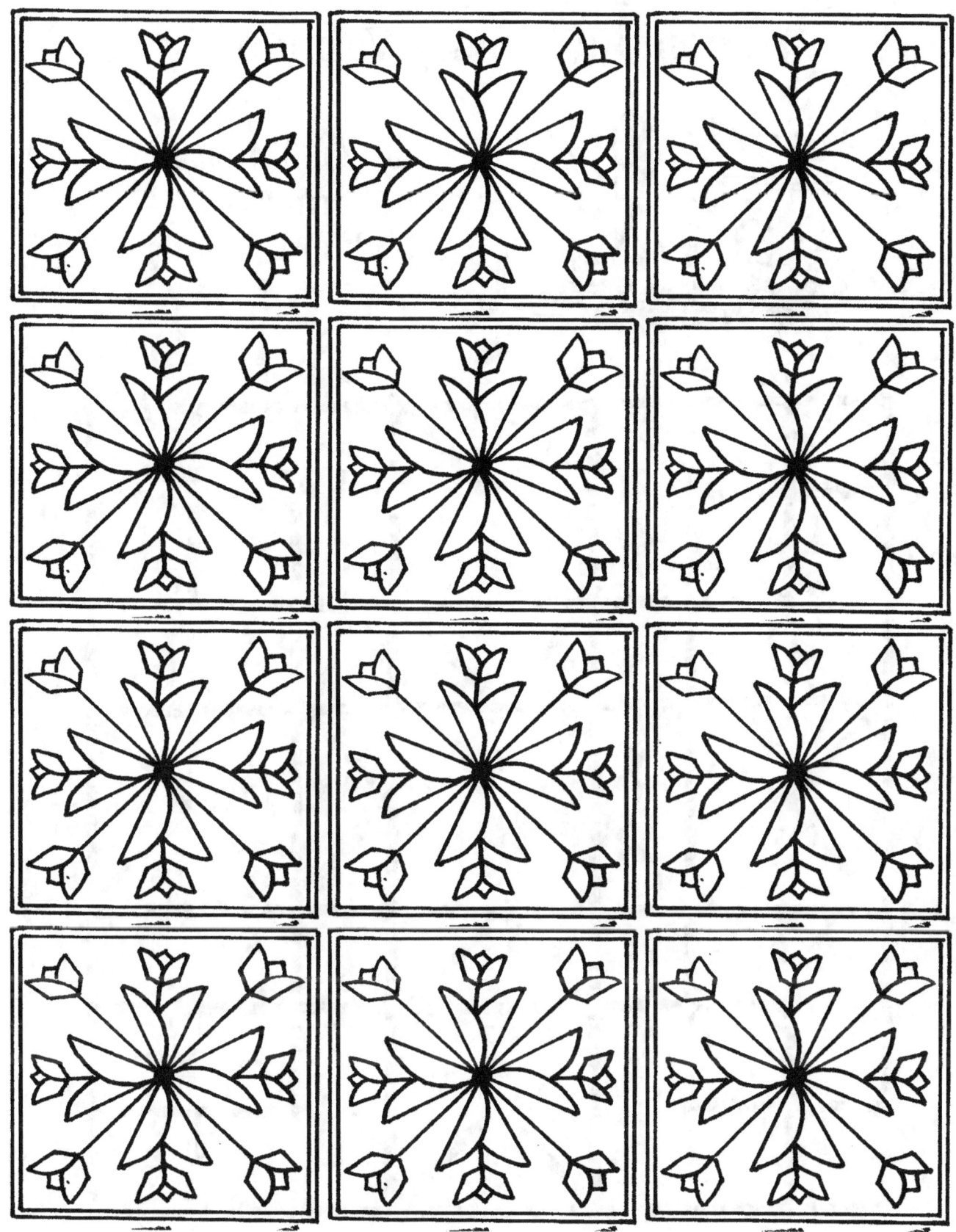

Barn Quilt Winter Stars
Franklin County Vermont

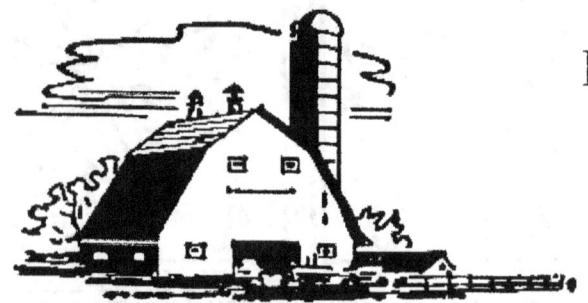

Barn Quilt Location
North Ave
Richford, Vermont

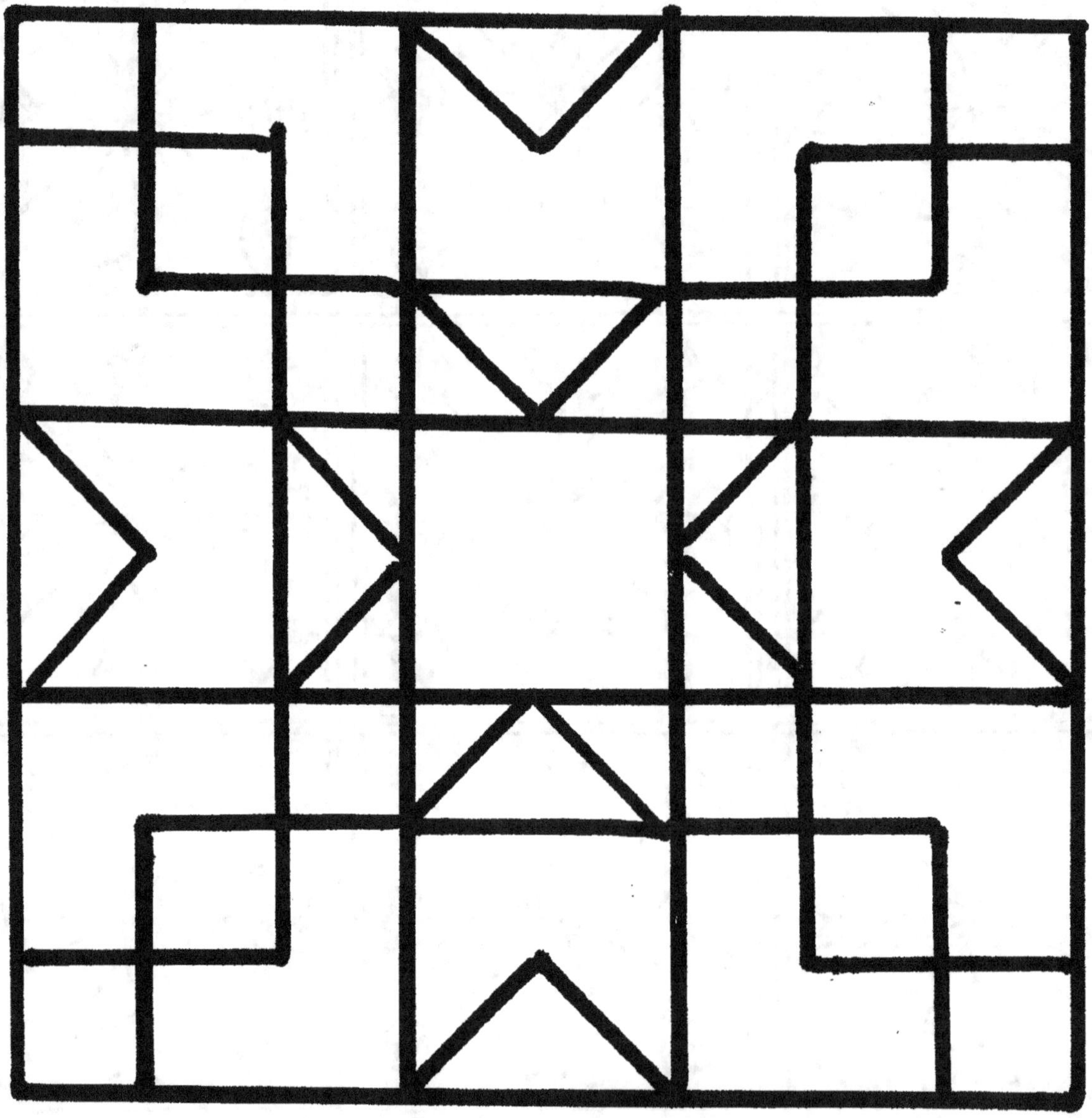

Franklin County Barn Quilt Winter Stars

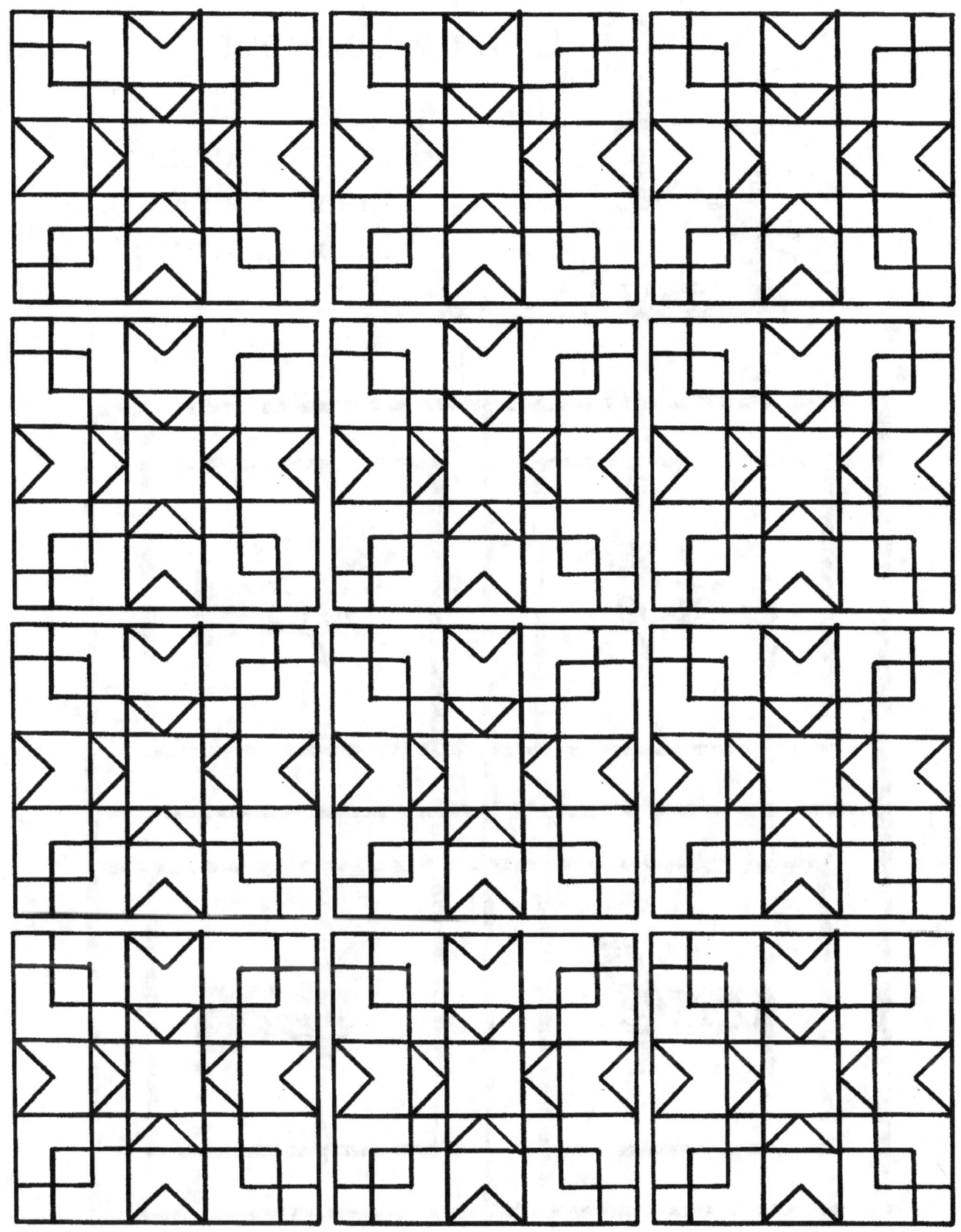

Barn Quilt Dachshunds
Franklin County Vermont

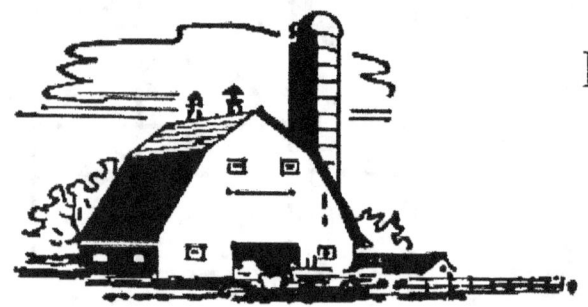

Barn Quilt Location
Grange Hall Rd
Enosburg, Vermont

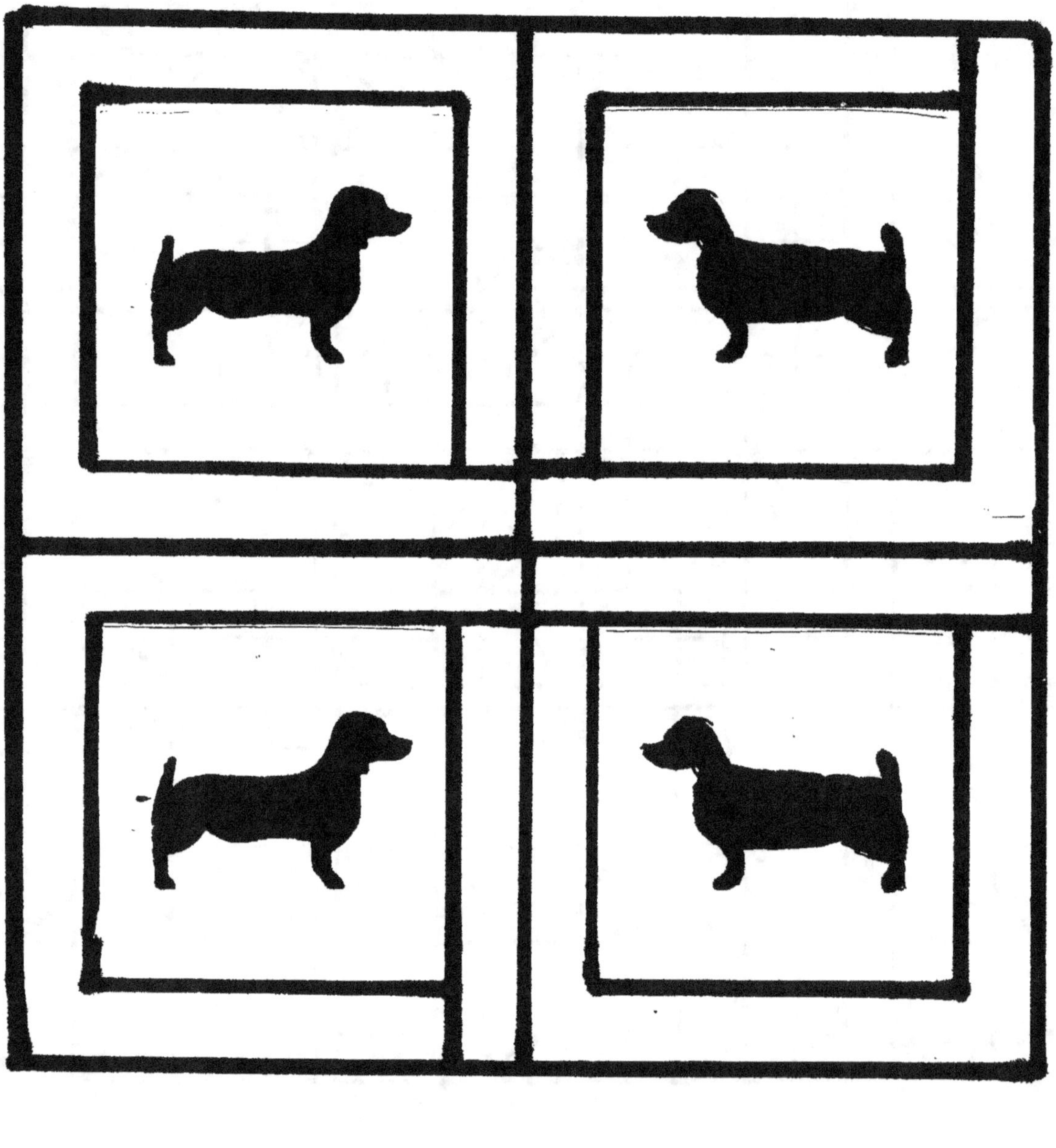

Franklin County Barn Quilt Dachshunds

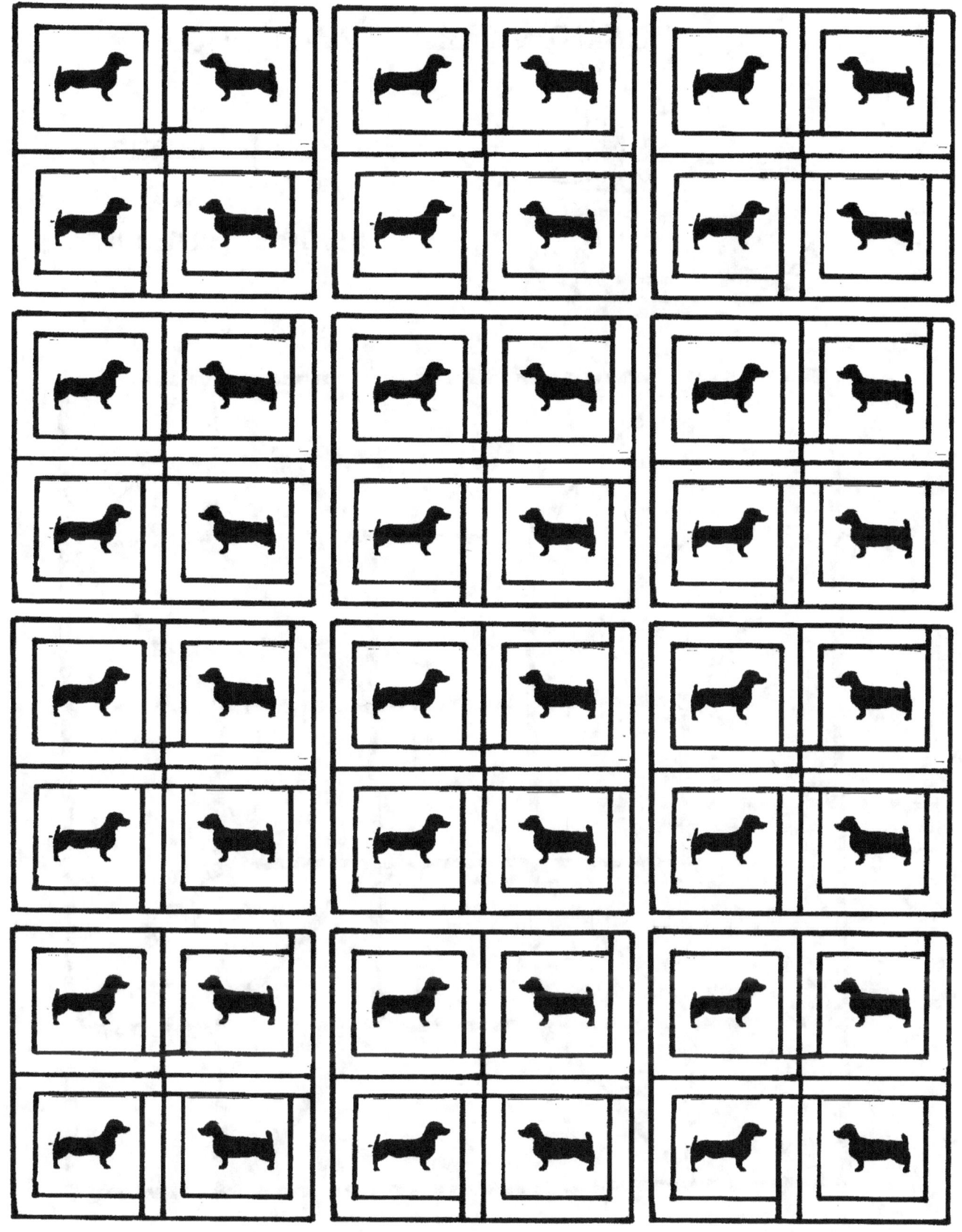

Barn Quilt Sister's Choice
Franklin County Vermont

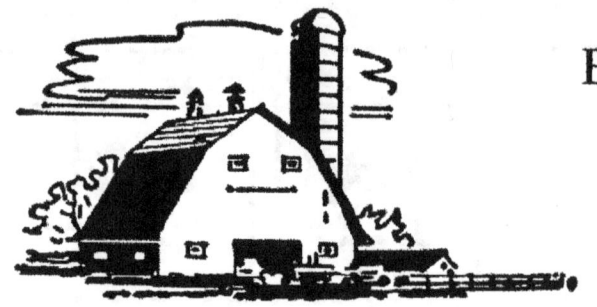

Barn Quilt Location
VT Rte 105
Sheldon, Vermont

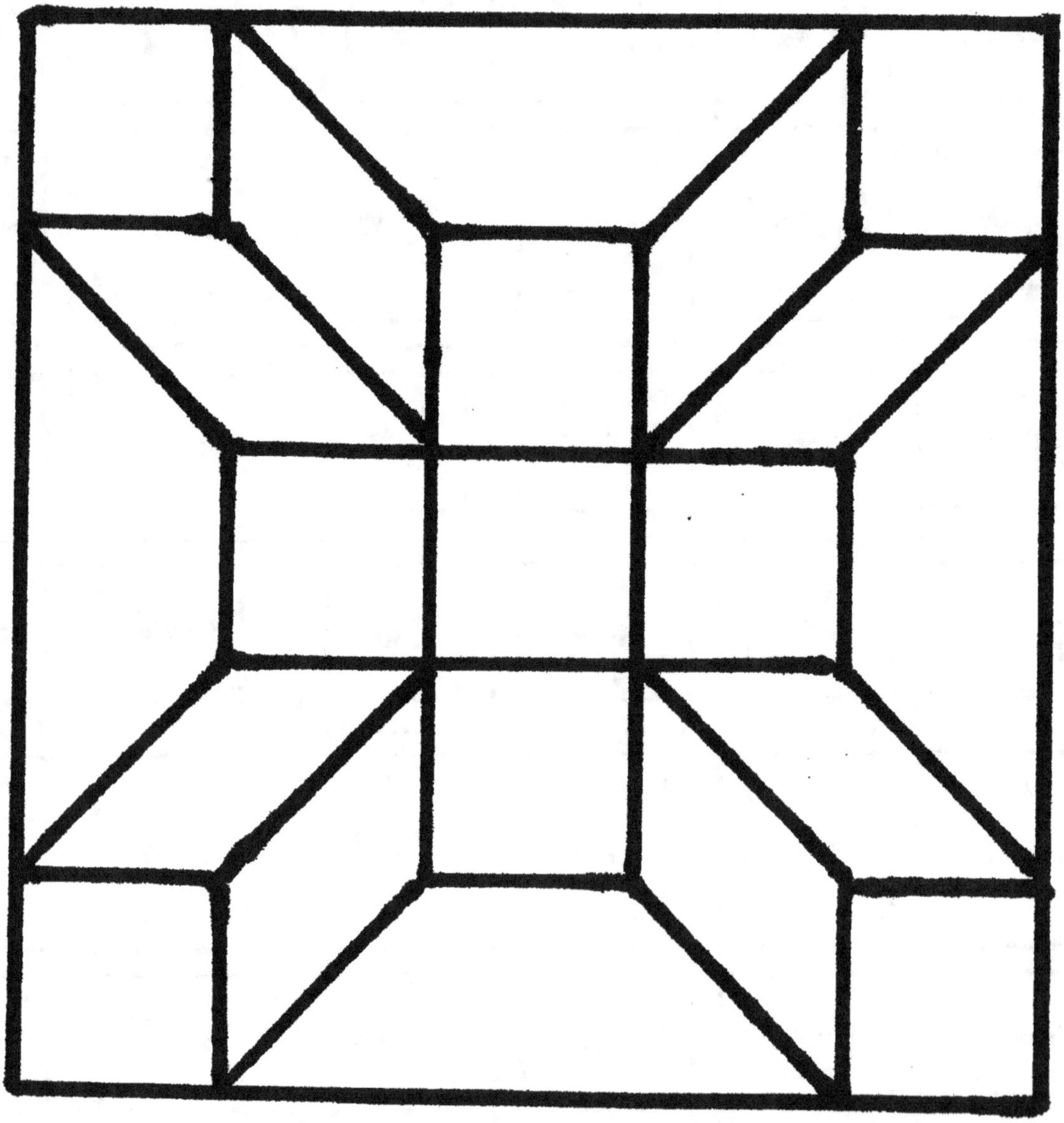

Franklin County Barn Quilt Sister's Choice

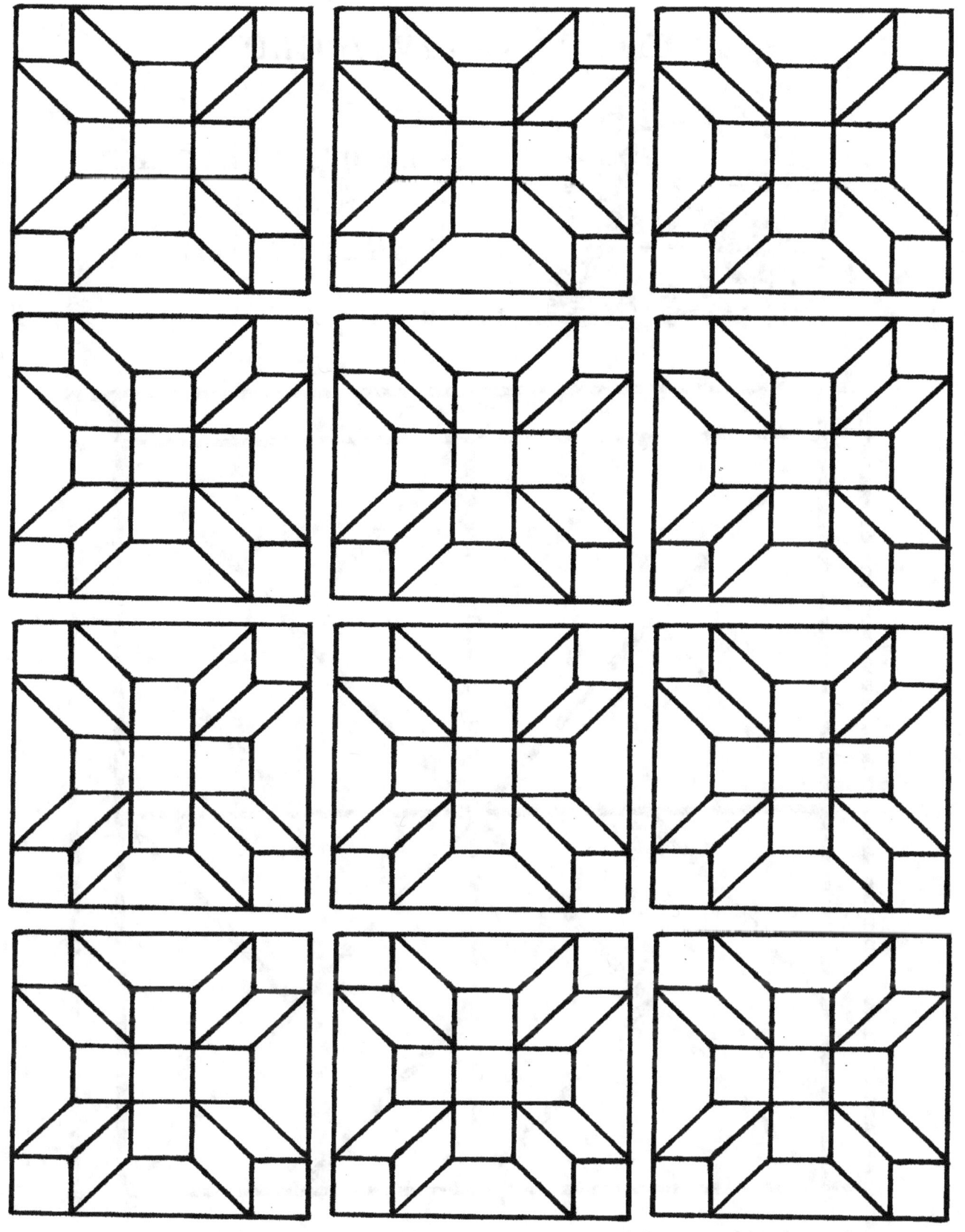

Barn Quilt Wheels
Franklin County Vermont

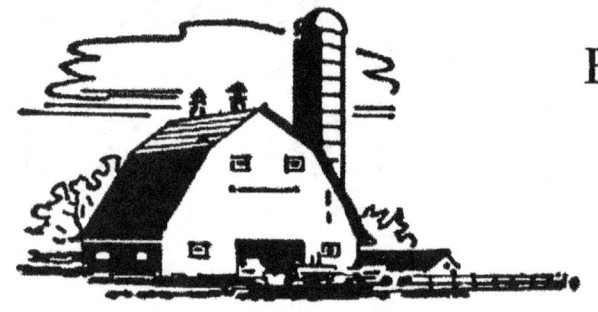

Barn Quilt Location
Richard Rd
Franklin, Vermont

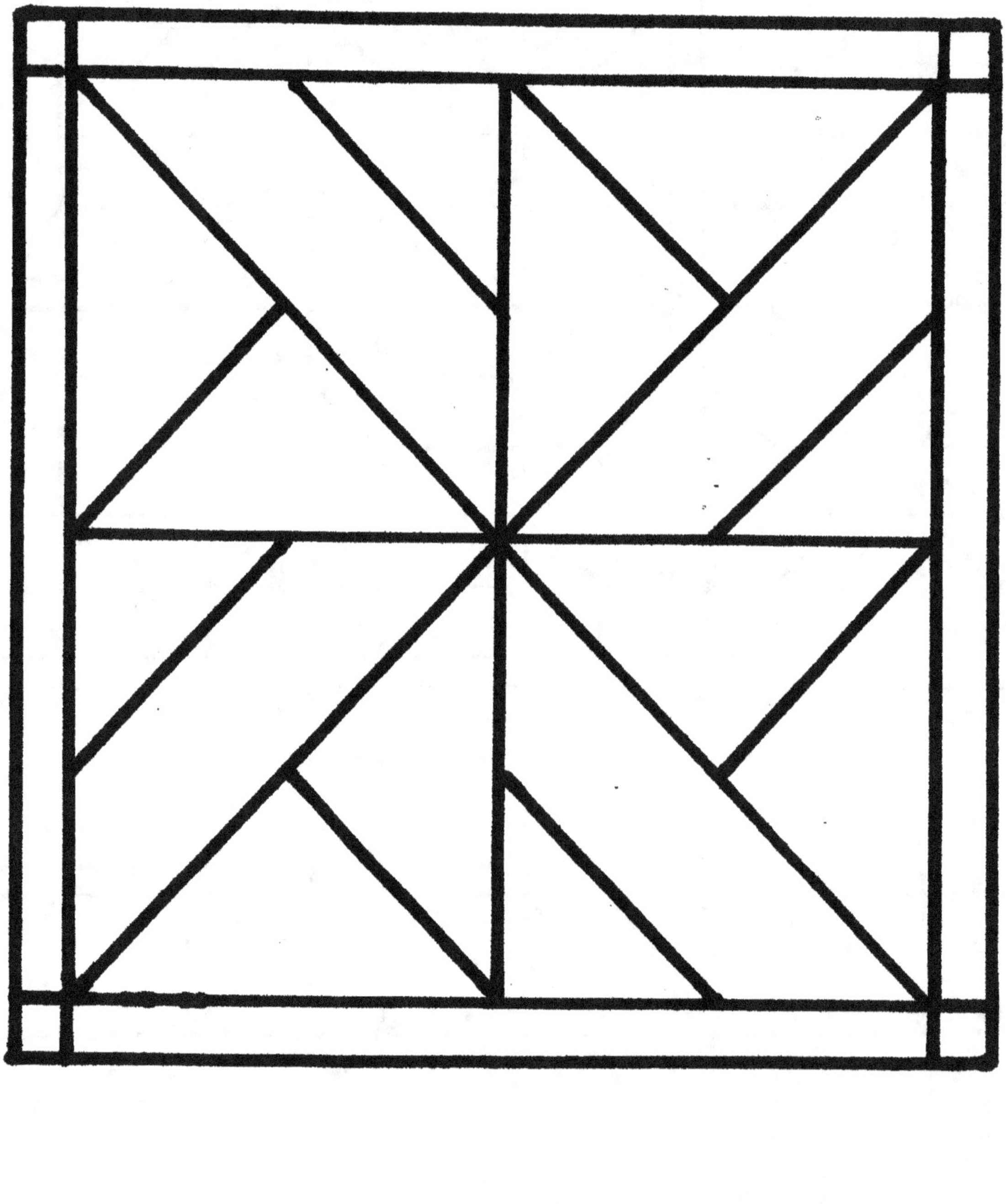

Franklin County Barn Quilt Wheels

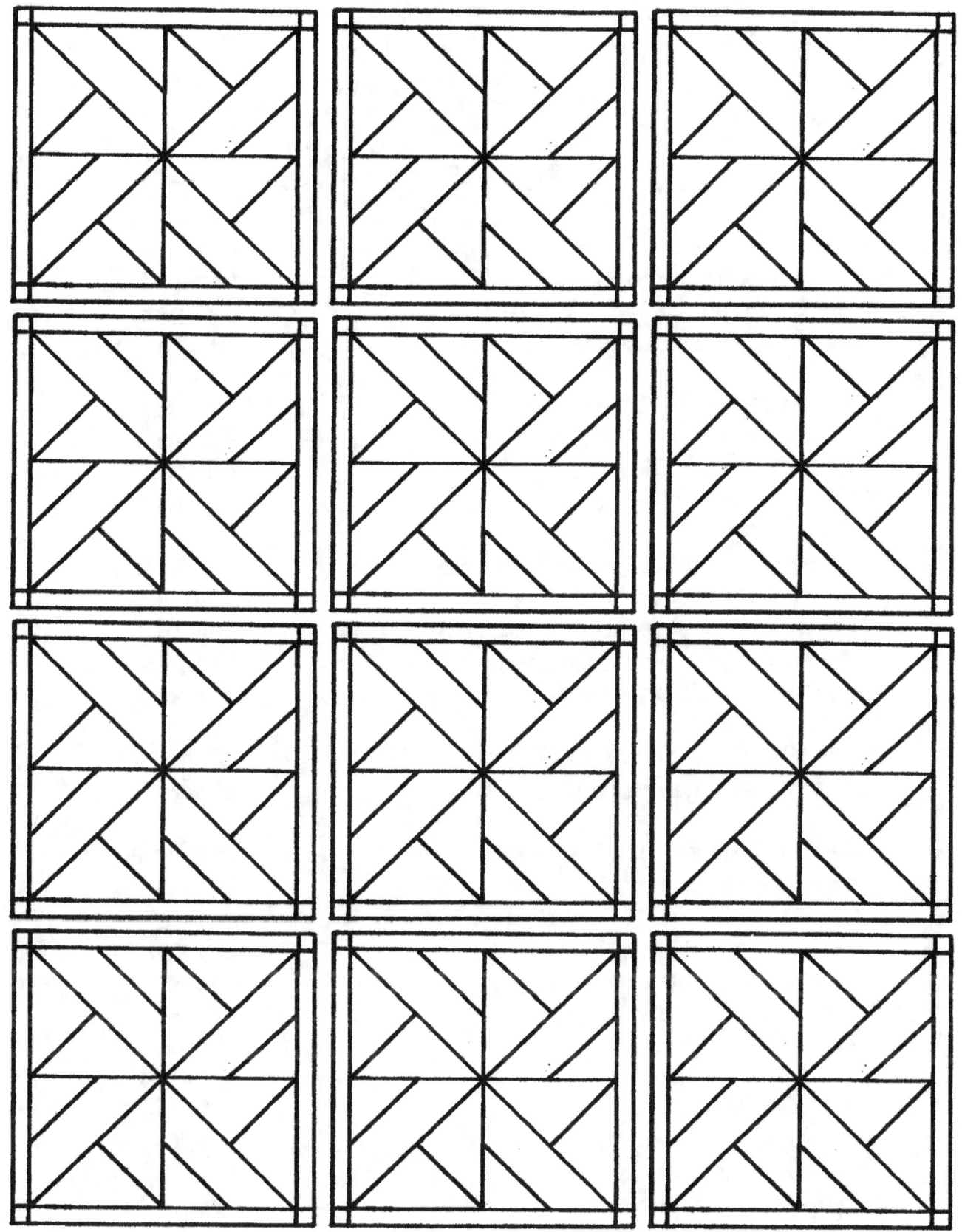

READING & MATH BOOKS by JOHN H. LETTAU

1st Dimension	Grades 3-6
2nd Dimension	Grades 3-6
Primary Dimension	Grades 1-4
Aztec Math Primary Book One	Grades 1-3
Aztec Math Primary Book Two	Grades 1-3
Aztec Math Intermediate Book One	Grades 3-6
Aztec Math Intermediate Book Two	Grades 3-6
Aztec Math Jr. High Book One	Grades 5-8
Aztec Math Jr. High Book Two	Grades 5-8
Aztec Math Decimal Book	Grades 4-8
Aztec Math Fraction Book	Grades 4-8
Sum-Action Number Puzzle Book One	Grades 3-6
Sum-Action Number Puzzle Book Two	Grades 3-6
Sum-Action Number Puzzle Primary Book One	Grades 1-3
Sum-Action Number Puzzle Primary Book Two	Grades 1-3
Multiplication Number Puzzles	Grades 3-6
Geometric Design Puzzle Book One	Grades 3-6
Geometric Design Puzzle Book Two	Grades 3-6
Aztec Reading Primary Book One	Grades 1-3
Aztec Reading Primary Book Two	Grades 1-3
Math in Action	Grades 3-6
A-Maze-ing Number Puzzles	Grades 3-6
Graph Paper Designs	Grades 2-6
Pick-A-Dilly Papers	Grades 3-6
Awards for All Reasons	Grades 1-6
Time Marches On	Grades 1-3
Pennies, Nickels & Dimes	Grades 1-3
Super-Sum Activity Cards	Grades 3-6
Learning Center Game Boards	Grades 1-3
Aztec Design Coloring Book	Grades 1-6

John Lettau Coloring Books

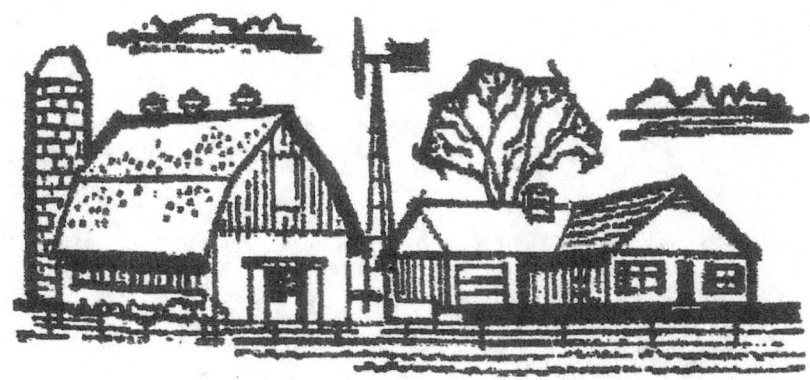

American Barn Quilt Coloring Books

Shawano County Wisconsin Barn Quilt Coloring Book 1
Shawano County Wisconsin Barn Quilt Coloring Book 2
Shawano County Wisconsin Barn Quilt Coloring Book 3
Green County Wisconsin Barn Quilt Coloring Book
Delaware County Iowa Barn Quilt Coloring Book
Tennessee Appalachain Barn Quilt Coloring Book 1
Tennessee Appalachain Barn Quilt Coloring Book 2
Franklin County Vermont Barn Quilt Coloring Book 1
Franklin County Vermont Barn Quilt Coloring Book 2
Gibson County Indiana Barn Quilt Coloring Book 1
Gibson County Indiana Barn Quilt Coloring Book 2
Lake County California Barn Quilt Coloring Book

Geometric Patterns

Geometric Design Coloring Book 1
Geometric Design Coloring Book 2
Geometric Design Coloring Book 3
Geometric Design Coloring Book 4
Geometric Design Coloring Book 5

Graph Paper Designs

Create your own geometric designs with Graph Paper Designs.

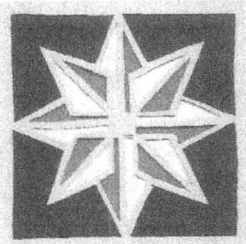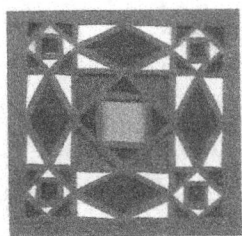

Order...John H. Lettau at Amazon.com

www.ingramcontent.com/pod-product-compliance
Lightning Source LLC
Chambersburg PA
CBHW082013230526
45468CB00022B/2118